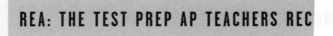

D0598649

AP ENGLISH
LANGUAGE & COMPOSITION

8th Edition

TestWare® Edition

Susan Bureau, B.A.
Alvirne High School
Hudson, New Hampshire

Stacey A. Kiggins, M.A.
Edison High School
Alexandria, Virginia

Katherine A. Nesselrode, B.A.
Mandarin High School
Jacksonville, Florida

Kristi R. McGauley, M.Ed.
Mandarin High School
Jacksonville, Florida

Research & Education Association
Visit our website at: www.rea.com

Research & Education Association
61 Ethel Road West
Piscataway, New Jersey 08854
E-mail: info@rea.com

 AP ENGLISH LANGUAGE & COMPOSITION
with TestWare®

Library of Congress Control Number 2011920126

ISBN-13: 978-0-7386-0901-0
ISBN-10: 0-7386-0901-3

CONTENTS

About Our Authors

Susan Bureau is the English Department Head at Alvirne High School in Hudson, New Hampshire where she has taught AP English Language and Composition for the past nine years. She has a B.A. in English from The University of New Hampshire.

Stacey A. Kiggins received her B.A. degree in Secondary English Education from the University of North Carolina at Greensboro, and her M.A. degree in Initiatives in Educational Transformation, from George Mason University, Virginia. She is the English department chair at Thomas A. Edison High School in Alexandria, Virginia. She has taught a variety of English disciplines, including: Advanced Placement Language and Composition, International Baccalaureate English, and Speech and Debate. Ms. Kiggins is the coach of a nationally recognized speech and debate team, and was the 2010 Virginia Association of Communications Arts and Sciences Speech Teacher of the Year.

Kristi McGauley is currently in her thirteenth year of teaching English. She joined Mandarin High School in November of 2005. Before arriving at MHS, she taught for seven years in a private school. Ms. McGauley graduated with a B.A. in English from Clearwater Christian College and earned her M.Ed. in Secondary English Education at the University of North Florida. She is chair of the school's literacy team.

Katherine A. Nesselrode graduated from the University of Tampa with a Bachelor of Arts in English. She was Nationally Board Certified in 2008. She has been teaching English for twenty-two years, currently at Mandarin High School in Jacksonville, Florida. She has taught high school English for 17 years and taught middle school English for the first five years of her teaching career. Each year she tries to challenge her students in a different and hopefully more interesting manner. Her ultimate plan is get her students to grow as thinkers and as writers and especially as readers.

About Research & Education Association

Founded in 1959, Research & Education Association (REA) is dedicated to publishing the finest and most effective educational materials—including software, study guides, and test preps—for students in elementary school, middle school, high school, college, graduate school, and beyond.

Today, REA's wide-ranging catalog is a leading resource for teachers, students, and professionals.

We invite you to visit us at *www.rea.com* to find out how "REA is making the world smarter."

Acknowledgments

In addition to our authors, we would like to thank Larry B. Kling, Vice President, Editorial, for his overall guidance, which brought this publication to completion; Pam Weston, Publisher, for setting the quality standards for production integrity and managing the publication to completion; John Cording, Vice President, Technology, for coordinating the design and development of REA's TestWare®; Diane Goldschmidt, Senior Editor, for project management; Alice Leonard and Kathleen Casey, Senior Editors, for preflight editorial review; Heena Patel, Technology Project Manager, for design contributions and software testing efforts; Christine Saul, Senior Graphic Designer, for designing our cover, and Fred Grayson of American BookWorks Corporation for overseeing manuscript development and typesetting.

We gratefully acknowledge Sonja Mix of Thomas Dales High School, Richmond, Virginia, for her incisive technical review of the manuscript.

CHAPTER 1
AP English Language & Composition

Introduction

About This Book and TestWare®

This test-preparation guide, along with the accompanying CD, will help you do well on the AP English Language & Composition Exam. You will become familiar with the requirements of the examination and be given a chance to prove your mastery of the AP exam on a series of specially developed practice exams. The introductory sections of the book are devoted to explaining the test, reviewing and expanding your critical reading skills, and helping you learn how to approach writing essays and answering multiple-choice questions in the very ways the AP examination will expect you to be able to do successfully.

This book provides three full-length practice exams with thorough explanations of every answer to help pinpoint your problem areas. By taking these practice exams and devoting time to going through our targeted subject review, you'll be well prepared to succeed on the AP English Language & Composition Exam. In addition, this book includes a glossary of key literary terms, all fully defined.

Two of the practice exams are also included on the enclosed TestWare® CD. The software provides timed conditions and instantaneous, accurate scoring, which makes it all the easier to establish your strengths and weakness.

How to Contact the AP Program

To obtain a registration bulletin or to learn more about the Advanced Placement Examinations, contact:

The College Board Advanced Placement Program
P.O. Box 6671
Princeton, NJ 08541-6671
Phone: (609) 771-7300
Website: *www.apcentral.collegeboard.com*
E-mail: *apexams@info.collegeboard.org*

About the AP English Language Exam

The AP English Language and Composition Examination is divided into two parts: Section 1, multiple-choice, or critical-reading, questions (45 per cent of your score) and Section 2, the free-response, or essay, questions (55 per cent of your score). The multiple-choice section has approximately 54 to 60 questions divided among four to six reading passages (the exact number varies from year to year), and there will be from nine to fifteen questions per reading passage. You are allowed 60 minutes for the objective portion. Although the test is geared so that most good students can finish within the time limits, the time constraints are also challenging. It is essential that you do some timed practice. Note two recent changes to the multiple-choice section of the exam:

- **Change in Content:** From 2007 onward, some items in the multiple-choice section refer to documentation and citation of sources. While examinees need not memorize any particular style (e.g., MLA, Chicago, APA, etc.), they will need to use information from citations that may indeed follow a given style. Some passages—"at least one," says the College Board—will be from a published work (book, journal, periodical, etc.) that incorporates footnotes or a bibliography; the documentation questions will be based on such passages.

- **Change in Scoring:** The method of scoring the multiple-choice section has changed. Beginning in 2011, the score on the multiple-choice section will be based only on the number of questions the student answers correctly. Points will no longer be deducted for incorrect answers, and, as always, no points will be awarded for unanswered questions. It is in your best interest to answer *all* multiple-choice questions.

The free-response section of the AP English Language and Composition exam is composed of three prompts, for which you are given 135 minutes in total to complete. Currently there are three types of free-response questions on the AP exam with some subset variations within these categories. These include the Synthesis Essay, the Rhetorical Analysis or Language Analysis Essay, and the Argument Essay.

- **New Directions for the Synthesis Essay:** Beginning with the May 2011 exams there will be new directions for the synthesis essay. The synthesis essay itself has not changed, but the new directions provide students with clearer and more concise guidelines for approaching the essay; the new directions clarify expectations about how students should synthesize, incorporate and cite the sources provided in the task.

AP English Language and Composition Test **Score Range 1-5** Generally, a score of 3 is considered "passing"	
SECTION 1	**SECTION 2**
Multiple-Choice (must use a No. 2 pencil)	Essays (must be written in blue or black ink)
55-60 questions based on four to six reading passages: • Fiction and nonfiction prose is divided into two categories: Pre-20th Century and 20th Century to the Present. • These categories include essays, letters, diaries, histories, biographies, sermons, speeches, literary works, satire, social criticism and all forms of journalism.	Three essays: each scored on a scale 0-9 • Rhetorical Analysis or Language Analysis Essay (suggested time—40 minutes) • Argument Essay (suggested time—40 minutes) • Synthesis Essay (reading time—15 minutes, suggested writing time—40 minutes)
Answer ALL questions (no deductions for incorrect answers).	You must write all three essays to pass. The essays do not have to be written in the order they appear on the test.
60 minutes	135 minutes
45% of the AP test score	55% of the AP test score

AP Scoring and Grade Distribution

The distribution of scores on the Advanced Placement tests ranges from 1 to 5. A test score of 3 is considered "passing"; however, keep in mind that colleges treat the scores differently. Some may accept a score of 2, while others will only accept a 4 or 5. You should contact the colleges directly or visit their websites to receive information about their AP score acceptance and credit policies.

You will complete the multiple-choice section of the test on a scan form, which is graded by a computer. You will write the essays on paper. College professors and teachers of Advanced Placement English grade the essays, using standardized procedures. The scores are usually released around mid-July.

Materials Needed for Test Day

The only materials you need to bring on test day are writing utensils: blue or black ink pens and two sharpened No. 2 pencils. You will not be able to use a dictionary, thesaurus, highlighters or colored pencils on the test. The College Board will provide you with all other materials, including paper for the essay portion of the test. However, it is highly recommend that you wear a watch. Timing is very important if you want to do well on this test. Although the test center will provide a clock, students find it easier and less distracting to use a watch than to look at a clock on the wall—especially if it is not directly in front of them.

Overview of Test Format and Content, Timing, and Annotation

It is possible to improve your score simply by being familiar with the test format and content, knowing how to use the time allotted effectively, and using annotation to stay focused and organized.

- **TEST FORMAT AND CONTENT**
  Multiple-choice questions are designed to test your skills in analyzing the rhetoric of prose passages. The passages included on the AP English Language test are usually not found in your typical high school textbooks. The College Board has designed the test so everyone will have an equal advantage. It is a test, not based on memorization, but based on application. In other words, the questions test how well you can apply your knowledge to new material. For both the multiple-choice passages and the essays, you should become acquainted with a wide variety of prose styles from many disciplines and historical periods: pre-20th Century and 20th Century to the present. These prose styles include essays, letters, diaries, histories, biographies, sermons, speeches, literary works, satire, social criticism and all forms of journalism.

  Not only will this knowledge help you analyze the passages, but you will become a better writer as well. The three essays that you will write for the free-response section of the test are briefly defined below:

  o **Rhetorical Analysis or Language Analysis Essay** (suggested time— 40 minutes): For this essay you will be asked to analyze the style of a passage; analyze the effect of the passage on the reader; define the author's attitude toward his or her topic; describe the rhetorical purpose of the passage; and/or identify the author's purpose or views and how he or she achieves that purpose or conveys those views. The skills needed for this particular essay are similar to the skills needed to answer the questions on the multiple-choice portion of the *AP English Language* test. Frequently, this question takes the form of two passages on the same topic but written in different styles and with different attitudes.

  o **Argument Essay** (suggested time—40 minutes): For this essay you are asked to write about a controversial topic. The topics tend to be broader, taking into account the variety of backgrounds students bring to the exam. Students who demonstrate knowledge and understanding of the world, have a diverse knowledge base, and can make connections across disciplines—i.e. history, literature, current events, science, economics—generally do better because they have more supports to draw from.

o **Synthesis Essay** (reading time—15 minutes, suggested writing time—40 minutes): For this essay you will be asked to read five to eight brief sources on a topic of some controversy in which differing sides will be presented. One of the resources you will have to analyze, and possibly use, in the synthesis essay is a visual image—a photograph, chart, editorial cartoon, graph, advertisement, etc.—found in texts published in print and electronic media. You will have to analyze the image as text. A 15-minute reading period is provided to accommodate the additional required reading for this prompt. The directions for the synthesis essay will ask you to explain a key idea or to argue a point. In other words, you will be writing another analytical/expository essay or another argumentative essay.

- **ANNOTATION**
Regardless of the section, multiple-choice or essay, you should begin annotating everything you read: the directions, the passages, the questions and answer choices in the multiple-choice section, the essay prompts, and the reading selections following the essay prompts. While reading the directions, underline key words, especially if the directions include background information about the passage. Marking the most important aspects of the passages and prompts will help you maintain focus on what you're answering or writing about. Just like the directions and the passages, you should mark the questions and answer choices in the multiple-choice section while you read. This technique will help you stay focused on the key words within the question, guide you to the correct answer, help you eliminate the obvious incorrect answers, and identify the questions you want to come back to later.

When you begin the essay section, reading and marking the key words in the prompt is essential. You could write a fabulous essay, but unless your essay addresses the prompt, your essay will not be scored. Unlike the first two essays, the synthesis essay will ask you to read several selections. Because you will have only 15 minutes to read, digest, and synthesize a lot of information, marking these selections is very important. Remember, you are not restating the sources; your task is to identify the information in the sources you plan to use in your response. Underlining and even labeling, key points that supports or refutes your thesis will save you time when you begin writing your essay. While writing your essay, you will want to incorporate direct quotations from the resources or reference specific material. You will be able to quickly identify these supports if they have been marked.

- **TIMING**
While taking the multiple-choice section of the AP test, you should know to how to pace yourself in the 60 minutes allotted and know the best method that will allow you to answer these questions efficiently. When it is time to

begin the multiple-choice section, quickly look through the test and count how many passages are included. Divide this number into 60 minutes; for example, if there are 5 passages, then you will divide 60 by 5. So, you should spend about 12 minutes on each passage. Use the practice tests in this book to help you practice your timing. You may find that you are more comfortable reading the questions and answers *before* reading the passage. This technique will help you know what to look for while reading the passage. Regardless of the approach you take, remember to annotate.

Do the easiest questions first. In other words, if you are sure you know the answer, mark it immediately on the scan form. If you find yourself spending too much time on a particular question, circle it in your test booklet, skip it, and come back to it later if you have the time. Most importantly, if you run out of time, fill in *all* answers; there will be no penalty for incorrect answers.

It is important that you feel comfortable to write three lengthy essays within a very short period of time. Learning to write analytical and argumentative essays without planning and revision takes practice. Months before taking the test, practice writing similar essays within a timed framework. Quantity does not mean quality; however, if the essay is too short then it will be difficult to explore the topic thoroughly. Most essays that have received high scores (7-9) usually range from five to seven paragraphs. You may write the essays in any order. Read all the choices and write the essays you feel the most confident about first. Save the most difficult essay for last, but don't skip it because you must answer all the essay questions in order to receive a 2 or higher on the test. You will have an extra 15 minutes for the synthesis essay. The extra 15 minutes gives you time to read the resources, seven passages and at least one image, and annotate key ideas from each resource. Instead of the 40 minutes you get to write the other essays, you will have 55 minutes to write the synthesis essay.

CHAPTER 2
AP English Language & Composition

Reviewing Rhetorical Devices

Terms to Know

You don't need to know as many terms as you might think. There has always been less terminology on the English Language and Composition exam than on the English Literature and Composition exam; in recent years, knowledge of terminology has been de-emphasized even further. That being said, there are some terms as well as some specific vocabulary that is important for you to know and will be mentioned in the subsequent discussion of both sections of the exam and are listed in the Glossary in the back of this book. This vocabulary will be useful to you as you continue your academic and professional career, as well as in the general sense of living your life as an informed, educated adult.

Types of Questions

There are two types of questions on the multiple-choice portion of the exam. Over-arching questions measure your understanding of the passage as a whole. The other kind of question asks you to focus on a very specific part of the passage, from a paragraph or sentence to a particular phrase or word. Again, the good news is that even if you don't completely understand the passage as a whole, you can still figure out the answers to many of the focused questions, and, even more good news, sometimes figuring out the focused questions can help you gain a better understanding of the passage as a whole.

One caution—some students don't want to believe that meaning is derived from a complex interplay of content, structure, and language, believing that this complexity is some kind of figment of their English teacher's imagination and not the intent of the writer. These students often have great difficulty with this test. Remember, good writing is purposeful writing, and very good writing feels effortless even when it's not. As you work through the multiple-choice section of the exam, approach every word, detail, image, figure of speech, allusion, syntactic construction—basically everything—as a choice, not as a happenstance. In addition, assume these elements not only exist in isolation but are inter-related: acting together, they combine to achieve the writer's purpose. Thus, diction and syntax affect style, style affects tone, etc.

Items to Notice as You Read

1. Main idea, argument, or purpose of the passage: Do you understand the point of the passage? The most basic and essential of questions, these can also be the most difficult and panic-inducing in students. Often, it is not stated explicitly in the passage, but needs to be inferred. While it is difficult on the free-response section of the exam to write about an excerpt you don't completely understand, the multiple-choice format of this section of the exam can help guide you to a deeper understanding of the text.

Sometimes you are asked to make predictions about the author outside the scope of the immediate text. These questions ask you to transfer what you understand the author to mean in this passage to an analogous situation or to infer things about the author's state of mind.

2. Audience: The audience is, of course, the intended reader of the piece. It would be difficult for a seventeenth-century writer to envision the world in which you would be reading his or her work hundreds of years later, but all writing has an intended audience, and it informs the writer's rhetorical choices. Occasionally, you will be told who the intended audience of the excerpt is, but often you will not, so you will need to make inferences about the intended audience.

Obviously, consider the writer's purpose, especially when it's persuasive, when you think about the audience. Also pay careful attention to diction and syntax. For example, the piece might be about a scientific subject, but if it lacks technical jargon, it's probably meant for a more general audience. Also, don't be thrown off by the time period. A pre-twentieth century piece may be difficult for you to read because of the differences in language and experience between you and the writer, but that doesn't mean it was difficult for the typical reader of that time period. For example, William Bradford's seventeenth-century *History of Plymouth Plantation* is a difficult text for the average American high school student because she is unfamiliar with the language of the time-period. Bradford wrote in what was called "plain style," meaning his work lacks the Latin expressions, figurative language, and allusions to classical literature common in the ornate style of writing of the highly educated of his time. His intended audience was the common folk, at least the literate common folk, so, while his work is filled with references to God and Biblical allusions, his assumption was that the average reader of his time was religious and well-versed in the Bible. He also used diction that would be offensive today, especially when referring to Native Americans as "savages," "barbarians," and "wild men." Keep in mind, there is language we use every day that will seem dated, if not completely incomprehensible, to an audience three hundred years in the future.

3. Imagery: The word *imagery* is derived from the Latin word *imago*, meaning "to image." There are five types of imagery that appeal to each of our senses: visual, auditory, kinesthetic, olfactory (smell), and gustatory (taste). Writers use sensory-rich details to reinforce the important points in the message and to connect with the audience.

- **visual imagery**: something seen in the mind's eye
    Example: "It's the answer told by lines that stretched around schools and churches in numbers this nation has never seen" (Barack Obama, presidential victory speech)

- **auditory imagery**: sound
    Example: "Buzzes its frightful F / And dies between three cannibals," (Karl Shapiro, "The Fly")

- **kinesthetic imagery**: touch
    Example: "These wretches, who ne'er lived,/ Went on in nakedness, and sorely stung/ By wasps and hornets, which bedew'd their cheeks/ With blood, that mix'd with tears dropp'd to their feet,/ And by disgustful worms was gather'd there." (Dante Alighieri, *Inferno* Canto III)

- **olfactory imagery**: smell
    Example: "That morning there was alfalfa on his pillow and cow manure embedded in his tennis shoes and the cuffs of his coveralls that lay by the bed. Those were sweet reminders of him. He had gone out as one shaft of searing light came through the window. He had put on clean clothes to milk the cows." (Jane Hamilton, *A Map of the World*)

- **gustatory imagery**: taste
    Example: "Let us not seek to satisfy our thirst for freedom by drinking from the cup of bitterness and hatred." (Martin Luther King Jr., "I Have a Dream")

4. Syntax: Syntax is defined as the "arrangement of words in meaningful patterns." Sentences, which are syntactical units composed by words, do not have meaning until they are put together. When we examine an author's use of syntax, we are examining devices which the author may have manipulated to create an emotional or intellectual effect. Sentence length and structure—repetition, rhythm, parallelism—all contribute to help the audience better understand the author's message. The items below are common techniques for manipulating syntax:

- **Sentence Length and Type:** Are the sentences simple, compound, complex, or compound-complex? Are they short or long? Shorter sentences imply a less formal style; for example, short sentences are used in the novel *The Catcher in the Rye*. Longer sentences imply a more formal style; for example, long sentences are used in The Declaration of Independence. A series of shorter sentences tend to quicken the pace of the writing, while longer sentences slow it down. As always, consider how sentence length and type works with the other elements of style to achieve the writer's purpose.

- **Sentence Variety:** Most writing is a combination of both long and short sentences as well as sentence types. Where does the author use sentence variety to create meaning? Are short sentences or fragments used for special emphasis? Are long sentences or run-ons used for a specific effect? Look (and listen) for the diversion from the pattern as a point of special meaning and emphasis.

- **Specialized Sentence Structures:** What specialized sentence structure does the author use? Sometimes this terminology makes it on to the exam, so it is helpful to you as a critical reader to be aware of these structures and their effects. Knowing these six sentence structures is beneficial: balanced, periodic, cumulative, inverted, imperative, and antithesis.

    o **Periodic Sentence:** A periodic sentence builds to a climactic statement in its final main clause or phrase. Herman Melville wrote this comment about Benjamin Franklin, "Printer, postmaster, almanac maker, essayist chemist, orator, tinker, statesman, humorist, philosopher, parlor man, political economist, professor of housewifery, ambassador, projector, maxim-monger, herb-doctor, wit: Jack of all trades, master of each and mastered by none—the type and genius of the land, Franklin was everything but a poet."

    o **Cumulative Sentence:** Cumulative sentences reverse the order of the periodic sentence. Instead of withholding the main idea until the last clause, the writer states it immediately and then expands on it with examples, details, and/or clarifications.

    o **Balanced Sentence:** In a balanced sentence, two coordinate but contrasting structures are placed next to each other like the weights on a balanced scale. Thus, a balanced sentence creates a contrasted thought: "Many are called but few are chosen" (Matthew 22:14), "I come to bury Caesar, not to praise him" (Shakespeare, *Julius Caesar*). When you read a balanced sentence out loud, you tend to pause between the balanced parts. That pause is marked by some kind of fulcrum: a coordinating conjunction, "not," or a mark of punctuation.

    o **Inversion:** In an inversion sentence the typical subject-verb order is reversed. Consider Jesus' last words, "Forgive them, Father, for they know not what they do." The typical word order would be, "Father forgive them…." Because inversion is infrequently used in prose, we should pay attention when it is used. Inversion calls attention to the part of the sentence that is out of typical order, so it creates a special emphasis.

    o **Imperative:** The imperative sentence is when the subject is the understood "you," telling or even commanding the audience to do something. There is no hedging or qualifying in the imperative, so the form is very strong and assertive: "Don't worry; be happy."

o   **Antithesis:** An antithesis balances two opposite or contrasting words, phrases, or clauses: "Ask not what your country can do for you; ask what you can do for your country." (John F. Kennedy). This quote is also an example of a balanced sentence.

- **Repetition:** Bad writing is repetitive; good writing effectively uses repetition to create meaning. Anyone who has ever heard or read Martin Luther King, Jr.'s famous 1963 speech at the Lincoln Memorial remembers the "I have a dream" refrain. As you read, consider the words and/or phrases that are repeated. Are certain sentence structures repeated? You will notice these repetitive words, phrases and sentences when you read; think about how these stylistic choices affect the meaning.

- **Rhythm:** Does the language have rhythm? Rhythm is not only a characteristic of poetry, but good prose is often rhythmic as well. Rhythm is created in a number of ways. Parallel syntax is the repetition of word order or form either within a single sentence or in several sentences that develop the same central idea. Consider this famous line from The Declaration of Independence: "We hold these truths to be self evident: that all men are created equal; that they are endowed by their creator with certain inalienable rights; that among these rights are life, liberty, and the pursuit of happiness; that to secure these rights, governments are instituted among men, deriving their just powers from the consent of the governed...." This is a long, complicated sentence (even this abridged form), but the parallel syntax and repetition of the relative clauses, not only creates the grammatical coherence necessary for comprehension, but it also creates equal emphasis on each clause as well as a rhythmic lyricism that distinguishes Thomas Jefferson's masterpiece. Rhythm can also be created by the repetition of words or sentences of similar length, especially short ones. Again, you may have been criticized for using this technique in your own writing, but good writers use these elements to make their writing "sing." Listen for patterns in syntax as you read, but also pay attention to breaks in the pattern. They are just as significant.

- **Sentence Beginnings and Endings:** Do any sentences begin or end with a significant word or phrase? Do any sentences have the main idea "hidden" in the middle, in an interrupter, so as to create surprise or suspense?

- **Fancy Stuff:** Allusions to Shakespeare or Greek philosophers? Latin words and/or phrases? A little French? These stylistic choices combined with elevated diction are usually characteristics of formal writing meant to appeal to an educated audience. But again, not always. Look for humor and incongruity—the audience probably still needs to be educated to understand it, but the style may not be formal. Is the language purposefully inflated to create irony, parody, or humor?

Again, even if these terms are not asked specifically on the test, understanding how these syntactic structures are used will support your understanding of the connection between style and meaning; and, they may be useful in the free-response section.

5. *Tone:* The tone is the writer's attitude toward the subject and the audience, a combination of the writer's diction, choice of details and examples, imagery, syntax, point of view, and figurative language. Tone can be obvious, but it also can be subtle and misleading in sophisticated prose. Developing your understanding of the elements that create tone will improve your ability to discern it. Consider the following as you analyze tone:

- Diction and Figurative Language: Diction and figurative language contribute to the tone of a piece. Many words have connotation, emotional impact, in addition to denotation or literal, dictionary-definition meaning, and you are expected to draw inferences from them. While a teacher might call a student "disruptive" on a misconduct report meant to precipitate disciplinary action for a classroom offense, he or she may call the same student "high-spirited" in a college recommendation the following year. The word *disruptive* has a negative connotation and is meant to evoke a critical response from the reader, while *high-spirited* has a positive connotation and is meant to cast the student in a positive light to the college. Likewise, figurative language is really just expanded, heightened diction. It too has both denotation, but more importantly, connotation. Thus, when Shakespeare uses the simile "My love's like a red, red rose," the audience knows he's being highly complimentary.

- Imagery: Imagery, language that appeals to the senses, also contributes to the tone. Images can be striking in their consistency as well as their incongruity. The old, clichéd opening "It was a dark and stormy night," creates an ominous tone leading us to expect bad things to happen. Also, consider the power of incongruous images to create tone, for example, the view of a passenger plane striking the World Trade Center against the backdrop of blue sky on a perfect September morning on September 11, 2001. Here we have a heightened sense of tragedy and helplessness developed through the imagery. Remember, if the writer chooses to include imagery, he or she is doing something with it. Pay attention.

- Support: Details and examples, like imagery, also help to create tone. Meaning is always formed by the details and examples the writer chooses to include, as well as the ones the writer chooses to exclude. Are objective details and examples used, or is the support personal, anecdotal, or hypothetical? Maybe it's a combination of both. In addition, logic and reasoning are also valid methods of support for an argument, and are often, but not always, combined with other methods of support. The character of the support will always contribute to the tone.

- Syntax: Syntax also influences tone. Often, groups of shorter sentences increase the pace and heighten the emotion of a piece, while longer sentences slow it down and make it more cerebral. A short sentence or fragment in a group of longer sentences will create emphasis and impact. The use of the imperative, a command created with the understood "you," can help to create an assertive tone. Also, consider the use of the active and passive voice in your reading. Active voice is where the subject of the sentence is performing the action: *The boy climbed the tree*. When the subject performs the action, the ideas in the sentence tend to be more alive and engaging to the reader. The passive voice is where the subject of the sentence is having the action performed upon it: *The tree was climbed by the boy*. The ideas in this sentence tend to create a greater distance and objectivity between the writer and the subject. This style is used in scientific writing such as lab reports, where the emphasis is placed on the observations from the experiment and not on the scientist/observer. Thus, the scientist writes, "The beaker of liquid was placed on the Bunsen burner," as opposed to "The scientist placed the beaker of liquid on the Bunsen burner."

- Satire is often included on the AP English Language and Composition exam. Satire uses humor and irony to criticize people or social institutions. It's related to, but not quite the same as, sarcasm. In satire, the writer takes on a role, so the voice of the writer and the voice of the narrator are often not the same. Thus, the satirist might criticize the excessive claims on late-night television infomercials by presenting an exaggerated, mocking version of one of those commercials. Here, the narrator is espousing the greatness of his product, while the writer disparages him with his own inflated language. Satire can sometimes be subtle and therefore difficult for inexperienced readers to hear. Think—is the writer being completely serious or is he or she teasing or mocking? If you observe something in the work that seems unusual or strange—especially if you sense hyperbole, inflated language, or understatement—consider satire.

- Identifying the tone will help you discern the writer's purpose. See where the tone questions lead you if you struggle with satire. You might begin making connections about the entire piece if you isolate the tone.

- Learning the vocabulary of tone will help you to identify satire, as well express it. The following words can be used to describe tone, and many communicate subtle distinctions in feeling. Though you may not know the meaning of some of these words, this is not an esoteric list—these are words commonly understood by educated people, and thus are valuable to you in your reading and writing. And, they appear in test questions. Learn them. Also, as you use these words to develop your vocabulary, get a sense of their connotation. Some words that have similar meanings are distinguished by degrees of feeling; for example, consider how being *pleased* is different from being *happy*, which is different from being *ecstatic*. In addition, many of these words can, and will be used to describe diction and style.

Useful Words in Describing Tone

admiring	detached	inflammatory	petty
angry	determined	informative	pretentious
apprehensive	didactic	insipid	respectful
bantering	diffident	insolent	restrained
benevolent	disdainful	ironic	sardonic
biting	disgusted	irreverent	satiric
bitter	dramatic	learned	scholarly
candid	ecstatic	lugubrious	scornful
clinical	effusive	mock-heroic	sentimental
colloquial	elegiac	mocking	solemn
compassionate	facetious	mock-serious	somber
complimentary	factual	moralistic	sympathetic
concerned	fanciful	mournful	taunting
condescending	flippant	neutral	threatening
confident	hopeful	nostalgic	turgid
contemptuous	impartial	objective	urbane
contentious	incisive	patronizing	urgent
cynical	indignant	pedantic	worshipful

6. *Language and Style:* Style is the habitual, repeated patterns that differentiate one writer from another (or, one singer or painter from the other, for that matter). Salvador Dali painted in the surrealist style, with his most famous painting being "The Persistence of Memory," which shows the clocks and watches dripping and oozing off the sides of tables and over a bare tree limb. Claude Monet painted in the impressionist style, with bits of color that blend together to form a coherent whole only if the viewer stands back from the picture. Monet was interested in the use of color to form an impression, rather than the absolute realistic portrayal of a scene. In literature, Hemingway is well known for his terse, sparse, objective style indicative of the isolation of people in the twentieth century; Hawthorne is well known for his flamboyant, exaggerated word "pictures" that create a mood of horror or fearful introspection.

So, one of the essential attributes of style is the repetition of patterns. The other component of style is deviation from the customary patterns. Hemingway, for example, deviates from his usual short sentences and few descriptive words when he describes nature. In those passages, you will find long, complex sentences and lyrical descriptions of nature, such as a river, to show the peace that people obtain when they escape the jarring, destructive effects of civilization and are comforted by the healing beauty of nature.

Expectation (the pattern) and surprise (the deviation from the pattern) are the component parts of style. A discussion of style is also a discussion of the well-chosen word or phrase. A discussion of the well-chosen word or phrase depends on your ability to be discriminating about language and to recognize good writing.

For example, colloquial word choice is not standard formal usage and employs idiomatic or slang expressions; this word usage develops a casual tone. Scientific, Latinate (words with Latin roots or origins), or scholarly language would be formal and employ standard rules of usage. Concrete words form vivid images in the reader's mind, while abstract language is more appropriate for a discussion of philosophy. Allusive style uses many references to history, literature, or other shared cultural knowledge to provoke or enlighten the reader. Appeals to the senses make the writing more concrete and vivid. Since prose does not have a natural rhythm, an obvious metrical pattern in a passage signals an important idea.

Authors employ other poetic devices in their writing to emphasize important ideas. When an author makes the choice to use similes or metaphors, or any of the other common poetic or rhetorical devices, usually, it is because the author wants to draw attention to that particular characteristic and perhaps suggest a more complex relationship to the implied or stated theme.

If the author suddenly or obviously varies sentence structure or length of a sentence, you should take note. Short sentences (seven or fewer words) or fragments usually signal important ideas. You should look out for them. If, in the midst of a variety of sentence structures and lengths, the author inserts two or three short, simple sentences, you should notice this change as being significant. Most certainly, a detail or action will appear in these sentences that the author considers crucial.

An author can choose from a variety of specialized sentence patterns or structures to create emphatic sentences. Most sentences in the English language are loose sentences; that is, the main idea appears at the beginning of the sentence (subject first, then predicate, then additional modifiers) and much of the predicate part of the sentence can be cut off without serious damage to the main idea. Any time an author wishes to call attention to an important idea, he or she can use a different sentence structure. These different structures are called "emphatic" because they emphasize the ideas contained therein.

The *most important* aspect about understanding style is to understand its relationship to the purpose or main idea of a passage. Memorizing lists of difficult terms will not get you a good grade on the AP English Language and Composition test; in fact, the most recent exams have de-emphasized the knowledge of specific terminology in favor of your understanding of how the elements of style work in the passage to enhance meaning. You will be asked to characterize the author's style in the passages. Like tone, an author's style is formed from the combining of rhetorical elements working together; style is always a reflection of the author's purpose and intended audience, as well as the specific occasion for the writing. When you think about style, consider the following:

- **Formal or informal:** As you read, try to quickly assess whether the writing is more formal or informal. While there are many degrees and subsets of these two categories, making this initial judgment will help you read the passage and answer the questions within the multiple-choice context. Just remember that archaic language in the passage, which makes it difficult for you to read, does not necessarily mean the writing is formal. Pay attention to all the elements of style discussed in this section.

- **Diction:** How would you characterize the author's choice of words? Is it colloquial, idiomatic, scientific, Latinate, concrete, abstract, scholarly, or allusive? Does the language include slang, jargon, or dialect? Is the word choice inflated or understated? Consider incongruity as well. Is a very informal or slang word used in an otherwise formal passage? What effect is the author trying to create with this contrast?

- **Figurative Language:** Which literary devices—personification, metaphor, simile, allusion, hyperbole—does the author use? Remember, figurative language has denotation, literal meaning, and connotation, the power to evoke feeling. Passages with figurative language tend to be more formal and/or lyrical; however, passages with slang would suggest an informal, colloquial style.

- **Imagery:** Does the author use imagery? If the author uses imagery, to what senses does the author appeal? Is the imagery pleasant or distasteful? Beautiful or frightening? Are there incongruous images—a dagger lying on a child's bed? A beautiful flower growing through the cracks in a sidewalk on a rough urban street? Does a particular sense dominate the description? Why?

- **Sound Effects:** Which literary devices of sound—alliteration, assonance, consonance, rhyme—does the author use? While you probably won't be asked specific questions using these terms on the test, it is important to know how these elements influence style. Both alliterative words and rhyming words become connected to each other as well as emphasized in the reader's mind. Consider the Ben Franklin maxim, "One today is worth two tomorrows." The connection in meaning between "today," "two," and "tomorrow" are emphasized by the alliterated "t" sound. Take another Franklin maxim, "If you would know the value of money, go and try to borrow some; he that goes a-borrowing goes a-sorrowing." Here of course the rhyming words become even more connected in meaning by their connection in sound. In addition, the repetition of sounds of words in close proximity, both initial sounds as well as sounds within words, contribute to the feeling of a passage. Soft words repeating soft sounds (*l, m, n, s, f* sounds) can create a calming effect while stronger sounds (*t, k, p* sounds) might create an exciting or harsh effect. Look at these lines from Washington Irving's short story "Rip Van Winkle." Rip is the fictional character who falls asleep in the Catskill Mountains for twenty years, and this is the line Irving uses to bring us in to the section of the story that will begin Rip's long slumber:

    "From an opening between the trees he could overlook all the lower country for many a mile of rich woodlands. He saw at a distance the lordly Hudson, far, far below him, moving on its silent but majestic course, with the reflection of a purple cloud, or the sail of a lagging bark, here and there sleeping on its glassy bosom, and at last losing itself in the blue highlands."

    Notice how Irving combines the repetition of the soft sounds here in the initial and internal syllables of the words in this sentence with the imagery to create this sleepy fantasy. As always, consider incongruity. Anytime the author deviates from the pattern, notice the deviation and consider its effect on the meaning.

7. *Definitions of Common Fallacies of Logic:* When taking a position, an author wants his or her audience to accept his or her argument. Arguments should follow a logical pattern. However, sometimes the author will use faulty logic—logic that is not logical—to present his/her position. This faulty logic is referred to as fallacies, which weaken an argument. Although you do not have to know all the types of fallacies, it is best to be aware of the main fallacies that authors use in their writing. Once you become comfortable with recognizing fallacies, you want to make sure you avoid using them in your own arguments. Some of the more common fallacies are presented below:

- **Ad hominem:** Latin for "against the man." When a writer personally attacks his or her opponents rather than attacking the arguments.

- **Ambiguity:** When a situation may be interpreted in more than one way.

- **Authority (also referred to as "Appeal to Authority"):** Arguments that draw on recognized experts or persons with highly relevant experience are said to rest on authoritative backing or authority. Readers are expected to accept claims if they are in agreement with an authority's view.

- **Begging the Question (often called "Circular Reasoning"):** Occurs when the believability of the evidence depends on the believability of the claim.

- **Common Knowledge (also referred to as *Ad Populum*):** Argues that if it is a shared belief or assumption, then readers should accept it.

- **Either-Or Reasoning (also referred to as "False Dichotomy"):** When the writer reduces an argument or issue to two polar opposites and ignores any alternatives.

- **Emotional Appeal (also referred to as "Appeal to Pity"):** When a writer appeals to readers' emotions (often through pathos) to excite and involve them in the argument.

- **Equivocation:** When a writer uses the same term in two different senses in an argument.

- **Ethical Appeal (also referred to as "Appeal to Pity"):** When a writer tries to persuade the audience to respect and believe him or her based on a presentation of image of self through the text. Reputation is sometimes a factor in ethical appeals, but in all cases the aim is to gain the audience's confidence.

- **False Analogy (also referred to as *Post Hoc*):** When two cases are not sufficiently parallel to lead readers to accept a claim of connection between them.

- **Generalization (also referred to as "Hast Generalization"):** When a writer bases a claim upon an isolated example or asserts that a claim is certain rather than probable. Sweeping generalizations occur when a writer asserts that a claim applies to all instances instead of some.

- **Non sequitur:** Latin for "it does not follow"; when one statement isn't logically connected to another.

- **Red Herring:** When a writer raises an irrelevant issue to draw attention away from the real issue.

8. *Organization:* A coherent piece of writing is a progression of ideas. Ask yourself, what is the progression of thought from each sentence and idea to the next, from each paragraph to the next? Try to follow how each sentence, or even clause or phrase, is related to and proceeds from the previous one. Try to follow as well the way in which one paragraph is related to and proceeds from the previous one. Sometimes, particularly in the older passages, our modern conceptions of paragraphing are lacking. If you are presented with an unusually long passage without conventional paragraph breaks, you will be challenged to look for shifts in ideas or tone to help you understand how the passage develops. Consider the following points about the organization of the passage:

- **If the passage is descriptive**, is it organized spatially or by order of importance? What is the overall effect?

- **If the passage is narrative**, is the chronological order of events interrupted by flashback, foreshadowing, or episodic events? Is the plot framed or circular?

- **If the passage is expository**, are any of the following devices or methods used: definition, cause and effect, deductive order, inductive order, comparison/contrast, division and classification, examples, extended example, analogy?

- **If persuasion is used**, what methods does the author use to bolster the argument? Does the author deal with opposing evidence? Where is the thesis—at the beginning or at the end? Does the author commit any logical fallacies?

- **Transitions:** In addition, look for transition words and phrases to help you understand the progression of ideas in the passage. Transitions tell us how words, phrases, clauses, sentences, paragraphs—essentially ideas—are related to each other. For example (and yes, *for example* is a transition), you know from my transition "for example" in this sentence, how the idea that came before this phrase is related to the idea that is about to come next; you know that I'm about to use an example to illustrate the point I just made. This strategy is especially useful in the denser, pre-twentieth century passages. Even if the passage seems like complete gibberish to you, if the transition to the second paragraph begins with the word *however*, you actually know quite a bit about that passage—you know the first gibberish contrasts with the second gibberish. In fact, frequently you will be asked, "How does the second paragraph develop from the first?" You need only to notice the *however* to get that question correct. Now, if you actually understand a little of the gibberish in the second paragraph—even understand the main idea of the second paragraph—then, you in turn, know more about the first paragraph than you originally thought. You may now be able to understand what was said in the context of its contrast to the second paragraph. The same rule applies to sentences, or even words, phrases, and clauses. Marking transitions in the text will help you understand the author's progression of thought.

Transition Words and Phrases

Words that can be used to show **location:**

above	behind	by	near	throughout
across	below	down	off	to the right
against	beneath	in back of	onto	under
along	beside	in front of	on top of	
among	between	inside	outside	
around	beyond	into	over	

Words that can be used to show **time**:

while	first	meanwhile	soon	then
after	second	today	later	next
at	third	tomorrow	afterward	as soon as
before	now	next week	about	when suddenly
during	until	yesterday	finally	

Word that can be used to **compare** two things:

likewise	also	while	in the same way
like	as	similarly	

Words that can be used to **contrast** two things:

but	still	although	on the other hand	though	while
however	yet	otherwise	even though	despite	

Words that can be used <u>to **emphasize a point:**</u>

again	truly	especially	for this reason
to repeat	in fact	to emphasize	

Words that can be used to <u>**conclude or summarize:**</u>

finally	as a result	to sum up	in conclusion
lastly	therefore	all in all	because

Words that can be used to <u>**add information:**</u>

again	another	for instance	for example
also	and	moreover	additionally
as well	besides	along with	other
next	finally	in addition	

Words that can be used to <u>**clarify:**</u>

that is	for instance	in other words

Words that show <u>**cause and effect:**</u>

therefore	because	thus

9. Methods of development: How are the author's ideas supported? He or she may rely on a primary method, or, more likely, the writer may combine a number of elements.

- **Examples:** These examples may be very specific, concrete examples or they may be hypothetical examples.

- **Anecdotes:** Anecdotes are short narratives, often personal, used to illustrate a point within a larger context of a piece that may not necessarily be narrative.

- **Narration:** The piece is developed as a story, usually ordered chronologically.

- **Description:** Descriptive pieces are supported by details and imagery, and—except in the most scientific, objective writing—meant to evoke an emotional response in the reader. Description is also often used to illustrate a point within a larger context of a piece where the dominant mode of exposition is not descriptive.

- **Figurative language:** Ideas are often supported through figurative language. In fact, an entire piece may develop through an extended metaphor or an analogy. Again, it is just as likely that these devises will be used in conjunction with other methods of development.

- **Logic or reasoning:** The author may use abstract reasoning to support the point. Some arguments are presented deductively—a general or universal idea is presented leading to a more specific point or application. Other arguments are presented inductively—specific points are provided leading to a more general or universal conclusion. Fallacies are errors in reasoning; they are presented as following the logic, but indeed don't. There is much terminology devoted to the rhetorical study of logic, but knowing a few key fallacies could help you with this test. Stay focused on the basics: deduction, induction, and fallacy.

CHAPTER 3

AP English Language & Composition

Chapter 3

Documentation and Citation

It is important that you are familiar with the rhetoric of documentation that you will find in the multiple-choice questions and for the essays. Although you will not have to memorize all the documentation styles, it is important that you have certain skills, such as the analysis of footnotes. In order to answer the documentation questions, your close reading of materials and familiarity with the nature of academic discourse with documentation will help you on the *AP English Language* test. Although there are different rules or guidelines, these documentation styles have similar elements: selection of headings, punctuation and abbreviations, citation of references, and many other elements that are a part of a manuscript.

- **Documentation styles:**
  o **APA – American Psychological Association:** used by psychologists, anthropologists, and business managers for scientific writing.

  o **MLA – Modern Language Association:** used in English and foreign language and literature courses, as well as in other disciplines in the humanities. MLA recommends the use of a parenthetical system of documentation. Citations are in parentheses within the text to point to sources in an alphabetized list of works cited that appears at the end of the essay.

  o **Turabian/Chicago:** used by different groups of scholars in the humanities, literature, history, and the arts, and scholars in the physical, natural, and social sciences. *The Chicago Manual of Style* presents two basic documentation systems: (1) notes and bibliography and (2) author-date.

  o **CSE – Council of Science Editors:** used by students in the Biological Sciences.

On the *AP English Language* test there are multiple-choice questions that address the footnoted nonfiction passages. When you read a researched essay with documentation, especially with footnotes, you should think about the questions below:

- What type of publication is it?

  Print:

  o book
  o encyclopedia

o journal article
o magazine article
o newspaper article
o anthology
o Government publication

Nonprint:

o online journal or magazine article
o online encyclopedia
o web-based images, videos or documents
o podcast
o online database
o TV or radio program
o film
o interview
o lecture
o speech

- What is the author's full name?

- Is there more than one author?

- What is the full title (including subtitle)?

- Who is the editor/s or translators (if there is one)?

- What is the edition (if the book is a second or later edition)?

- What is the number of the volume and the total number of volumes (if the book is a multivolume work) in the series?

- What is the series name (if the book is part of a series)?

- What is the city of publication?

- Who is the Publisher?

- What is the year of publication?

- When was the webpage last updated and date viewed?

- Is it a Subscription Online Database Services (Grolier or Britannica encyclopedias, Gale Literature Resources, ABC-CLIO Social Studies, SIRS, Facts.com, CQ Library, Li, etc.)?

Questions About Annotated Material

For questions about annotated material, you need to be able to identify the information the notes reveal about the meaning of the passage and the nature of the support used. You might not recognize the format in the selection (APA, MLA, Chicago style, CSE), but knowing the exact style is not important. These questions usually appear in the following format:

- The purpose of footnote ___ is to inform the reader ____.

- The number ___ in the footnote most probably indicates ____.

- Taken as a whole, the footnotes suggest that ____.

- In line ___ of the footnote, the word ___ refers to ____.

- According to footnote ____, which of the following is the source for the quotation: ____?

- The footnotes imply all of the following about the passage EXCEPT ____.

- Which of the following is an accurate reading of footnote ____?

CHAPTER 4

AP English Language & Composition

How to Approach Multiple-Choice Questions

The multiple-choice section of the AP English Language and Composition exam is a test of your critical reading skills; the breadth and depth of the knowledge you bring to the test—vocabulary, grammar, rhetorical strategies—are measured only in your ability to apply them in your reading. The good news is that all of the answers to critical reading questions are in the excerpt; the difficulty lies in finding those answers, extracting meaning from complex, often dense, and sometimes archaic passages, and doing so under the pressure of time and without the aid of dictionaries or the Internet. Most good readers, which you probably already are, apply critical reading strategies intuitively—they deconstruct text without thinking much about what they are actually doing. It is also no accident that strong readers read a lot, almost always because they enjoy it, but the beneficial byproduct of that practice— besides the pleasure and knowledge they derive from it—is that they become very good at it. Consider a study on the role of practice in the creation of musicians. The research found that it takes 10,000 hours of practice to become an expert at playing a musical instrument, and that innate talent was only a secondary element, far less important than those hours of focused, purposeful practice. The implications of this research have been expanded to other skills: athletics, computer programming, math, dance, etc. What video game whiz kid isn't the product of thousands of hours of bleary-eyed, glued-to-the-screen practice? Just think of what he could do if those hours had been applied to practicing the piano, hitting tennis balls—or reading. Increase your reading practice and you will become a better reader, and probably a better writer as well.

This book will help you to do well on the *AP English Language and Composition* exam by helping you to become a better reader, that is, by heightening your ability to apply critical reading strategies and by focused reading practice. This may require you to fill in some of the holes in your knowledge base, increase your vocabulary, as well as work on your ability to focus and concentrate in a timed assessment. Yes, there are some test-taking strategies, even tricks, that will help you; familiarity with the types of questions on the exam will give you an advantage and a feeling of preparedness. But even these "tricks" are still really about becoming a better reader, someone who has developed the mental discipline to know what to do when faced with challenging text.

The Format of the Multiple-Choice Section

The AP English Language & Composition examination is divided into two parts: **Section I, Multiple Choice** or **critical reading** questions (45 per cent of your score) and **Section II, the Free Response** or **essay** questions (55 per cent of your score). The multiple-choice section has approximately 54 to 60 questions divided among four to six reading passages (the exact number varies from year to year), and there will be from nine to fifteen questions per reading passage. You are allowed 60 minutes for the objective portion. Although the test is geared so that most good students can finish within the time limits, the time constraints are also challenging. It is essential you do some timed practice. Note two recent changes to the multiple-choice section of the exam:

- **Change in Content:** From 2007 onward, some items in the multiple-choice section refer to documentation and citation of sources. While examinees need not memorize any particular style (e.g., MLA, Chicago, APA, etc.), they will need to use information from citations that may indeed follow a given style. Some passages—"at least one," says the College Board—will be from a published work (book, journal, periodical, etc.) that incorporates footnotes or a bibliography; the documentation questions will be based on such passages.

- **Change in Scoring:** The method of scoring the multiple-choice section has changed. Beginning in 2011, the score on the multiple-choice section will be based only on the number of questions the student answers correctly. Points will no longer be deducted for incorrect answers, and, as always, no points will be awarded for unanswered questions. Though this change certainly has implications for test-taking strategies, the formula for calculating the scores has also changed, and The College Board is expecting the distribution of scores (on the 1 to 5 final scale) to remain the same.

The Passages

The AP English Language and Composition exam is decidedly not "literary" in the sense that its sister test, the AP English Literature and Composition exam, is; thus you will **NOT** be asked to analyze fiction, poetry, or drama on Section I of the exam. The multiple-choice section of the test measures your ability to read nonfiction. It may include essays, speeches, letters, journal entries, journalistic writings, biographies, or memoirs. Other important passages on the exam include types of criticism (literary, historical, cultural, political—including satire) as well as academic writing on various subjects (history, science and nature, the social sciences, etc.). Of course you won't be reading grocery lists, the phone book, or other informational types of writing. Most of what you will read on the exam will be on some level persuasive—meant to make you think or feel a certain way, or at least make you understand how the author thinks or feels about a particular subject. Also expect the range of expository modes: description, narration, definition, cause and effect, argument, process analysis, and compare/contrast. One passage will be research-based with notes, and you may be asked a question or two about those notes.

This test is also, what a musician would call, a sight-reading test. The College Board looks for materials obscure enough not to be typically read or studied by high school students in order not to give anyone an unfair advantage on the test. While you may see a familiar writer on the test, it is highly unlikely that you will recognize an excerpt on the multiple-choice section, so you need to gain the experience necessary to approach a wide variety of reading in your preparation. In addition, it is important to understand that most of what you will see in the objective section of the exam is excerpted material, meaning that there is text that comes before and text that comes after what you are reading. This structure poses obvious difficulties for the reader, but again, always remember that the answers are in the passage. Everything you need to know about context for the purpose of this exam is provided for you; you just need to find it in the content and language of the passage. The other contextual difficulty is that the passages are almost all anonymous and obscure, so you usually don't know the writer or the time period of the piece. Anything of vital importance to the reader that can't be gleaned from the passage will be footnoted for you or presented in a brief introduction.

Finally, expect to be challenged and expect to be bored. At least one of the excerpts will be pre-twentieth century text and is extremely archaic even to avid readers. Expect difficult and archaic vocabulary. Being a twenty-first century student, you may wonder why you should be expected to know a word that was used in the seventeenth century and no longer used today. Certainly, strong readers have good vocabularies, but they also have an advanced ability to derive the meaning of a word from the context in which it is used, and the exam tests how well you do this. In addition, the length of the test, as well as the archaic and esoteric nature of some of the pieces, may challenge your ability to focus and concentrate. The exam is designed to measure your ability to read critically at the college level. Most people can read about subjects they are interested in, even if the reading level is advanced. College-level reading and research will require you to read beyond your comfort zone and apply strategies to make sense of difficult material. Reading outside one's comfort zone is a mental discipline that most of us need practice and patience to attain.

Practice

> **DIRECTIONS:** Consider the following letter written in the early 18th century by the Native American leader Canassatego, in response to an offer of free education at the College of William and Mary presented to his people by the Virginia colony. Think about how all the elements discussed in this section come together to inform your understanding of purpose, audience, style, and tone.

We know you highly esteem the kind of learning taught in these colleges, and the maintenance of our young men, while with you, would be very expensive to you. We are convinced, therefore, that you mean to do us good

5

by your proposal; and we thank you heartily. But you who are so wise must know that different nations have different conceptions of things; and you will not therefore take it amiss, if our ideas of this kind of education happens not to be the same with yours. We have had some experience of it. Several of our young people were formerly brought up in the colleges of the northern provinces; they were instructed in all your sciences; but, when they came

10

back to us, they were bad runners, ignorant of every means of living in the woods, unable to bear either cold or hunger, know neither how to build a cabin, take a deer, or kill an enemy, spoke our language imperfectly, were therefore neither fit for hunters, warriors, nor counselors, they were totally good for nothing. We are however not the less obliged for your kind offer,

15

tho' we decline accepting it; and to show our grateful sense of it, if the gentlemen of Virginia shall send us a dozen of their sons, we will take great care of their education, instruct them in all we know, and make men of them.

1. What can we infer about the intended audience? We know by the introductory material that the leaders of the Virginia colony, who had made this offer, are the intended audience. What assumptions does Canassatego make about his audience?

Canassatego assumes by their offer that they value their culture and education over his, and even more arrogantly, they assume he does as well. His knowledge and assumptions about his audience along with his purpose inform his approach to this piece.

2. His explicit purpose is to reject the offer; however, what is the implied purpose of this letter?

Canassatego asserts his cultural pride here, challenging the ethnocentric paradigm of the European colonists who assume the Native Americans will quickly accept the opportunity to become more like them. He wants the colonists to see their arrogant offer for what it is.

3. How does Canassatego craft his tone to achieve his purpose?

Canassatego's letter is satiric; in other words, he uses humor to make his point. He begins his letter in the form of a thank-you note. Using the most cordial and polite language and noting the generosity of the offer by acknowledging how highly the colonists "esteem the kind of learning taught in these colleges" and how "very expensive" their education is, he thanks them "heartily." He maintains this cordiality and respect, referring to his audience as "you who are so wise," even as he begins to point out the differences in the two cultures. When he lists the specific examples of the proud skills the young men were deficient in, the true purpose of the letter becomes apparent, his mocking assertion that "they were totally good for nothing." He concludes his letter—still maintaining the polite, but now clearly mocking tone— by offering to educate the sons of the colonists and "make men of them" and implying that their education is a less than masculine attainment. Canassatego achieves his purpose through his use of tone; his criticism of the Colonists' education is clear, yet relatively gentle, when placed in this humorous context. He certainly chooses his language and tone carefully, possibly thinking that expressing anger or outrage might offend or provoke the colonists.

4. How does Canassatego's style help him to achieve his purpose?

As mentioned above, Canassatego outwardly maintains the formal, yet gracious style, of the official thank-you letter from the leader of one great nation to another. He presents himself as an equal by referring to the differences between people of "different nations" and using the first-person plural *"we."* Using the word *"we"* establishes to his audience that he is a leader, a representative of his people. Canassatego's command of sophisticated syntax and other stylistic elements demonstrates to his audience that, though he does not see the value of his people acquiring a European education, they are in no way incapable of acquiring it. In addition, he uses syntax to emphasize two very important points. The first, "they were totally good for nothing," occurs as the culminating point after he catalogues a long list of the deficiencies of a college education for his young men. While it might not be essential to know that this construction is a periodic sentence, it is important to understand how this structure works to create meaning here. The other example is, of course, in the last line, another periodic sentence, where the final parallel construction concludes the final insult, "and make men of them."

Grammar on the Multiple-Choice Section

The AP English Language and Composition exam does ask you to apply some grammar skills, but it has de-emphasized much of the terminology you learned in school. What the test measures is your ability to apply your understanding of English grammar and syntax in context and deciphering complex language. Good readers intuitively understand sentence structure, but anyone can be challenged by a hundred-word sentence written over three-hundred years ago, or even a Faulkner line written in the twentieth century. An understanding of some grammatical elements and applying them as a reading strategy will help you when faced with what feels like impossibly complex syntax.

- Find the subject and the verb of the main (or independent) clause. The subject and the verb, often just two words, is the grammatical essence of all sentences. If you can isolate them, work from there to decide what the other words, phrases, and clauses are telling you about the subject and verb. Since the independent clause is grammatically the most important part of the sentence, it is often rhetorically the most important part of the sentence as well. If you have a compound sentence, you will have more than one main clause of grammatically equal value. If you have a complex sentence—one with at least one subordinate (dependent) clause in addition to an independent clause—the subordinate (dependent) clause is *subordinated* structurally in the sentence, so it usually plays a subordinate or dependent role in meaning as well. Let's take that complicated (technically *complex* if you know the grammar jargon) sentence from The Declaration of Independence. I'll write it out completely for you this time:

> "We hold these truths to be self evident: that all men are created equal; that they are endowed by their creator with certain inalienable rights; that among these rights are life, liberty, and the pursuit of happiness; that to secure these rights, governments are instituted among men, deriving their just powers from the consent of the governed; that whenever any form of government becomes destructive of these ends, it is the right of the people to alter or to abolish it, and to institute new government, laying its foundation on such principles, and organizing its powers in such form, as to them shall seem most likely to effect their safety and happiness."

This sentence contains 112 words! So, where do you begin? Well, what is the main clause? "We hold these truths to be self-evident...." The rest of the sentence following the colon is a series of subordinate or dependent clauses that lists the "truths" Jefferson says are "self-evident." Jefferson organizes the clauses for you, using parallel structure as we discussed earlier; but, he clearly separates the clauses from each other with semi-colons as well. Now, some of the subordinate clauses contain other complicating phrases, but you can look at these subordinate clauses as separate units now, separate units that all exist in service to illustrating the self-evident truths. Will they ask you to identify the phrases and clauses in the technical way I just described? No, but what they might ask you is a question such as this one: How do the clauses beginning with "that" function in the sentence? And now you know; they illustrate the "truths." You also might see a question such as this one:

The series of dependent clauses beginning with "that" do all of the following EXCEPT

(A) They create a parallelism that adds coherence to the sentence.

(B) They present a list of items exemplifying the "truths."

(C) They assert the concepts Jefferson says that declaration will assume.

(D) They incorporate abstract nouns and adjectives to help illustrate the truths.

(E) They employ a series of metaphors to illustrate the "truths."

And **(E)** is the bad choice, or in this case good choice, because you are looking for the one that *doesn't* belong. Notice that the grammar you employed to deconstruct the sentence in order to understand it was exactly the grammar you needed to answer the questions.

- **Pronoun reference:** It is essential when you read that you know what nouns the pronouns are referring to in the selection. These nouns are technically called the antecedents. Though it is not important you know this term for this test, you do need the skill it represents. If you are finding, as you work through complicated syntax, that the pronouns are confusing, slow down and puzzle them out. Let's again look at the line from The Declaration of Independence. The antecedent of the first two pronouns, "they" in line 2 and "their" in line 2, can easily be identified; they both refer back to "men." It is the pronoun "their" in the fifth line, "governments are instituted among men, deriving their just powers from the consent of the governed," that presents a problem. The pronoun refers to "governments" (not "men") who are "deriving their just powers from the consent of the governed"; if you do not identify this concept, it will be difficult to understand the passage. The pronouns, "it" and "its" in line 8, may also be problematic. The "it" refers back to the "form of government," the one that becomes "destructive of these ends," while the "its" refers to the "new government." Take the time when you are reading to sort these out to support your comprehension, and be aware that there may be questions about pronoun reference on the multiple-choice section of the test.

- **Phrases:** Phrases are groups of words that go together but do not have subjects and verbs like clauses do. We could talk all day about phrases, but it is important to know that often phrases have modifiers. And when placed correctly, phrases are usually near the word they are modifying. For example, "laying its foundation" modifies "government" and "on such principles" modifies "foundation." Appositive phrases occur right after a noun and rename or describe that noun. It is recommended that you draw an arrow back to the noun modified. This annotation will help you stay focused on the passage and makes it easier to identify if you want to refer to it later when you are answering the questions.

- **Punctuation:** Use punctuation to help you understand what you read. For example, colons introduce clarifying material or a list illustrating the text before the colon. The colon after the main clause in the line from the Declaration introduces clarifying material in the form of a list of subordinate clauses. You can usually replace a colon with the phrase "in other words: "We hold these truths to be self-evident" *in other words* "that all men are created equal," etc. The semi-colons are useful here because they create a strong separation between each subordinate clause. Semi-colons connect independent clauses that are closely related in meaning. When faced with very dense text, use all the punctuation to help you hear what you are reading in your mind. Practice reading difficult text out loud with the expression the punctuation implies, and you will improve your reading comprehension.

Types of Questions

Overall Meaning, Purpose, or Style

Often, one of the first few questions following the passage test your understanding of the passage as a whole: why did the author write the work? what is he or she attempting to accomplish? Questions about the overall style of writing often come at the end of the piece. These questions usually appear in the following format:

- As a whole, the passage can best be described as ____.

- The passage in its entirety can best be described as ____.

- The author's primary concern in this passage is to ____.

- The passage describes ____.

- The primary function of the passage is to ____.

- The primary goal of the passage is to ____.

- What is the point of the statement in line ___ as it applies to the passage as a whole?

- All of the following can be said about the author's purpose EXCEPT ____.

- Which of the following are true according to the passage? (The question will state three possibilities and you will be asked which combination of these choices is true.)

- The style of the passage can best be characterized as _____ (often the answers will include two words, i.e., formal and pedantic, lyrical and ceremonial, erudite and allusive, etc.).

- All of the following can be said about the author's style EXCEPT _____.

- Which of the following sentences (from the passage) best represents the author's main point in the passage?

- Which of the following is true about the author's style? (The question will state three possibilities and you will be asked which combination of these choices is true.)

- All of the following is true about the passage EXCEPT ____.

- The passage characterizes _____ as ____.

- The passage implies all of the following about ____ EXCEPT ____.

- The overall effect of the passage is to ____.

- The passage is meant to ____ (define, explain, examine, refute, persuade, describe).

Questions About the Author or Audience

For questions about the author or audience, you are asked to make observations about the speaker or author and his or her audience. You are asked to judge how the author views himself or herself, what effect the subject has on the author, what is important to the author, and how he or she obtains/has obtained information about the world. Questions about the audience ask you to draw inferences about the text to decide who specifically is being targeted, what assumptions the author is making about the audience, and what strategies the author uses to appeal to this audience. These questions usually appear in the following format:

- In lines _____ the author depicts himself/herself as _____.

- The author believes that ____.

- In lines _____ the author depicts himself/herself as all of the following EXCEPT _____.

- For the author, _____ (subject) has the effect of _____.

- For the author, _____ (subject) is _____ (evaluation of meaning or importance).

- Which of the following is probably the main source of the author's knowledge of ____?

- In "____" (quotation containing action or description) the author is _____ (conclusion about that action or description).

- The author would probably consider himself to be which of the following? (The choices might include these following adjectives: a cynic, skeptic, romantic, realist, idealist, pragmatist, etc.)

- The author probably assumes the audience is ____.

- This piece would most likely appeal to (or is meant to appeal to) ____.

- The author uses _____ to appeal to the audience's ____ (emotions, sense of justice, patriotism, etc.)

- Which of the following does the author probably assume about the audience? (The question will state three possibilities and you will be asked which combination of these choices is true.)

- The author probably assumes all of the following about the audience EXCEPT ____.

Questions About Tone or Attitude

For questions about tone or attitude, you are asked to determine or make judgments about the attitude of the speaker or author toward the subject being described or discussed. You may be asked to do the following:

- identify a shift

- analyze the effect of the author's attitude

- decide what the author believes

- determine the atmosphere/mood

- determine the tone/atmosphere

These questions usually appear in the following format:

- The tone of the passage can best be described as _____ (often the answers include two words, i.e., supercilious and scornful, reverent and respectful, scholarly and didactic, apathetic and cynical, etc.).

- The shift in point of view has the effect of _____.

- The author's attitude toward _____ can be described as _____.

- The speaker assumes that the audience's attitude will _____.

- The author believes/apparently believes _____.

- The point of view indicated in _____ is that of _____.

- The atmosphere is one of _____.

- In "_____" which of the following most suggests a humorous attitude on the part of the author?

- The passage is an appeal for _____.

Questions About Word Choice and Selection of Details

For questions about word choice and details, you are asked to analyze the fine points of language and specific word choice. You are asked to determine the meaning of a word/phrase/sentence, identify elements of fiction, analyze important details or quotations, determine meaning of a word or phrase from the context, identify parts of a sentence, such as subject of a verb or antecedent of a pronoun, or analyze the style of a passage.

Sometimes, you will be asked to identify the meaning of a word in the context of the paragraph. You may not have seen the word before, but from your understanding of the writer's intent, you should be able to infer the author's implied meaning.

For example, read the following paragraph:

> Paris is a beautiful city, perhaps the most beautiful on Earth. Long, broad avenues are lined with seventeenth and eighteenth century apartments, office buildings, and cafés. Flowers give the city a rich and varied look. The bridges and the river lend an air of lightness and grace to the whole urban landscape.
>
> In this paragraph, "rich" most nearly means
>
> (A) wealthy
>
> (B) polluted
>
> (C) prismatic
>
> (D) dull
>
> (E) abundant

If you chose (C), "prismatic," you would be right. Although the word *rich* literally means "wealthy" ("wealthy" is its denotation, its literal meaning), here the writer means more than the word's literal meaning and seems to be highlighting the variety and color that the flowers add to the avenues—that is, richness in a figurative sense.

The writer is using a non-literal meaning, or connotation, that we associate with the word *rich* to show what s/he means. When we think of something "rich," we also think of abundance and variety and color. If the word you are being asked to define is a common word, suspect the meaning is either a non-literal or a secondary meaning of a word. Don't make assumptions; always refer back to the passage for vocabulary in context questions. These questions usually appear in the following format:

- Which of the following best describes what _____ symbolizes?

- The _____ sentence/paragraph/section is unified by metaphors of _____.

- "_____" signals a shift from _____ to _____.

- The _____ paragraph employs which of the following?

- The statement "_____" is best described as _____.

- The use of "_____" instead of "_____" accomplishes which of the following?

- In line _____ the author emphasizes "_____" because _____.

- The use of "_____" suggests most strongly _____.

- The major purpose of the word/phrase/statement "_____" is to make clear that _____.

- By "_____," the speaker means/most probably means _____.

- The mention of _____ is appropriate to the development of the argument because _____.

- In the sentence/paragraph/section, the speaker seeks to draw attention to _____ by stressing _____.

- In the context of the passage as a whole, the _____ (paragraph/word/phrase/sentence) "_____" is best interpreted to mean _____.

- In relation to _____, which of the following best describes the function of the ___ (word/phrase/sentence/paragraph)?

- Which of the following best describes the _____ (word/phrase/sentence)?

- Which of the following is an example of "_____" mentioned in line _____?

- All of the following qualities are present in the passage EXCEPT _____.

- The primary purpose of ____ (selection of details) is to ____.

- The author uses the word ____ in order to ____.

- In line __, "____" modifies "____." (Might be an adjective or adverb, or might be an adjective or adverb phrase or clause.)

Questions About Grammar and Sentence Construction

For questions about grammar and construction, you are asked to identify how words work together in groups. You are asked to analyze syntax, identify sentence construction, or analyze relationships of sentences or phrases. These questions usually appear in the following format:

- The syntax of sentence/sentences beginning with _____ in lines __ serves to _____.

- The phrase/clause _____ in line ___ are describing _____.

- "_____" (pronoun) in line __ refers to _____ (the antecedent).

- What is the function of the two (or three) _____ (words/phrases/clauses)?

- Despite its length, the _____ sentence remains coherent chiefly because of its use of _____.

- The subject of the verb "_____" is which of the following?

- The sentence beginning ___ in lines __ is characterized by all of the following EXCEPT _____. (The question might reference parallelism, complex structure, active verbs, etc. These terms might be mixed with choices that speak to meaning rather than structure.)

- Which best describes the syntax of lines ___.

- Which of the following is grammatically parallel to _____?

- Which of the following best describes the function of the _____ (phrase, clause, parenthetical comment, series of phrases, parallel construction) in lines __?

Questions About Progression of Thought and Organization

- In relation to the first sentence, the second sentence serves to _____.

- The (particular sentence) moves from _____.

- In relation to the rest of the passage, the _____ paragraph provides/serves to _____.

- The passage develops from _____ (a specific example to a universal truth, a universal truth to its specific examples, a universal truth to a discussion of its exception, an idea or event and its causes, an idea or event and its effects).

- Which of the following best describes the relationship between the first paragraph and the second paragraph?

- Paragraphs _____ and _____ are unified by _____.

Questions About Development

- The rhetorical purpose of lines __ is to ____ (assert, suggest, contrast, encourage, prompt, qualify, provide, etc.)

- The primary imagery of the passage is that of ____.

- The passage is developed through ____ (a series of anecdotes, an extended metaphor, a description, an analogy, etc)

- The development of the passage can best be described as the ____ (process of…, examination of…, presentation of…, illustration of…).

- The ____ paragraph is significant in that the author ____ (cites, outlines, traces, describes, utilizes, qualifies, etc.)

- The examples in the passage are meant to illustrate ____.

- The allusion in lines __ serves to ____.

- The purpose of the questions beginning in lines __ is to ____.

- All of the following antitheses may be found EXCEPT ____.

- The relationship between ____ and ____ is explained primarily by the use of ____.

- The author uses ____ as an example of ____.

- The author's discussion of ____ depends on which of the following?

- The type of argument employed in ____ by ____ is ____.

- The pattern of exposition exemplified in the passage is best described as ____.

- In describing ____, the author emphasizes ____.

- The principal contrast (or comparison) in the passage is between ____.

- The author mentions ____ as examples of ____.

- Which of the following does the author use to illustrate ____?

- Which of the following best explains/supports the author's claim that ____?

Questions About Inferences

For questions about inferences, you are asked to draw conclusions based on context clues. You are asked to determine relationships or identify references. These questions usually appear in the following format:

- It can be inferred that ____ is/are ____.

- It can be inferred from the description of ____ that ____ is ____.

- It can be inferred that _____ refers to _____.

- It can be inferred from the passage that _____ occurs for which of the following reasons.

Questions About General Conclusions

For questions about general conclusions, you are asked to predict outcomes and make inferences. You are asked to determine what the author would think about a certain subject, what the author wants us to do, or what the author would/would not advise us. These questions usually appear in the following format:

- The author believes that we should _____.

- According to the author, _____ should _____ because _____.

- Which of the following would the author be LEAST/MOST likely to encourage?

- If one were to take the author's advice, one should _____.

- The effectiveness of the final paragraph (sentence) is primarily the result of _____.

Tricky Question Formats

There are two formats specific to this test that sometimes causes the student to misread the question: the "EXCEPT" questions and the questions that provide you with three possibilities for your evaluation. The "EXCEPT" questions are only tricky if you miss the word *EXCEPT*. Though the screaming uppercase presentation might suggest otherwise, students often miss the "EXCEPT" and choose an answer that is true of the passage, rather than one that is not. Here is an example using the famous Jefferson quotation:

In lines ___ of The Declaration of Independence, Jefferson incorporates all of the following EXCEPT

    (A)   parallel syntax
    (B)   a complex sentence
    (C)   a cumulative sentence
    (D)   abstract diction
    (E)   figurative language

The answer is (E); there is no figurative language in the line. If you missed the word *EXCEPT*, you might have chosen (A) because the line includes parallel syntax. Be aware that this format is a frequent question style because it is used to assess your understanding of various aspects of the passage. If you find yourself missing these questions in your practice, discipline yourself to mark them as they occur. This annotation will help you pay closer attention so you will not misread the questions or help you identify the question quickly if you choose to return to the questions later.

The "three possibilities" questions are just like any other question, except they offer you three possibilities about an aspect of the passage to consider in isolation or in combination. These questions are problematic because several of the answers may be correct, not just the best answer. Here is an example, again, from Jefferson.

Jefferson uses which of the following in lines __ of The Declaration of Independence?

    I.   parallel syntax
    II.   abstract diction
    III. figurative language

    (A) I only
    (B) II only
    (C) III only
    (D) I and II only
    (E) I, II, and III

The correct answer is (D), I and II only; however, the question is tricky because (A) and (B) are not completely wrong, but they are not the *best* answer. Any answer that included III cannot be correct because it is not *completely* correct. These questions consume the most time. Most students find it helpful to initially skip these questions and return to them later. It is not worth missing several questions that you can easily answer for the possibility of answering one, difficult, time-consuming question correctly.

Multiple-Choice Test-Taking Preparation and Strategies

Anticipate and Annotate: Annotating the test helps you focus and actively engage with the reading. Now that you have read the preparation material, you should begin developing a sense of the types of questions you will be asked on the multiple-choice section of the test. While you read the passages, mark items that will support your comprehension and may be useful later. You'll be surprised as you work on the practice tests, how interrelated these objectives are, especially if you are a visual or a kinesthetic learner. But, just underlining items is not useful—develop your own shorthand to mark the important concepts and comment on what you are highlighting in the margins. The following are items you should mark in the text:

- **Important points:** Briefly paraphrase or mark explicit statements of purpose, assertions, or conclusions.

- **Transition words and phrases:** Transition words and phrases are essential to your understanding of the writer's progression of thought. It is important to isolate words and/or phrases with a special mark (a circle or box perhaps). When asked how one paragraph or idea relates to another, the answer will be obvious and quick to find if you use this technique.

- **Expository modes:** Be looking for these expository modes—description, definition, narration, cause and effect, process analysis. They may be the dominant mode or they may be a secondary mode used in combination with others.

- **Figurative Language:** Mark all examples of simile, metaphor, analogy, and obvious hyperbole and label them in the margins near the place they occur. If you are not sure the type of figurative language, just write your shorthand abbreviation for figurative language.

- **Tone:** Did the writer move from humorous to serious? Understanding to critical? Mark the place where a shift in tone occurs.

- **Imagery:** Mark imagery and comment on the character of the imagery in the margins.

- **Allusions:** Similarly, mark all allusions.

- **Anecdotes:** Mark them

- **Examples:** Number them if your author offers you several examples to support the point.

- **Alliteration, repetition of words, onomatopoeia:** Mark them.

- **Parallel Syntax:** Mark the beginning of each parallel item and write a parallel symbol in the margin.

- **Incongruity:** Mark examples of diction, sentence lengths or structures, images, etc., which are strikingly different from the rest of the passage, and comment in the margin.

- **Grammar:** Mark grammar that will help you. Find the subject and verb in long, dense sentences if you are having difficulty understanding the key ideas in the passage. Find the antecedents to any confusing pronouns.

- **Specialized sentence forms:** Periodic, cumulative, balanced, inverted sentences—mark them if you recognize them. More importantly, be aware that the writer made a conscientious decision to use stylized sentence forms; ask yourself why.

Keep in mind that not all of these items will be important in every passage. The more you practice annotation, the better you will get at it, and the more useful your marking will become. Marking can be especially helpful in the "EXCEPT" questions because they may require you to reread a big portion of the passage. If you have already marked items in the text, you will be able to quickly eliminate choices without rereading. Before they read the passage, some students have found it helpful to look at the questions that refer to specific line numbers and mark those lines, so they know to give them special attention as they read. You may want to experiment with this approach as you complete the practice tests to see if it works for you.

Process of Elimination: Every guide that prepares you for a multiple-choice test will tell you to eliminate those answers that you are sure are wrong. Every answer you eliminate raises your odds of answering correctly by twenty percent.

Distracters: Every good multiple-choice test has distracters meant to test your critical reading skills. Here are some typical distracters on this test.

- *Opposites:* There is often an answer choice that is the exact <u>opposite</u> of what you are looking for. Students will choose these answers because they misread the question, they misread the answers, or they misread the passage. There is probably not much you can do about a passage misreading at this point, but be careful to read the question as carefully as you read the passage. The test is difficult enough without making these kinds of errors. Again, practice will train you to avoid making this mistake. Try marking key words in the questions to keep you focused.

- *Almost right:* Most likely your answer choices will include items that are true about the passage, but are not the answer to the specific question being asked. Again, familiarity with and careful reading of the questions is essential.

- *Vocabulary in context:* Don't assume you know the meaning—always check back in the passage. If the word you are being asked about is easy, suspect they are looking for the secondary or archaic meaning of the word.

Know thyself: One of the benefits of preparation is that it allows you to learn about yourself as a reader and as a test taker. Are you a person who falls for the distracters? Taking practice tests will help you understand your strengths and weaknesses. If you consistently choose the distracter, be aware of this habit and analyze the problem. Are you missing questions because you don't know the rhetorical terms? If so, you need to learn them. Also, if you find yourself changing your mind from the right to a wrong answer, trust your first instinct.

Review the practice tests: Remember, quality over quantity. Don't just take the tests and consider yourself to have practiced. After you finish taking and correcting a practice test, read the answer explanations carefully to understand your mistakes and delve back into the passage to deepen your understanding of the questions and the passage. In fact, read the explanations for the questions you answered correctly, making certain you fully understand why they are correct. It will be helpful to be able to intellectualize the reason for an answer that you merely intuit correctly on the practice test. Use this opportunity to improve your test-taking vocabulary. Know your terms as well as the general vocabulary that occurs in the questions and answer choices (don't worry so much about the vocabulary in the passage). Look up words you don't know after you have corrected the test—even on the questions you answered correctly—and learn those words. Finally, you shouldn't try to complete an entire test at once early in your preparation. Complete one multiple-choice passage in a sitting and spend quality time with it, learning it deeply. You should be increasing your knowledge and skill with every passage you read. Keep a vocabulary notebook and spend time learning the words you don't know.

Timing: When you begin the test, quickly look to see how many passages and how many questions there are, so you can pace yourself appropriately. Some passages are longer and more difficult than others, but in general you should divide your time evenly between the number of passages on the test. **Do not spend too much time on one question.** All the questions, the easy and the difficult, count the same, so it is a waste of valuable time to labor too long over one question. Do your best and move on. Practice will greatly improve your ability to do this; but remember, if you can't understand the passages and answer the questions without the pressure of time, you will never be able to with a time pressure. So, when you first start practicing, do so untimed. Focus on understanding the text, annotating, and familiarizing yourself with the questions. Then, as the test date gets closer, practice with the time constraint.

If you are running out of time: If you only have a few minutes left, but you have read the passage, skim the questions to find the ones you can answer most easily without having to go back into the passage. Make your best guess on the others. If you haven't read the passage and you don't have time to, look for the questions that ask you about specific line numbers, vocabulary in context, grammar, etc., and try to answer some of those. Guess on the rest, but don't leave any blank.

If you have almost completely run out of time: For the first time on the 2011 exam, there will be no deduction for wrong answers, so do not leave any questions blank. This change should alter your strategy in only one situation, when you are running out of time. If you have a minute left and you have questions you cannot possibly get to, randomly fill in the blanks so that all the questions are answered.

Get in a reading state of mind: You should spend a year reading to prepare for this test, but in the last few months before the big test day make sure your brain is engaged at full capacity. Turn off the TV, the iPod, your cell phone, and video games and set aside time every day to read, beyond your normal school requirements. Sit in a quiet place, without interruptions, for at least a half hour (an hour would be better) and read. Be focused—**no electronics!** This practice will improve your speed, comprehension, and ability to concentrate.

Be well-rested and well-fed: This is a long, grueling test that demands stamina. Get some rest the entire week before. Even if your normal routine is to wake up only a few minutes before you leave for school, get up early on test day. Take a brisk walk and eat a good breakfast. You want to be wide awake, ready for the adrenaline to kick in when you start the test. Most schools will break after the multiple-choice section, so bring a light snack and drink for that short break.

CHAPTER 5

AP English Language & Composition

Chapter 5

The Essays

The free-response section of the English Language and Composition exam is composed of three prompts, for which you are given 135 minutes in total to complete. Currently there are three types of free-response questions on the AP exam with some subset variations within these categories. These include the **Synthesis Essay**, the **Rhetorical Analysis** or **Language Analysis Essay**, and the **Argument Essay**.

Just like reading, writing is a skill that needs to be developed and practiced. Ideally, your English classes have been a continuous cycle of writing, editing, revising, and feedback, and your other content area courses have emphasized writing as well. There is no substitute for this kind of instruction and practice in your development as a writer. However, the time constraints on the AP exam add an extra level of difficulty because the exam asks you to address complex prompts without the benefit of the writing process most good writers rely on. So, while you may be a fine writer—truly advanced for your grade—on-demand, timed writing is challenging and stressful for most people, and it is a skill that needs to be practiced before the exam.

The English Language and Composition exam assumes that you are fluent in standard English syntax and grammar and that you are able to organize your thoughts in coherent, well-expressed expository prose. Most students will be amply familiar with the standard thesis and support essay with its introduction, body paragraphs, and conclusion. Beyond an ability to use this basic form, however, students need to be aware of the different stylistic effects created by different syntactic and lexical choices. That is to say, when you choose a particular word or construct a very short or very complex sentence, you need to be in control of your choices, realizing how these choices affect your reader. This awareness is useful in both the analysis *and* creation of expository prose.

Scoring the Essays

Essays on the English Language and Composition exam are scored on a scale of 0 to 9 points, with the point count and standards being tailored to suit each essay question. Two trained readers score each paper. If the scores of the two readers differ by more than one point, a third reader is brought in. Many hours are spent training readers so that they can score different kinds of responses to the essays with great consistency. Though the essays are read quickly, they are read accurately and thoroughly!

The readers understand that these are first-draft essays, so they are not expecting perfection. Content counts much more than grammar, word choice, or spelling;

however, seldom does an essay with even as few as three or four significant errors receive the top score. It is wise, therefore, to proofread and correct your writing before going on to the next topic. Recasting (rewording) some of your sentences is acceptable, but make sure your paper is legible. You must address the given task carefully: do not deviate from the topic or dwell too long on one point. You should attend to subtle nuances of language in your essay. The mediocre paper fails to identify and to analyze subtleties of meaning. Better-quality papers recognize and respond to the emotional shadings of the topic. The scores are usually given as follows:

Scores of 9–8: These are superior essays. They have a clear statement of position, thoughtful support, convincing examples, and stylistic maturity (sentence structure, diction, organization). Although there may be a few minor grammar or spelling errors, the author demonstrates a superior control of language in writing the essay.

Scores of 7–6: These are proficient essays. They have a clear thesis which is supported by specific and convincing proof, but these essays are less nuanced, sophisticated, and/or original than the 8/9 essays. The author's writing is less mature and thus has occasional lapses of diction, tone, syntax, or organization. Although there may be errors of grammar and spelling, the author demonstrates a solid control of language. Very well-written papers with "6" content may earn a 7, and "7" content essays with weaker writing may earn a 6.

Score of 5: These are mediocre, but adequate, essays. The thesis may not be quite clear, the argument not as well developed, and/or the organization may not be especially effective. The writing generally conveys the author's ideas, but the style is less mature and there are some grammatical and spelling errors. A score of 5 is considered the lowest passing score an AP Reader can give an essay.

Score of 4: These essays are judged as not adequate. Though 4 essays tend to follow a standard multi-paragraph thesis and support format, the paragraphs tend to be short (three or four sentences) indicating a lack of adequate development. Essays will receive a score no higher than 4 if they do *any one* of the following:

  (a) oversimplify or overgeneralize the issues;

  (b) present a misreading or a partial misreading of the presented text;

  (c) substitute simpler tasks such as paraphrasing rather than arguing a point or analyzing a problem or a text;

  (d) write only in general terms, ignoring fine distinctions;

  (e) fail to discuss the issue completely satisfactorily;

  (f) mismanage the evidence;

(g) contain insufficient details;

(h) fail to establish the importance to the writer;

(i) treat only one aspect of a two-sided issue;

(j) cite examples but fail to consider the consequences;

(k) cite stylistic techniques but fail to explain their effect or impact on the author's purpose;

(l) characterize the passage without analyzing the language;

(m) display immature or inconsistent control of syntax, diction, and/or mechanics. Though the prose in these essays generally conveys the writers' ideas, the syntax may be awkward, repetitive, and/or overly simplistic; the diction may be immature or inappropriate; and basic spelling and punctuation rules are at times lacking.

Scores of 3–2: These are weak essays. They lack clear organization and adequate support, the writing style is simplistic, and there are frequent grammar and spelling errors.

Score of 1: These are poor essays. Although they may mention the question, they lack clarity, have little or no evidence, and contain consistent grammar and spelling errors. They are badly written, unacceptably brief, or off topic.

Your Score

You need to score an average of 5 on your three essays and at least score 50% correct on the multiple-choice section to earn an overall score of 3, or "qualified," on the AP English Language and Composition exam. Many schools accept a 3 for college credit, but some do not.

Types of Essays

The Synthesis Essay

From 2007 onward, the free-response section of the exam contains, as one of three mandatory questions, an essay that asks students to synthesize ideas from various sources to either support an argument or analyze an issue. To synthesize means to combine various components into a new whole, so for the synthesis prompt, you will be asked to read five to eight brief sources on a topic of some controversy in which differing sides will be presented. At least one of the sources will be visual: a photograph, chart, editorial cartoon, graph, advertisement, etc. Essentially, this is meant to be a facsimile of a research paper, without the actual research since you are provided with the sources. A 15-minute reading period is provided to accommodate the additional required reading for this prompt. The synthesis prompt runs the entire content-area gamut, so expect just about any topic that might be controversial. Recent topics have included the funding of space exploration, the proposed abolishment of the penny, and the use of information technologies in schools.

We see two basic types of questions on the synthesis prompt. The first is primarily persuasive: you will be asked to defend, challenge, or offer a qualified position on an argument. A qualified position is one in which you fall somewhere in-between the two extremes, accepting merit and problems with both sides, and offering a compromise of the two. Qualified positions show off your ability to understand the complexity of an issue; however, they can be tricky. If not handled skillfully, a qualified response can sound weak and ambivalent rather than nuanced. A strong thesis statement asserting your intent to pursue a qualified position is essential. Here is an example of this kind of prompt:

> In most states, the legal age for obtaining a driver's license is sixteen, but in response to a recent increase in accidents caused by teen drivers, some state legislatures are considering the merits of raising the driving age to eighteen.
>
> Read the following sources (including the introductory information) carefully. Then, in an essay that synthesizes at least three of the sources, develop an argument that agrees, disagrees, or offers a qualified position on raising the driving age to eighteen.

A second type of synthesis prompt asks you to analyze and/or evaluate the issues surrounding a controversy. A sample prompt would look something like this:

> In most states, the legal age for obtaining a drivers license is sixteen, but in response to a recent increase in accidents caused by teen drivers, some state legislatures are considering the merits of raising the driving age to eighteen.
>
> Read the following sources (including the introductory information) carefully. Then, in an essay that synthesizes at least three of the sources, develop a position about what issues should be considered most important in making a decision about raising the driving age to eighteen.

Notice that we have the same topic, but a very different kind of prompt. Your number one objective on this (and any other AP free-response question) is to **address the prompt.** If you are asked to do B, but you instead do A, you are dead in the water before you even start, no matter how inspired your essay is.

In addition to not addressing the specific prompt, the other trap students fall into is merely summarizing the sources rather than using them to support a position. Don't just take your reader on a tour of the sources—your argument needs to be central in this essay. Finally, make sure you cite your sources either by their titles or by the descriptions in the parentheses.

Questions about the Synthesis Prompt

May I draw on my own knowledge and experience in my essay? Yes you may, but you still need to cite at least three of the provided sources in your essay. Consider using a personal experience, local issue, or historical or literary example as an interesting introduction to your essay if the perfect one comes to you. If not, don't worry about it; you will get a high score if you do a good job with the sources you have on the exam.

Should I use more than three sources in my response? You can but you don't need to. Discussing fewer sources well is better than giving us just a cursory glance at all of the sources. Remember, time is a factor as well. You have three essays to write and only 135 minutes to write them.

Should I read all the sources, or just focus on the ones that support the position I want to take to save time? The College Board advises you to read all the sources, reserving judgment until you have completed all of them. This makes sense for a couple of reasons. First, you likely will not know enough about the topic to have an informed position, so you will need the sources to develop one—as much as you can in an hour anyway. Second, the best available sources might not be the ones that support the position you want to take. Given your limited time to think and respond, it might be safer to just go where the sources lead you. Remember, this essay is essentially an exercise—it is not a measure of your value system, nor is it a forum for your political or social views, so it is perfectly acceptable to argue something you don't necessarily believe in this context. Unlike the people who read your college admissions essay, the AP readers are not trying to get to know you here; they are evaluating your ability to read, think, and write critically.

Should I acknowledge the sources that contradict my opinion? Higher-scoring papers often acknowledge the complexity of the issue by including some discussion of the opposing side. The danger is that less mature writers can produce papers that appear indecisive and unfocused rather than nuanced and sophisticated. Do this, but only if you have practiced it and are confident you can do it well. Try this approach:

- **Introduction:** State your thesis statement. "While concern for public safety is a compelling reason to consider raising the driving age from sixteen to eighteen, we should keep the law the way it is because raising the driving age is unlikely to ultimately reduce the number of serious accidents on the road."

- **First Body Paragraph:** Briefly discuss motivation for the discussion— probably the number of sixteen and seventeen year olds involved in accidents as well as the damage to innocent people and property. Be sure, however, to not overdo it. Just show that you understand why the public is concerned.

- **Second Body Paragraph and Beyond:** Discuss the reasons why raising the age won't improve safety. I don't know what those are, but I'm sure they are in the sources.

- **Conclusion:** Offer a compromise, perhaps. Don't change the age but improve driver education and place more restrictions on young drivers.

Things to keep in mind:

- Make sure the thesis statement is strong and emphatic, keeping your main point in the independent clause and the acknowledgment of the other side in the subordinate clause.

- Emphasize the shift to your main point with a strong topic sentence in the third paragraph. For example: "Despite these legitimate concerns for public safety, the evidence shows that raising the driving age is not the answer."

- Make sure you spend significantly more time on your main point that on the opposing side.

- Stay focused on the task at hand. If you decide to go in a particular direction, you are restricted in the evidence you can use. For example, with this particular thesis statement, you need to focus on the safety issue. While the argument that teens need to drive to get to after-school jobs supports your desire to keep the law the same, it muddies your safety argument, so it doesn't really fit. In fact, this evidence implies that teens really are problematic drivers, but that the benefits outweigh the risks. If you want to use this evidence, make sure your thesis statement supports its inclusion in your essay.

What style issues should I consider? This is an academic essay, so write in an academic style, meaning no first-person singular, slang, abbreviations, or other kinds of casual language here. Of course, if you are using a strong example from your own experience, the first-person is acceptable.

What should I document and what format should I use? Just like research papers you have written in school, document any material you have taken from the sources through direct quotation or paraphrasing. Here it is better to document too much rather than too little, so when in doubt, document. The directions for this essay say: "You may refer to the sources by their titles (Source A, Source B, etc.) or by the description in the parentheses." This means that you can embed the source in your own prose or you can follow the cited material with the title or description in parentheses. For example a source listing will look like this:

> Source A (The American Highway Safety Task Force)
> Source B (Photo)
> Source C (Collins)
> Source D (Denis)
> Source E (U.S. Department of Transportation)

Here are some options for documentation.

- The American Highway Safety Task Force data shows....

- Source B asserts....

- There is a strong causal relationship between accidents and inexperience that applies to drivers regardless of age (Source C). In fact, eighteen-year-old new drivers are involved in accidents at almost identical rates as sixteen-year-old new drivers. The increased risk of accidents subsides after three years, and goes away completely after five years (Source E). Thus, we can conclude that raising the driving age will only delay the spike in accident statistics to eighteen-year-old new drivers.

Notice also, that the third example does not merely paraphrase the sources, but also discusses their broader implications as they apply to your thesis, your primary task on this paper.

How much time should I take for this essay? You are allotted 135 minutes to complete all three essays; that means 40 minutes for each essay plus an extra 15 minutes to complete the reading for the synthesis essay. However, despite concern amongst AP teachers and students over the introduction of this new type of prompt, recent test takers have performed significantly better on the synthesis essay than on the rhetorical analysis essay, which requires a greater depth of reading of more difficult text. Therefore, you may find that using some of that 15 minutes of reading time on the rhetorical analysis essay may be your best strategy. This is where practice is key. Familiarity with the prompts will allow you to develop a rhythm for maximum success: reading time, planning time, writing time, editing time.

The Argument Essay

The argument essay is similar to the synthesis essay in that you are asked to take a position on a topic of controversy. It differs from the synthesis essay in that you will not be provided with the sources to support your argument; thus the topics tend to be broader taking into account the variety of background students bring to the exam. Recent topics have included academic honesty, the ethics of offering incentives for charitable acts, and the role adversity plays in the creation of a person's character. You are unlikely to get a question that would require specialized knowledge of a subject. That being said, students who bring more knowledge and understanding of the world to the table (i.e., history, literature, current events, science, economics, etc.) generally do better because they have a deeper pool of support to draw from. Good writers have something to say. While personal experience is a valid method of support, it rarely gets you all the way there on your essay. The list of potential topics is endless and very few teens have enough life experience to speak to every issue intelligently. In addition, most life experience is anecdotal. It can be emotionally compelling, but it is still just your own experience and not necessarily relevant to others. If you can connect your experience to broader, more objective evidence, you will present a more convincing and sophisticated argument and earn a higher score. Of course, there are exceptions: if the question is about the homeless and you have spent time living or working in a homeless shelter, you will clearly have a great deal to say about that issue, and you should go for it. But most teens, on most topics, need to reach beyond their immediate world.

The good news is you know more than you think you do. As you practice writing these essays, take time to consider books you have read, interesting places you have visited, and subjects you have learned about in school. In addition, get into the habit of following the news. Newspapers and news magazines are great ways to practice and improve your critical reading skills for this exam, and news commentary provides models of professional argument. Also, try listening to the news on the car radio or watch it on television when you exercise. This commitment is guaranteed to make you a smarter, better-informed person—the kind of student most colleges are looking for. This learning may also come in handy on that other College Board writing assignment: the persuasive essay on the writing section of the SAT.

What do the questions look like? This type of question takes two forms. Most recently, the questions have asked you to take a position on an issue. Sometimes you are provided with up to several paragraphs of text to help frame the issue and place it in context. Read all the material prior to forming your response. Often, you will be asked to defends, challenges, or qualifies a position presented in the prompt, often in a quotation or a short excerpt. Remember, qualified responses can be tricky, so practice this skill before you try it on the actual test. Presenting a compromise solution in your conclusion (sometimes you are asked to do just that) can show that you understand the complexity of the issue as well as providing you with a neat way to close your essay. No matter what you do, make sure you provide a strong, clear thesis statement in your introduction: the rubric demands it.

The other type of question asks you to analyze the argument of another writer—sort of a combination of the argument essay and the rhetorical analysis essay. It has been dormant for a few years, but it may be due for a return. Here you are asked to discern the author's position on a particular topic, and analyze and evaluate the approach he uses to persuade his audience.

Things to Keep in Mind

- Make sure you address the prompt.

- No matter how strongly you feel about an issue, present a reasonable position supported by solid evidence. This is an essay, not a diatribe. Don't be inflammatory and don't resort to heavy sarcasm or name calling, no matter how emotional the subject is for you. In fact, showing you understand the concerns of the opposing side in your response will show you have a sophisticated understanding of the complexity of the issue and earn you a higher score.

- If you don't have strong feelings about the topic, just pick the side you can support in the most compelling and interesting way, and go with it. Remember, this is a test of your reading, writing, and thinking skills—you will not be judged on your views or personality. That being said, AP readers are human beings: silly, outrageous, racist, or overtly cruel views will be difficult to effectively support and will not earn you a good score.

- Avoid hypothetical examples. Some very good writers can use them to good effect, but most students cannot. In addition, hypothetical examples often lead to the dreaded "generic you," a characteristic of weak style. Good writing is specific writing. One exception would be the use of the hypothetical example in order to make an analogy, but that analogy should lead to more specific support.

- Of all the essays, this is the one where your personal voice and writing style can shine. The first-person point of view is completely acceptable here as is humor appropriate for the situation. But, keep in mind, this is not your Facebook page; you are writing for an audience of adult English teachers, not your peers, and your purpose is to impress them as a student who is already thinking and writing at the level of a college sophomore.

The Rhetorical Analysis Essay

Another type of essay asks you to analyze the language used in a passage and to explain how the language achieves the author's purpose. In recent years, this has been the statistically most difficult essay for students on the exam because it is different from most of the writing they have done in school up to this point. This essay is most closely aligned with the skills in the multiple-choice section of the exam, except that on the rhetorical analysis essay you are tasked to analyze the author's purpose and use of language in the passage without the benefit of the questions to guide you. Do not oversimplify the author's position or attitude. Even if the essay is satirical in tone, take care not to exaggerate the tone and classify it as "bitter" or "biting" unless you are certain this is the author's intention. Remember, the makers of the test are looking for subtle gradations of analysis in your answer, and subtlety is difficult to achieve if you are analyzing a simplistic piece of literature, one with an obvious, one-sided, or "cut-and-dried" approach or tone.

Frequently, this question takes the form of two passages on the same topic but written in different styles and with different attitudes. Again, if you are asked to discuss the differences between two passages, do not oversimplify or exaggerate the differences.

This question expects you to analyze the style of a passage. The question directs you to read the passage carefully. Then, you are instructed to write an essay that (1) analyzes the effect of the passage on the reader; or (2) defines the author's attitude toward his or her topic (usually, the AP test question will name the topic of the passage for you); or, (3) describes the rhetorical purpose of the passage; or (4) identifies the author's purpose or views and how he or she achieves that purpose or conveys those views.

A List of Typical Instructions

Below, you will find a list of the most common directions used for writing essays. Become familiar with these directions, since they have been used frequently on past exams.

Analyze the language and rhetorical devices; consider such elements as narrative structure, selection of detail, manipulation of language, and tone;

Analyze how the author uses juxtaposition of ideas, choice of details, and other aspects of style;

Analyze stylistic, narrative, and persuasive devices;

Analyze the figures of speech and syntax;

Consider word choice, manipulation of sentences, imagery, and use of allusions;

Consider the rhetorical devices such as arguments, assumptions, attitudes, and diction.

Don't let the wording intimidate you: "rhetoric" and "rhetorical devices" refer to word choice and such things as poetic devices; "diction" refers to word choice; "syntax" refers to sentence structure and placement of words within the sentence; "juxtaposition" refers to unlike ideas or details that appear side-by-side or in close proximity to each other.

Basically, this type of question asks you to examine (with attention to nuance) these stylistic devices:

Word choice
Imagery
Figures of speech
Selection of detail
Sentence structure
Tone

"Word choice" or "diction" refers to individual words. "Imagery" refers to vivid pictures that appeal to the senses. "Figures of speech" refers to common devices, such as simile, allusion, alliteration, etc. "Selection of detail" is not exactly the same as word choice; rather, it is a significant piece of information about the character or location. "Sentence structure" or "syntax" is the arrangement of words in the sentence; sentence structure also includes types of sentences. "Tone" is the author's attitude toward the character, or location, and the author will use all of the devices above to generate that tone or attitude.

The question may ask you to consider these items in your answer:

Narrative structure
Persuasive devices
Rhetorical devices

"Narrative structure" refers to plot structure, or how the details are arranged. "Persuasive devices" refers to valid arguments the author uses, or perhaps logical fallacies. "Rhetorical devices" refers to imagery, word choice, figurative language, sentence structure.

Things to Keep in Mind:

- Misreading the excerpt is impossible to recover from on this essay, so you must read carefully, bringing all your critical reading skills to the task. If you are a weak reader, you need to address this issue through focused practice using the approaches discussed in Chapter 3 as a guideline.

- Discuss what's important. Don't treat this prompt as a literary terms scavenger hunt. You need to pick out the rhetorical devices that are playing an important role in the support of the author's purpose. For example, if the piece is focused around an extended metaphor or lush imagery, you need to discuss those things.

- Don't define the rhetorical devices. The readers know what figurative language and parallel syntax are; instead, show *how* the rhetorical devices support the author's purpose. For example, in *Walden*, Henry David Thoreau says, "If a man does not keep pace with his companion, perhaps it is because he hears a different drummer. Let him step to the music which he hears, however measured or far away." Show *how* Thoreau uses this metaphor as an explanation of his own life choices and, more importantly, to his views on the autonomy of the individual.

- Don't offer any discussion of language unless you connect it back to the author's purpose. No exceptions. This purpose should be asserted explicitly in your thesis statement at the beginning of your essay. Your thesis statement should be similar to or a close variation of this formula:

> author's name + author's attitude/purpose + subject + devices.

Example:

In "The Gettysburg Address" by Abraham Lincoln, the ninth President
    [Title of work]   [author]

uses the setting of the Battlefield and the emotional diction of democratic
    [device]   [device]

ideals ironically to promote a new idea of rebirth of government in the
                       [thesis]

United States.

The elements of the formula can be re-arranged in any order comfortable for you, but leaving out one of the elements is not advised unless you are an advanced writer. Beginning with this thesis makes you focus on the essential problem and gives your essay a specific direction.

    In your essay answer it is useful, but not necessary, to name the specific term ("metaphor," "inverted sentence," "parallelism"). Superior essay writers will, of course, know and use the basic devices of style in a smooth, mature manner. However, remember that your essay answer must include specific examples in the form of short, direct quotations and your answer should explain.

Strategies for Answering Essay Questions

1. Read the question carefully before you read the passage. Know what you are looking for before you read. As you read the question, underline the directions. Make sure you understand what you are looking for as you read. In the passage underline significant details, words with connotative meaning, reasons, logical structure, notable sentence beginnings or endings, unusual sentence structures, sentences that are noticeably short or long, vivid imagery, figures of speech, and words or phrases that may indicate the author's attitude.

2. Plan your response before you start writing. The English Language and Composition essay answers are graded as "first draft" papers. You are not given enough time to do prewriting, rough draft, and final copy—prewriting and one draft are really all you have time for in a 40-minute time period. Therefore, prewriting—organizing in advance of writing, in which you decide on content and order of ideas—is critical to your success. Give yourself about 5-10 minutes to read the essay question, write a working thesis sentence, and list 3-5 points in order of importance or logical development. The remaining time (15-20 minutes) should be spent writing, with 5 minutes to correct/revise and proofread.

3. You are pressed for time, so you should never use long introductory or long concluding remarks. Long introductions and conclusions take valuable time away from your main argument. Remember that you have only about 40 minutes to read the question, read the passage, plan your strategy, write your answer, and proofread and revise. Another argument against lengthy introduction and conclusions is that your central development will be shorter, and therefore most probably weaker in development. One or two sentences of introduction and conclusion are adequate. If you have a eureka moment and a good idea for an introduction that you can accomplish quickly just comes to you, go for it, but don't labor your introduction or you won't have time to write the paper. Also, a silly introduction that says nothing is worse nothing. (i.e., "Rhetorical strategies are an important part of writing." Ugh!) Some students like to leave a little space at the top of the page above the thesis. Then, if a good idea for an introduction comes to you later and you have time, you can add it. If not, the important part of the essay, the part that earns points for you on the rubric, is written. The same applies to conclusions.

4. Ideas should lead from one to the other in a smooth, logical progression. Organization of ideas in prewriting and composing will depend on the type of essay, but organize before you write. The multi-paragraph, thesis and support essay structure is adequate for answering many of the AP essay prompts as long as you make sure to shorten the introduction and conclusion. In particular, remember that the introduction should generally be no more than one sentence long! Further, it is often a good idea to

start your essay by answering the prompt in the first sentence you write. In case you are most comfortable with the five-paragraph structure, the basic components are: introduction, first paragraph, second paragraph, third paragraph, and finally, the conclusion.

5.   Use strong transition topic sentences to emphasize your progression of thought and assert the specific aspect of the thesis statement to be discussed in the upcoming paragraph. Never start a body paragraph with a quotation or example. Quotations and examples support points. You cannot introduce support unless you have made an assertion.

6.   Likewise, each quotation and example should be followed by interpretation and analysis connecting it back to the thesis statement. Always ask yourself "Why is this significant?" It is essential to answer this question for your reader after each point of support in your essay.

7.   Although it is possible to use the five-paragraph structure effectively, it is much more important simply *to write persuasively and logically.* If you can, *you should answer the prompt in the essay directions in your first sentence*—or, at the very latest, in the second sentence. The AP graders will be reading your essays rapidly, and it is critical to show them right away that you know the answer to the question they ask. In addition, as mentioned before, the longer you spend writing an introduction, the less time you'll have to write a convincing body of the essay. Make sure you have *specific* supports, referring to the text of the essay whenever possible. General observations or vague references to the reading material will usually cause your score to be in the mediocre range at best.

8.   Though there won't be time for any major revision, save yourself some time to read over your responses. Listen to your prose fixing awkward sentences, run-ons, and fragments, and look for the spelling and punctuation errors you are bound to make when you are writing in a hurry. You know (or you should know) your writing better than anyone. If you have chronic issues with pronoun/antecedent agreement or apostrophes, assume you will have made some of these errors and be on the lookout for them. A few lucky people compose relatively flawless first drafts, but the rest of us mere mortals need to proofread.

Preparing for the Essay Questions

1.   Research questions from previous years. The College Board website offers you many past questions along with scored sample student essays (called anchor papers) with explanations of the scoring (*http://apcentral. collegeboard.com/*). Spend time reading these questions and responses and develop an understanding of how they were scored. It is unproductive to expend energy disagreeing with the score; learn what the graders expect on the different types of questions and reconcile yourself to these standards.

2. Practice writing essays for the sample questions from the website. Then, read the anchor papers and try to score your essays according to how the rubric aligns with the student exemplars. Does yours look more like a "2" paper, a "5" paper, or an "8" paper? If you are having trouble, ask a teacher to help you evaluate your papers or work with a friend who is also taking the test.

3. At first, write your practice papers in one sitting but don't otherwise apply any time constraint. Take as long as you need to do a good job. Then, as you gain more confidence, begin timing yourself. Also, always hand write your practice papers.

4. Good writers use this trick to improve their fluency. Read your essays out loud, with expression, and listen to your prose. If you are stumbling over your own words, there is a problem. Do this for everything you write and your style will improve.

5. Build your skills and confidence by writing "fake" papers. Take a question from the website and allow yourself 5-10 minutes to write a thesis statement and plan out your response. You can do many of these in the weeks leading up to the exam!

6. If you have issues with basic grammar and spelling, put yourself on a self-improvement plan. The AP readers understand the limitations of timed, first-draft writing and expect a few mistakes on even the "9" papers, but if you are still misspelling "your and you're" and "there, their, and they're," it is time to address these problems. Know how to spell the words you probably will need to use on AP English Language and Composition exam—imagery, parallel syntax, simile, rhetorical, and persuasive—to name a few.

7. You will improve your writing if you read more, especially good contemporary prose. Reading examples of the kind of writing you will be asked to do on the exam is even better.

CHAPTER 6

AP English Language & Composition

Glossary of Literary and Rhetorical Terms

Abstract Language
Language describing ideas and qualities rather than observable or specific things, people, or places. The observable or "physical" is usually described with concrete language. Examples: love, honor, integrity, evil.

Ad hominem
Latin for "against the man." When a writer personally attacks his or her opponents instead of their arguments.

Allegory
A story, fictional or nonfictional, in which characters, things, and events represent qualities or concepts. The interaction of these characters, things, and events is meant to reveal an abstraction or a truth. The characters and other elements may be symbolic of the ideas referred to.

Alliteration
Repetition of initial sounds of words in close proximity to each other.

Allusion
Indirect reference to something (usually a literary text, mythology, folklore, fairy tales, the Bible, etc.) with which the reader is supposed to be familiar. Allusion is used with humorous intent, to establish a connection between writer and reader or to make a subtle point.

Anecdote
Short narrative used to illustrate a writer or speaker's point.

Ambiguity
Event or situation that may be interpreted in more than one way. Also, the manner of expression of such an event or situation may be ambiguous. Artful language may be ambiguous. Unintentional ambiguity is usually vagueness.

Analogy

A comparison to a directly parallel case. When a writer uses an analogy, he or she argues that a claim reasonable for one case is reasonable for the analogous case.

Analysis

Breaking down of something to see how the parts come together to form the whole. Thus, in rhetorical analysis, we consider how the rhetorical devices and strategies come together to support the author's purpose.

Anecdote

A brief recounting of a relevant episode. Anecdotes are often inserted into fictional or nonfictional texts as a way of developing a point or injecting humor.

Annotation

Explanatory notes added to a text to explain, cite sources, or give bibliographical data.

Antithesis

Balancing of two opposite or contrasting words, phrases, or clauses.

Apostrophe

Direct address to an absent or imaginary person or to an object, quality, or idea.

Assonance

Repetition of a vowel sound within two or more words in close proximity.

Authority

Arguments that draw on recognized experts or persons with highly relevant experience are said to rest on authoritative backing or authority. Readers are expected to accept claims if they are in agreement with an authority's view.

Backing

Support or evidence for a claim in an argument.

Balance

Construction in which both halves of the sentence are about the same length and importance.

Begging the Question

Often called "circular reasoning," begging the question occurs when the believability of the evidence depends on the believability of the claim.

Causal Relationship

A writer asserts that one outcome results from another. To show how one outcome produces or brings about another is often relevant in establishing a logical argument.

Circumlocution

Circumlocution is indirect, wordy language used to avoid stating it simply and directly.

Clause

Group of words containing a subject and a verb. An independent (or main) clause can stand alone grammatically as a complete sentence. A subordinate (or independent) clause begins with a subordinating conjunction and is considered a sentence fragment unless attached to an independent clause. Example: While we worked on our essays (subordinate clause), our teacher tutored the struggling students (independent clause).

Colloquial Language

Everyday, informal language; conversational language.

Common Knowledge

Shared beliefs or assumptions are often called "common knowledge." A writer may argue that if something is widely believed, then readers should accept it.

Concrete Language

Language that describes specific, observable things, people or places, rather than ideas or qualities.

Connotation

Rather than the dictionary definition, the associations suggested by a word. Implied meaning, connotation, rather than literal meaning, denotation.

Consonance

Repetition of a consonant sound within two or more words in close proximity.

Conventional

Following certain conventions, or traditional techniques of writing. An overreliance on conventions may result in a lack of originality. The five-paragraph essay is considered conventional.

Cumulative Sentence

Sentence which begins with the main idea and then expands on that idea with a series of details or other particulars.

Deduction

Begins with a general statement and then applies that statement to specific examples to arrive at a conclusion.

Dialect

Characteristics of language particular to a specific region or culture.

Diction

Word choice, particularly as an element of style. Different types and arrangements of words have significant effects on meaning. An essay written in academic diction would be much less colorful, but perhaps more precise than street slang.

Didactic

Term used to describe fiction or nonfiction that teaches a specific lesson or moral or provides a model of correct behavior or thinking.

Dramatic Irony

When the reader is aware of an inconsistency between a fictional or nonfictional character's perception of a situation and the truth of that situation.

Either-Or Reasoning

When the writer reduces an argument or issue to two polar opposites and ignores any alternatives.

Emotional Appeal

When a writer appeals to readers' emotions (often through pathos) to excite and involve them in the argument.

Equivocation

When a writer uses the same term in two different senses in an argument.

Ethical Appeal

When a writer tries to persuade the audience to respect and believe him or her based on a presentation of image of self through the text. Reputation is sometimes a factor in ethical appeals, but in all cases the aim is to gain the audience's confidence.

Euphemism

Pleasant or sanitized expression used to describe something unpleasant or negative. Example: "Passing away" is a euphemism for "dying".

Evoke

To transmit a particular feeling, emotion, or sensory image.

Example

Individual instance taken to be representative of a general pattern. Arguing by example is considered reliable if examples are demonstrably true or factual as well as relevant.

Explication

Act of interpreting or discovering the meaning of a text. Explication usually involves close reading and special attention to figurative language.

False Analogy

When two cases are not sufficiently parallel to lead readers to accept a claim of connection between them.

Figurative Language

Word or words that are inaccurate literally, but describe by calling to mind sensations or responses that the thing described evokes. Figurative language may be in the form of metaphors or similes, both non-literal comparisons. Shakespeare's "All the world's a stage" is an example of non-literal, figurative language (metaphor, specifically).

Footnote

Information provided outside and in addition to the main text of a piece of writing.

Generalization

When a writer bases a claim upon an isolated example or asserts that a claim is certain rather than probable. Sweeping generalizations occur when a writer asserts that a claim applies to all instances instead of some.

Hyperbole

Conscious exaggeration used to heighten effect. Not intended literally, hyperbole is often humorous.

Hypothetical Example

Example that is not specifically factual but is fashioned to imitate a possible real situation to support the writer or speaker's purpose.

Idiom

Common expression that has acquired a meaning different from its literal meaning. Example: window shopping.

Image

Word or words, either figurative or literal, used to describe a sensory experience or an object perceived by the senses. An image is always a concrete representation.

Imagery

Use of images, especially in a pattern of related images, often figurative, to create a strong, unified sensory impression.

Implication

Hint given but not stated explicitly.

Incongruity

Juxtaposition of ideas or images that seem inconsistent, incompatible, or out of place.

Induction

The opposite of deduction, induction moves from specific to general. Inductive reasoning takes the available information to derive a general conclusion that connects it.

Imperative Sentence

Sentence making a call to action or command where the understood "you" is the subject. Example: Go forth and multiply.

Inference

Drawing a conclusion from the available evidence.

Inversion

Variation of the normal word order (subject first, then verb, then complement) which puts a modifier or the verb as first in the sentence. The element that appears first is emphasized more than the subject.

Irony

When a reader is aware of a reality that differs from a character's perception of reality (dramatic irony). The literal meaning of a writer's words may be verbal irony.

Jargon

Technical language of a profession or skill, not typically understood or used by other people. Example: military jargon.

Juxtaposition

Purposeful placement of ideas, images, or language (often incongruous) to heighten their effect.

Logic

Implied comparison resulting when one thing is directly called another. To be logically acceptable, support must be appropriate to the claim, believable and consistent.

Metaphor

Comparison of two things, often unrelated. A figurative verbal equation results where both "parts" illuminate one another. I.A. Richards called the literal term in a metaphor the "tenor" and the figurative term the "vehicle." An *extended metaphor* carries that comparison beyond the initial statement and extends it further. A *mixed metaphor* is a metaphor that presents an inconsistent comparison. Example: We were drowning in an avalanche of paper. Tidal waves drown and avalanches bury—the metaphor is therefore inconsistent or mixed.

Mood

Atmosphere created by a writer's word choice (diction) and the details selected. Syntax is also a determiner of mood because sentence strength, length, and complexity affect pacing.

Moral

Lesson drawn from a fictional or nonfictional story. A heavily didactic story.

Non-sequitur

Latin for "it does not follow." When one statement isn't logically connected to another.

Objectivity

Writer's attempt to remove himself or herself from any subjective, personal involvement in a story. Hard news journalism is frequently prized for its objectivity, although even fictional stories can be told without a writer rendering personal judgment.

Onomatopoeia

Use of a word whose pronunciation suggests its meaning. *Buzz, hiss, slam,* and *pop* are frequently used examples.

Oversimplification

When a writer obscures or denies the complexity of the issues in an argument.

Oxymoron

Paradoxical construction juxtaposing two contradictory terms, like "wise fool" or "eloquent silence" to reveal a truth.

Paradox

Seemingly contradictory statement which is actually true. This rhetorical device is often used for emphasis or simply to attract attention.

Parallelism

Sentence construction which places in close proximity two or more equal grammatical constructions. Parallel structure may be as simple as listing two or three modifiers in a row to describe the same noun or verb; it may take the form of two or more of the same type of phrases (prepositional, participial, gerund, appositive) that modify the same noun or verb; it may also take the form of two or more subordinate clauses that modify the same noun or verb. Or, parallel structure may be a complex blend of single-word, phrase, and clause parallelism all in the same sentence.

Parody

Exaggerated imitation of a serious work for humorous purposes. The writer of a parody uses the quirks of style of the imitated piece in extreme or ridiculous ways.

Pathos

Qualities of a fictional or nonfictional work that evoke sorrow or pity. Over-emotionalism can be the result of an excess of pathos.

Periodic Sentence

Sentence that places the main idea or central complete thought at the end of the sentence, after all introductory elements.

Personification

Figurative language in which inanimate objects, animals, ideas, or abstractions are endowed with human traits or human form.

Phrase

Group of words that combine to create meaning but do not have a subject and verb, and therefore cannot stand alone as a sentence. Types of phrases include prepositional, participial, infinitive, gerund, verb, etc.

Point of View

Perspective from which a fictional or nonfictional story is told. First-person, third-person, or omniscient points of views are commonly used.

Pun

Play on words that exploits the similarity in sound between two words with different meanings, usually for a humorous effect.

Qualification

Condition, limitation, or restraint placed on an idea or argument. A qualified argument takes a position somewhere between the two opposing sides.

Red Herring

When a writer raises an irrelevant issue to draw attention away from the real issue.

Refutation

When a writer musters relevant opposing arguments.

Repetition

Word or phrase used two or more times in close proximity.

Rhetoric

Art of effective communication, especially persuasive discourse. Rhetoric focuses on the interrelationship of invention, arrangement, and style in order to create felicitous and appropriate discourse.

Rhetorical Devise

Any characteristic of language used to achieve the writer or speaker's purpose.

Rhetorical Strategy

Purposeful approach writers and speakers use to achieve their purpose. It can include any characteristic of language, development, and organization.

Rhetorical Question

Question with an obvious, understood answer.

Satire

Work that reveals a critical attitude toward some element of human behavior by portraying it in an extreme way. Satire doesn't simply abuse (as in invective) or get personal (as in sarcasm). Satire targets groups or large concepts rather than individuals.

Sarcasm

Type of verbal irony, the purpose of which is to denigrate the subject.

Simile

Figurative comparison of two things, often dissimilar, using the connecting words *like* or *as.*

Slang

Very informal or course language.

Source

Resource from which information has been drawn.

Style

Choices in diction, tone, and syntax that a writer makes. In combination they create a work's manner of expression. Style is thought to be conscious and unconscious and may be altered to suit specific occasions. Style is often habitual and evolves over time.

Subjectivity

Opinions based on personal preference or prejudice and not completely on objective fact.

Syllogism

Stylized deductive argument where two minor premises lead to a logical conclusion. Example: All men are mortal. Socrates is a man. Therefore, Socrates is mortal.

Symbol

Thing, event, or person that represents or stands for some idea or event. Symbols also simultaneously retain their own literal meanings.

Syntactic Fluency

Ability to create a variety of sentence structures, appropriately complex and/or simple and varied in length.

Theme

Central idea of a work of fiction or nonfiction revealed and developed in the course of a story or explored through argument.

Thesis

Central argument an author makes in a work of nonfiction sometimes stated explicitly or sometimes implied.

Tone

Writer's attitude toward his or her subject matter revealed through diction, figurative language, selection of details, imagery, and organization on the sentence and global levels.

Unity

A work of fiction or nonfiction is said to be unified if all the parts are related to one central idea or organizing principle. Thus, unity is dependent upon coherence.

Verbal Irony

Occurs when the reader is aware of a discrepancy between the real meaning of a situation and the literal meaning of the writer's words.

PRACTICE EXAM 1

AP English Language & Composition

PRACTICE EXAM 1

AP English Language & Composition

Section 1

TIME: 60 Minutes
        58 Questions

(Answer sheets appear in the back of this book.)

DIRECTIONS: This test consists of selections from literary works and questions on their use of language. After reading each passage, choose the best answer to each question and blacken the corresponding oval on the answer sheet.

Questions 1–11 are based on the following passage. Read the passage carefully before choosing your answers.

In the theatre itself—we were then located at the Maxine Elliott—the atmosphere resembled that of the actors' quarters. Its old star dressing room, right off the stage, had become the Group office. There was hardly any privacy at all. Everyone wandered in at will. There we conducted a little business, interviewed
5   actors, chatted, carried on controversies, prepared publicity, discussed policy.

Performances were kept at a high level, however, except when Luther Adler was overcome by lassitude. On such occasions we pepped him up by inventing distinguished guests in the audience. Stella Adler was almost always at top form, owing to her craft integrity and to her unusual energy. This energy, with
10 which she jolted her brother, often shocked him into fierce resistance. They quarreled at least four times a week, and the curtain calls amused, amazed, and terrified the company because between bows they turned on each other to resume their cat-and-dog fight.

Carnovsky regarded the Adlers' conduct as undisciplined. Besides their
15 quarrels they sometimes delayed the curtains by their tardiness in coming from

their dressing-rooms. But one night Carnovsky himself failed to appear for his entrance. Luther and Stella had to ad lib. for an unconscionable time. Finally Carnovsky appeared and instead of speaking his usual line: "I am five minutes too early," he confessed: "I am five minutes late." Hilarity followed the tension

20 backstage. When I inquired into the cause of this late entrance, something almost without precedent in Carnovsky's career, someone misinformed me, with a touch of malice, that he had been reading the *Communist Manifesto* of Marx and Engels in his dressing-room and had thus forgotten his entrance cue.

For the rest, the actors, insufficiently occupied, demanded more opportu-
25 nity to work at whatever duties we could find for them. Walter Coy alternated with Bill Challee in a small part in the play, as did Grover Burgess with Russell Collins. The graduate apprentice Elia Kazan, or "Gadget," as he was called for unspecified reasons, served as an example of enterprise by painting display signs, typing and aiding our harassed, underpaid press agent, whose office was
30 a dressing-room with a privy, around which a screen had been placed, a screen that perversely fell whenever visitors appeared.

Some of the actors began to seek an outlet for their energies outside our circle. There were, as noted, occasional performances of our experimental work at workers' clubs. But more than that, certain new groups were forming, and
35 they asked some of our actors to help them, perhaps to give talks or classes. Besides Gorelik's new Theatre Collective—which, according to him, was to be a "realistic" organization in contrast to our "romantic" Group—Charles and Adelaide Walker had spoken to me of a project on a larger, more professional basis than the modest Collective, a "proletarian theatre," which was to develop
40 into the Theatre Union, which opened on West Fourteenth Street in the spring of 1933.

At this time the Theatre Collective and the Theatre Union were holding formative meetings for discussion, some of which I attended. I noticed the presence of a few Group Theatre actors, notably Joe Bromberg. When word
45 about these meetings was reported back to our people, a certain suspicion, even resentment, manifested themselves among some of them, because they feared that people like Bromberg would be estranged from us. Actors like Carnovsky spoke for a moment, without meaning to, as if these new organizations were upstarts, with no right to divert serious actors from their legitimate work in the
50 still struggling Group. Bromberg pointed out, quite properly, that there was not enough for him to do around the Group then. He drew himself up to his full height (unfortunately insufficient for the occasion) and announced in an

almost defiant voice: "Besides, I like workers," a statement that struck everyone as a bewildering *non sequitur*.

55   Though no official policy had been announced by the Group directorate, it was now established that our actors were free to use their extra time as they would; and if some were interested in contributing to the development of new groups, amateur or professional, no one would gainsay them in any way.

Clurman, H.R., *The Fervent Years: The Group Theatre And The Thirties*

1.   In the last paragraph, "gainsay" (line 58) probably means

(A)   support   (D)   report

(B)   ignore   (E)   banish

(C)   oppose

2.   One of the reasons the actors sought a place in other groups is that they

(A)   wanted to challenge the Group

(B)   were insufficiently occupied

(C)   needed to raise capital for the Group

(D)   admired the directors of the Theatre Collective and the Theatre Union

(E)   sought to create disharmony within the Group

3.   The reader may infer, for the most part, that the actors enjoyed each other since

(A)   there was hardly any privacy

(B)   everyone wandered into the office at will

(C)   performances were kept at a high level most of the time

(D)   both (A) and (C)

(E)   (A), (B), and (C)

4.   Paragraph 2 can best be described as

(A)   anecdotal   (D)   rhetorical

(B)   allegorical   (E)   paradoxical

(C)   metaphorical

5. In context, the term, *non sequitur* (line 54) probably means

    (A)   a rude comment   (D)   an irrelevant statement

    (B)   an insightful retort   (E)   an unabashed remark

    (C)   a thoughtful reply

6. Which is the best example of a shift in tone?

    (A)   "...privacy at all. Everyone..." (lines 3–4)

    (B)   "...fierce resistance. They quarreled..." (lines 10–11)

    (C)   "...forgotten his entrance. For the next..." (lines 23–24)

    (D)   "...some of which I attended. I noticed..." (line 43)

    (E)   "...bewildering *non sequitur*. Though no official policy..." (lines 54–55)

7. The sentence, "There we conducted a little business, interviewed actors, chatted, carried on controversies, prepared publicity, discussed policy" (lines 4–5) contains all of the following EXCEPT

    (A)   alliteration   (D)   characterization

    (B)   caesura   (E)   verisimilitude

    (C)   frame

8. The principal contrast in paragraph 3 is between

    (A)   good and bad   (D)   triviality and gravity

    (B)   wit and stupidity   (E)   honesty and artifice

    (C)   humor and staidness

9. In paragraph 4, the third sentence beginning with "The graduate apprentice Elia Kazan...." (lines 27–31) remains coherent chiefly because of its use of

    (A)   parallel syntactical structure

    (B)   colloquial and idiomatic images

    (C)   a series of prepositional phrases

    (D)   periodic sentence structure

    (E)   retrospective point of view

10. One prominent stylistic characteristic of the passage is the use of

    (A) ethical appeal   (D) irony

    (B) sarcasm   (E) jocularity

    (C) analogy

11. The parenthetical aside in line 52 can best be described as

    (A) apologetic   (D) facetious

    (B) morbid   (E) obsequious

    (C) superficial

Questions 12–23 are based on the following passage. Read the passage carefully before choosing your answers.

    THE Number of Souls in *Ireland* being usually reckoned one Million and a half; of these I calculate there may be about Two hundred Thousand Couple whose Wives are Breeders; from which Number I subtract thirty thousand Couples, who are able to maintain their own Children; although I apprehend
5 there cannot be so many, under *the present Distresses of the Kingdom*; but this being granted, there will remain an Hundred and Seventy Thousand Breeders. I again subtract Fifty Thousand, for those Women who miscarry, or whose Children die by Accident, or Disease, within the Year. There only remain an Hundred and Twenty Thousand Children of poor Parents, annually born:
10 The Question therefore is, How this Number shall be reared, and provided for? Which, as I have already said, under the present Situation of Affairs, is utterly impossible, by all the Methods hitherto proposed: For we can *neither employ them in Handicraft* or *Agriculture*; we neither build Houses, (I mean in the Country) nor cultivate Land: They can very seldom pick up a Livelyhood
15 by *Stealing* until they arrive at six Years old; except where they are of towardly Parts; although, I confess, they learn the Rudiments much earlier; during which Time, they can, however, be properly looked upon only as Probationers; as I have been informed by a principal Gentleman in the County of *Cavan*, who protested to me, that he never knew above one or two Instances under the Age
20 of six, even in a Part of the Kingdom *so renowned for the quickest Proficiency in that Art.*

    I AM assured by our Merchants, that a Boy or a Girl before twelve Years old, is no saleable Commodity; and even when they come to this Age, they will not yield above Three Pounds, or Three Pounds and half a Crown at most,

25 on the Exchange; which cannot turn to Account either to the Parents or the Kingdom; the Charge of Nutriment and Rags, having been at least four Times that Value.

I SHALL now therefore humbly propose my own Thoughts, which I hope will not be liable to the least Objection.

30 I HAVE been assured by a very knowing *American* of my Acquaintance in *London*; that a young healthy Child, well nursed, is, at a Year old, a most delicious, nourishing, and wholesome Food; whether *Stewed*, *Roasted*, *Baked*, or *Boiled*; and, I make no doubt, that it will equally serve in a *Fricasie*, or *Ragoust*.

35 I DO therefore humbly offer it to *publick Consideration*, that of the Hundred and Twenty Thousand Children, already computed, Twenty thousand may be reserved for Breed; whereof only one Fourth Part to be Males; which is more than we allow to *Sheep*, *black Cattle*, or *Swine*; and my Reason is, that these Children are seldom the Fruits of Marriage, *a Circumstance not much regarded*

40 *by our Savages*; therefore, *one Male* will be sufficient to serve *four Females*. That the remaining Hundred thousand, may, at a Year old, be offered in *Sale to the Persons of Quality* and *Fortune*, through the Kingdom; always advising the Mother to let them suck plentifully in the last Month, so as to render them plump, and fat for a good Table. A Child will make two Dishes at an Entertain-

45 ment for Friends; and when the Family dines alone, the fore or hind Quarter will make a reasonable Dish; and seasoned with a little Pepper or Salt, will be very good Boiled on the fourth Day, especially in *Winter*.

I HAVE reckoned upon a Medium, that a Child just born will weigh Twelve Pounds; and in a solar Year, if tolerably nursed, encreaseth to twenty eight

50 Pounds.

I GRANT this Food will be somewhat dear, and therefore *very proper for Landlords*; who, as they have already devoured most of the Parents, seem to have the best Title to the Children.

INFANTS Flesh will be in Season throughout the Year; but more plentiful

55 in *March*, and a little before and after: For we are told by a grave Author, an eminent *French* Physician, that *Fish being a prolifick Dyet*, there are more Children born in *Roman Catholick Countries* about Nine Months after Lent than at any other Season: Therefore reckoning a Year after *Lent*, the Markets will be more glutted than usual; because the Number of *Popish Infants*, is, at

60 least three to one in this Kingdom; and therefore it will have one other Collateral Advantage, by lessening the Number of *Papists* among us.

I HAVE already computed the Charge of nursing a Beggar's Child (in which List I reckon all *Cottagers*, *Labourers*, and Four fifths of the *Farmers*) to be about two Shillings *per Annum*, Rags included; and I believe, no Gentleman would
65 repine to give Ten Shillings for the *Carcase of a good fat Child*; which, as I have said, will make four Dishes of excellent nutritive Meat, when he hath only some particular Friend, or his own Family, to dine with him. Thus the Squire will learn to be a good Landlord, and grow popular among his Tenants; the Mother will have Eight Shillings net Profit, and be fit for Work until she produceth
70 another Child.

12. The passage "I GRANT this Food will be somewhat dear, and therefore *very proper for Landlords*; who, as they have already devoured most of the Parents, seem to have the best Title to the Children" (lines 51–53) does all of the following EXCEPT

    (A) understate the cost of the "Food"

    (B) reverse the metaphor which dominates the passage

    (C) sarcastically indict the children's parents

    (D) reveal the speaker's attitudes toward landlords and tenants in a seeming aside

    (E) suggest persons who may play a role in giving the children better out-comes to their lives

13. Throughout the passage, poor children and their parents are metaphorically described using images of

    (A) urban decay   (D) scientific analysis

    (B) animal husbandry   (E) religious rituals

    (C) business transactions

14. What does the word "Popish" (line 59) mean?

    (A) Tiny   (D) Fish Eating

    (B) Unruly   (E) Irish

    (C) Roman Catholic

15. What effect does the construction of the argument in lines 1–47 have upon the reader?

    (A) Its seemingly rational progression makes the startling proposal even more jarring.

    (B) The emphasis upon "Souls" (line 1) initiates an atmosphere of religious reverence.

(C)   The references to animal breeding in the first and fifth paragraphs detract from the passage's main point.

(D)   The use of census-like statistics before the proposal confuses the issue and makes the reader more susceptible to persuasion.

(E)   The emphatic first person opening of each paragraph except the first underscores the speaker's reasonableness.

16.   The word "many" (line 5) refers to

    (A)   "Children" (line 4)   (D)   "Wives" (line 3)

    (B)   "Number" (line 3)   (E)   "Couples" (line 4)

    (C)   "Souls" (line 1)

17.   Which of the following can be inferred to be the intent of the passage?

    I.   To rebuke landlords for their callousness

    II.   To force a reexamination of other proposals

    III.   To offer a measured solution to a crisis

    IV.   To build the speaker's reputation as a civic-minded person

    (A)   I only   (D)   I, II, and III only

    (B)   I and II only   (E)   I, II, III, and IV

    (C)   III and IV only

18.   Stylistically, the passage may best be described as

    (A)   philosophical   (D)   hortative

    (B)   lyrical   (E)   satirical

    (C)   scientific

19.   The chief effect of the word "Breeders" (line 3) as it relates to "Wives"

    (A)   depersonalizes the women

    (B)   praises the women's fertility

    (C)   describes the women's occupation

    (D)   distinguishes the women from the men

    (E)   criticizes the women for having children

20.   The passage "I SHALL now therefore humbly propose my own Thoughts, which I hope will not be liable to the least Objection" (lines 28–29) is an example of

(A)   hyperbole   (D)   metaphor

(B)   oxymoron   (E)   digression

(C)   understatement

21.   In the context of the passage as a whole, the references to women as "Breeders" and children as a "saleable Commodity" (line 23) serve as

(A)   digressions from the course of the argument

(B)   statements of fact

(C)   summaries of the argument

(D)   omens of the proposal to come

(E)   objections to the proposal itself

22.   The rhetorical function of the sentence, "I have reckoned upon a Medium, that a child just born will weigh twelve pounds; and in a solar year, if tolerably nursed, encreaseth to twenty eight pounds" (lines 48–50) is to

(A)   show the author is trustworthy

(B)   demonstrate the author understands the audience

(C)   use emotionally charged diction

(D)   show the author has pondered the topic

(E)   cite commonly held beliefs

23.   Which of the following is NOT an appeal to reason?

(A)   "we can neither employ them in Handicraft or Agriculture" (lines 12–13)

(B)   "a young, healthy child, well nursed, is, at a year old, a most delicious, nourishing and wholesome food." (lines 31–32)

(C)   "these children are rarely the fruits of marriage" (lines 38–39)

(D)   "Infants flesh will be in season throughout the year" (line 54)

(E)   "The mother will have 8 shillings net profit" (line 69)

Questions 24-36 are based on the following passage. Read the passage carefully before choosing your answers.

We are apt to shut our eyes against a painful truth, and listen to the song of that siren till she transforms us into beasts. Is this the part of wise men, engaged in a great and arduous struggle for liberty? Are we disposed to be of the number of those who, having eyes, see not, and, having ears, hear not, the
5   things which so nearly concern their temporal salvation? For my part, whatever anguish of spirit it may cost, I am willing to know the whole truth; to know the worst, and to provide for it.

I have but one lamp by which my feet are guided; and that is the lamp of experience. I know of no way of judging of the future but by the past. And
10 judging by the past, I wish to know what there has been in the conduct of the British ministry for the last ten years, to justify those hopes with which gentlemen have been pleased to solace themselves, and the House? Is it that insidious smile with which our petition has been lately received? Trust it not, sir; it will prove a snare to your feet. Suffer not yourselves to be betrayed with a kiss. Ask
15 yourselves how this gracious reception of our petition comports with these war-like preparations which cover our waters and darken our land. Are fleets and armies necessary to a work of love and reconciliation? Have we shown ourselves so unwilling to be reconciled, that force must be called in to win back our love? Let us not deceive ourselves, sir. These are the implements of war and
20 subjugation; the last arguments to which kings resort. I ask, gentlemen, sir, what means this martial array, if its purpose be not to force us to submission? Can gentlemen assign any other possible motive for it? Has Great Britain any enemy, in this quarter of the world, to call for all this accumulation of navies and armies? No, sir, she has none. They are meant for us; they can be meant
25 for no other. They are sent over to bind and rivet upon us those chains which the British ministry have been so long forging. And what have we to oppose to them? Shall we try argument? Sir, we have been trying that for the last ten years. Have we anything new to offer upon the subject? Nothing. We have held the subject up in every light of which it is capable; but it has been all in vain.
30 Shall we resort to entreaty and humble supplication? What terms shall we find which have not been already exhausted? Let us not, I beseech you, sir, deceive ourselves. Sir, we have done everything that could be done, to avert the storm which is now coming on. We have petitioned; we have remonstrated; we have supplicated; we have prostrated ourselves before the throne, and have implored
35 its interposition to arrest the tyrannical hands of the ministry and Parliament.

Our petitions have been slighted; our remonstrances have produced additional violence and insult; our supplications have been disregarded; and we have been spurned, with contempt, from the foot of the throne. In vain, after these things, may we indulge the fond hope of peace and reconciliation. There is no longer any room for hope. If we wish to be free if we mean to preserve inviolate those inestimable privileges for which we have been so long contending if we mean not basely to abandon the noble struggle in which we have been so long engaged, and which we have pledged ourselves never to abandon until the glorious object of our contest shall be obtained, we must fight! I repeat it, sir, we must fight! An appeal to arms and to the God of Hosts is all that is left us!

They tell us, sir, that we are weak; unable to cope with so formidable an adversary. But when shall we be stronger? Will it be the next week, or the next year? Will it be when we are totally disarmed, and when a British guard shall be stationed in every house? Shall we gather strength by irresolution and inaction? Shall we acquire the means of effectual resistance, by lying supinely on our backs, and hugging the delusive phantom of hope, until our enemies shall have bound us hand and foot? Sir, we are not weak if we make a proper use of those means which the God of nature hath placed in our power. Three millions of people, armed in the holy cause of liberty, and in such a country as that which we possess, are invincible by any force which our enemy can send against us. Besides, sir, we shall not fight our battles alone. There is a just God who presides over the destinies of nations; and who will raise up friends to fight our battles for us. The battle, sir, is not to the strong alone; it is to the vigilant, the active, the brave. Besides, sir, we have no election. If we were base enough to desire it, it is now too late to retire from the contest. There is no retreat but in submission and slavery! Our chains are forged! Their clanking may be heard on the plains of Boston! The war is inevitable and let it come! I repeat it, sir, let it come.

It is in vain, sir, to extenuate the matter. Gentlemen may cry, Peace, Peace but there is no peace. The war is actually begun! The next gale that sweeps from the north will bring to our ears the clash of resounding arms! Our brethren are already in the field! Why stand we here idle? What is it that gentlemen wish? What would they have? Is life so dear, or peace so sweet, as to be purchased at the price of chains and slavery? Forbid it, Almighty God! I know not what course others may take; but as for me, give me liberty or give me death!

24. The author's main purpose in this piece can best be described as

    (A) a summons for rational thinking and peace

    (B) a demand for immediate freedom

    (C) a series of unwarranted claims

    (D) hyper-emotional preaching for equality

    (E) a patriotic call to action

25. The phrase, "listen to the song of that siren" (lines 1–2) is an example of

    (A) simile   (D) aphorism

    (B) hyperbole   (E) parallel construction

    (C) allusion

26. The intended audience of this piece is

    (A) the British government   (D) all oppressed people

    (B) Democrats   (E) British citizens

    (C) Americans

27. What is the author's main style of persuasion?

    (A) Asking questions and waiting for answers

    (B) Asking rhetorical questions

    (C) Demanding answers to his questions

    (D) Asking rhetorical questions and providing argumentative responses

    (E) Providing evidence for the questions asked

28. Which of the following is the best example of emotional appeal?

    (A) "Is this the part of wise men, engaged in a great and arduous struggle for liberty?" (lines 2–3)

    (B) "Trust it not, sir; it will prove a snare to your feet." (lines 13–14)

    (C) "We have held the subject up in every light of which it is capable; but it has been all in vain." (lines 28–29)

    (D) "But when shall we be stronger?" (line 48)

    (E) "Is life so dear, or peace so sweet, as to be purchased at the price of chains and slavery?" (lines 69–70)

29. In the sentence, "They are meant for us; they can be meant for no other," the word "they" refers to

    (A) "navies and armies" (lines 23–24)

    (B) "warlike preparations" (line 16)

    (C) "war and subjugation" (lines 19–20)

    (D) "kings" (line 20)

    (E) "last arguments" (line 20)

30. The audience probably feels liberty is

    (A) worthy of war

    (B) a valuable commodity

    (C) desirable but not attainable through war

    (D) an issue only governments can negotiate

    (E) an incredibly slow process

31. The tone in the passage shifts from _____ to _____.

    (A) caustic; didactic   (D) informative; sarcastic

    (B) pleading; cynical   (E) haughty; forthright

    (C) conventional; intimate

32. The speaker's diction is best described as

    (A) colloquial   (D) idiomatic

    (B) abstract   (E) pretentious

    (C) insipid

33. The speaker uses _____ to convince the audience

    I.   martyrdom

    II.   morbid language

    III. logical construction

    (A) I only   (D) I and III only

    (B) II only   (E) II and III only

    (C) III only

34. Which is NOT an example of hyperbole?

    (A) "I repeat it, sir, we must fight!" (lines 44–45)

    (B) "Will it be when we are totally disarmed, and when a British guard shall be stationed in every house?" (lines 49–50)

    (C) "There is no longer any room for hope." (lines 39–40)

    (D) "…we have prostrated ourselves in front of the throne…" (line 34)

    (E) "Give me liberty or give me death!" (lines 70–71)

35. The sentence, "Shall we acquire the means of effectual resistance, by lying supinely on our backs, and hugging the delusive phantom of hope, until our enemies shall have bound us hand and foot?" (lines 51–53) is best described as an example of

    (A) passive voice   (D) sarcasm

    (B) ethical appeal   (E) understatement

    (C) figurative language

36. Which metaphor extends throughout the piece?

    (A) "Chains" (line 25)   (D) "Storm" (line 32)

    (B) "Lamp" (line 8)   (E) "Arms" (line 45)

    (C) "Kiss" (line 14)

Questions 37-48 are based on the following passage. Read the passage carefully before you choose your answers. This passage is a portion of the National Institute of Mental Health Publication No. 01-4929, *entitled "Teenage Brain: A work in progress."*

New imaging studies are revealing—for the first time—patterns of brain development that extend into the teenage years. Although scientists don't know yet what accounts for the observed changes, they may parallel a pruning process that occurs early in life that appears to follow the principle of "use-it-or-lose-
5   it:" neural connections, or synapses, that get exercised are retained, while those that don't are lost. . . . While it's known that both genes and environment play major roles in shaping early brain development, science still has much to learn about the relative influence of experience versus genes on the later maturation of the brain. . . . Nonetheless, it's tempting to interpret the new findings as
10 empowering teens to protect and nurture their brain as a work in progress.

The newfound appreciation of the dynamic nature of the teen brain is emerging from MRI (magnetic resonance imaging) studies that scan a child's brain every two years, as he or she grows up. . . . In the first such longitudinal study of 145 children and adolescents, reported in 1999, NIMH's Dr. Judith

15   Rapoport and colleagues were surprised to discover a second wave of overproduction of gray matter, the thinking part of the brain—neurons and their branch-like extensions—just prior to puberty.[1] Possibly related to the influence of surging sex hormones, this thickening peaks at around age 11 in girls, 12 in boys, after which the gray matter actually thins some.

20   Prior to this study, research had shown that the brain overproduced gray matter for a brief period in early development—in the womb and for about the first 18 months of life—and then underwent just one bout of pruning. Researchers are now confronted with structural changes that occur much later in adolescence. The teen's gray matter waxes and wanes in different functional

25   brain areas at different times in development. For example, the gray matter growth spurt just prior to puberty predominates in the frontal lobe, the seat of "executive functions"—planning, impulse control and reasoning . . . Unlike gray matter, the brain's white matter—wire-like fibers that establish neurons' long-distance connections between brain regions—thickens progressively from

30   birth in humans. A layer of insulation called myelin progressively envelops these nerve fibers, making them more efficient, just like insulation on electric wires improves their conductivity.

Advancements in MRI image analysis are providing new insights into how the brain develops. UCLA's Dr. Arthur Toga and colleagues turned the NIMH

35   team's MRI scan data into 4-D time-lapse animations of children's brains morphing as they grow up—the 4th dimension being rate-of-change.[2] Researchers report a wave of white matter growth that begins at the front of the brain in early childhood, moves rearward, and then subsides after puberty. Striking growth spurts can be seen from ages 6 to 13 in areas connecting brain regions

40   specialized for language and understanding spatial relations, the temporal and parietal lobes. This growth drops off sharply after age 12, coinciding with the end of a critical period for learning languages.

While this work suggests a wave of brain white matter development that flows from front to back, . . . studies have suggested that gray matter

[1] Giedd JN, Blumenthal J, Jeffries NO, et al. Brain development during childhood and adolescence: a longitudinal MRI study. *Nature Neuroscience*, 1999; 2(10): 861-3.

[2] Thompson PM, Giedd JN, Woods RP, et al. Growth patterns in the developing brain detected by using continuum mechanical tensor maps. *Nature*, 2000; 404(6774): 190-3.

45   maturation flows in the opposite direction, with the frontal lobes not fully maturing until young adulthood. . . . increased myelination in the adult frontal cortex likely relates to the maturation of cognitive processing and other "executive" functions. Parietal and temporal areas mediating spatial, sensory, auditory and language functions appeared largely mature in the

50   teen brain.

     Another series of MRI studies is shedding light on how teens may process emotions differently than adults. Using functional MRI (fMRI), a team led by Dr. Deborah Yurgelun-Todd at Harvard's McLean Hospital scanned subjects' brain activity while they identified emotions on pictures of faces displayed on

55   a computer screen.[3] Young teens, who characteristically perform poorly on the task, activated the amygdala, a brain center that mediates fear and other "gut" reactions, more than the frontal lobe. As teens grow older, their brain activity during this task tends to shift to the frontal lobe, leading to more reasoned perceptions and improved performance. Similarly, the researchers saw a shift in

60   activation from the temporal lobe to the frontal lobe during a language skills task, as teens got older. These functional changes paralleled structural changes in temporal lobe white matter.

     While these studies have shown remarkable changes that occur in the brain during the teen years, they also demonstrate what every parent can confirm:

65   the teenage brain is a very complicated and dynamic arena, one that is not easily understood.

37.   Which of the following best reflects the subject of this article?

    (A)   Research on the changing behavior of teenagers

    (B)   Research on brain development during adolescence

    (C)   Comparison of adult brain matter and adolescent brain matter

    (D)   The use of MRIs in brain research

    (E)   Functional and structural changes in the brain throughout life

38.   To which of the following does the term "pruning" refer in lines 3 and 22?

    (A)   The loss of unused synapses

    (B)   Parallel roles of genes and environment in brain development

---

[3] Baird AA, Gruber SA, Fein DA, et al. Functional magnetic resonance imaging of facial affect recognition in children and adolescents. *Journal of the American Academy of Child and Adolescent Psychiatry*, 1999; 38(2): 195-9.

(C)   Gray matter growth spurts that occur at specific growth phases

(D)   Progressive thickening of the brain's white matter

(E)   The contrasting flow of gray and white matter in the brain

39.   The tone of this passage can best be described as mainly

(A)   humorous   (D)   urbane

(B)   informative   (E)   candid

(C)   sarcastic

40.   Which of the following is an accurate reading of the first footnote?

(A)   The article *Nature Neuroscience* appeared on page 861 of "Brain Development During Childhood and Adolescence: A Longitudinal MRI Study" in 1999.

(B)   The article "Brain Development During Childhood and Adolescence: A Longitudinal MRI Study" by Giedd, Blumenthal, Jeffries and others can be found on page 10 in *Nature Neuroscience*.

(C)   The second of ten articles about brain development during childhood and adolescence was published in *Nature Neuroscience* in 1999.

(D)   An article by Giedd, Blumenthal, Jeffries and others begins on page 861 in a 1999 issue of *Nature Neuroscience*.

(E)   *Nature Neuroscience* is an article that Giedd, Blumenthal, Jeffries, and others wrote in 1999 for a longitudinal study on brain development.

41.   Based on the information given in this article, what did the studies by Dr. Rapoport and Dr. Toga have in common?

(A)   Both focused on time-lapse animations of the brains of children.

(B)   Both focused on the pruning process of the brain.

(C)   They used one another's research findings in their studies of the brain.

(D)   They focused on the differences between the brain development of females and that of males during the adolescent years.

(E)   Both involved the changes that a brain undergoes as a person ages.

42.   The last two sentences in paragraph 4 (lines 39–42) imply that we should learn foreign languages before reaching what age?

(A)   Six years   (D)   Sixteen years

(B)   Eleven years   (E)   Adulthood

(C)   Twelve years

43. References to a "wave" in lines 15, 37, and 43 serve to

    (A) remind the reader that the brain contains water

    (B) highlight the steady development of the brain's gray and white matter

    (C) highlight the fact that some parts of the brain do not grow steadily and continuously

    (D) detail the size limitations of the brain's gray matter

    (E) detail the size limitations of the brain's white matter

44. Which of the following statements about footnote 2 is correct?

    (A) P. M. Thompson and colleagues interviewed Dr. Toga about the UCLA 4-D study

    (B) More information about the UCLA 4-D study may be available in a *Nature* article written by P. M. Thompson and colleagues

    (C) P. M. Thompson and colleagues worked with Dr. Toga and his associates on the UCLA 4-D study

    (D) Thompson, Giedd, Woods, and others wrote an article titled "Nature" for a journal that was published in 2000

    (E) an article about growth patterns in the developing brain appears on page 404 in a 2000 issue of *Nature*

45. The structure of lines 23–32 ("Researchers...conductivity") can best be described as

    (A) general statement followed by examples

    (B) general statement followed by other general statements

    (C) specific examples followed by general statement

    (D) easily understood statement followed by more technical terminology

    (E) technical terminology that an average reader probably could not understand

46. Lines 24 and 25 state, "The teen's gray matter waxes and wanes in different functional brain areas at different times in development." Which of the following is a different way to say "waxes and wanes"?

    (A) Progresses

    (B) Predominates

    (C) Becomes increasingly efficient with maturity

    (D) Is "wishy-washy"

    (E) Has growth spurts

47. In context, the word "dynamic" (line 65) is best interpreted to mean

    (A) ever-changing   (D) moving

    (B) emphatic   (E) strenuous

    (C) forceful

48. After a close reading of the three footnotes in this article, the reader might conclude that

    (A) the articles contain much more technical terminology than the passage does

    (B) brain research was a popular topic of many magazines in 1999 and 2000

    (C) not much brain research was conducted prior to 1999

    (D) research on the brain's development occurred during 1999 and 2000

    (E) J. Giedd wrote articles in collaboration with other scientists

Questions 49-58 are based on the following passage. Read the passage carefully before choosing your answers.

Between me and the other world there is ever an unasked question: unasked by some through feelings of delicacy; by others through the difficulty of rightly framing it. All, nevertheless, flutter round it. They approach me in a half-hesitant sort of way, eye me curiously or compassionately, and then, instead
5 of saying directly, How does it feel to be a problem? they say, I know an excellent colored man in my town; or, I fought at Mechanicsville; or, Do not these Southern outrages make your blood boil? At these I smile, or am interested, or reduce the boiling to a simmer, as the occasion may require. To the real question, How does it feel to be a problem? I answer seldom a word.

10 And yet, being a problem is a strange experience, – peculiar even for one who has never been anything else, save perhaps in babyhood and in Europe. It is in the early days of rollicking boyhood that the revelation first bursts upon one, all in a day, as it were. I remember well when the shadow swept across me. I was a little thing, away up in the hills of New England, where the dark
15 Housatonic winds between Hoosac and Taghkanic to the sea. In a wee wooden schoolhouse, something put it into the boys' and girls' heads to buy gorgeous visiting-cards – ten cents a package – and exchange. The exchange was merry, till one girl, a tall newcomer, refused my card, – refused it peremptorily, with a glance. Then it dawned upon me with a certain suddenness that I was different
20 from the others; or like, mayhap, in heart and life and longing, but shut out

from their world by a vast veil. I had thereafter no desire to tear down that veil, to creep through; I held all beyond it in common contempt, and lived above it in a region of blue sky and great wandering shadows. That sky was bluest when I could beat my mates at examination-time, or beat them at a foot-race,

25 or even beat their stringy heads. Alas, with the years all this fine contempt began to fade; for the words I longed for, and all their dazzling opportunities, were theirs, not mine. But they should not keep these prizes, I said; some, all, I would wrest from them. Just how I would do it I could never decide: by reading law, by healing the sick, by telling the wonderful tales that swam

30 in my head, – some way. With other black boys the strife was not so fiercely sunny: their youth shrunk into tasteless sycophancy, or into silent hatred of the pale world about them and mocking distrust of everything white; or wasted itself in a bitter cry, Why did God make me an outcast and a stranger in mine own house? The shades of the prison-house closed round about us all: walls

35 strait and stubborn to the whitest, but relentlessly narrow, tall, and unscalable to sons of night who must plod darkly on in resignation, or beat unavailing palms against the stone, or steadily, half hopelessly, watch the streak of blue above.

After the Egyptian and Indian, the Greek and Roman, the Teuton and
40 Mongolian, the Negro is a sort of seventh son, born with a veil, and gifted with second-sight in this American world, – a world which yields him no true self-consciousness, but only lets him see himself through the revelation of the other world. It is a peculiar sensation, this double-consciousness, this sense of always looking at one's self through the eyes of others, of measuring one's soul by the
45 tape of a world that looks on in amused contempt and pity. One ever feels his twoness, – an American, a Negro; two souls, two thoughts, two unreconciled strivings; two warring ideals in one dark body, whose dogged strength alone keeps it from being torn asunder.

The history of the American Negro is the history of this strife, – this longing
50 to attain self-conscious manhood, to merge his double self into a better and truer self. In this merging he wishes neither of the older selves to be lost. He would not Africanize America, for America has too much to teach the world and Africa. He would not bleach his Negro soul in a flood of white American-ism, for he knows that Negro blood has a message for the world. He simply
55 wishes to make it possible for a man to be both a Negro and an American, without being cursed and spit upon by his fellows, without having the doors of Opportunity closed roughly in his face.

49. The "veil" (line 21) is

    (A) a symbol that represents the anger of Negroes

    (B) a conceit that unifies the passage

    (C) a metaphor that portrays the genre

    (D) a simile that describes a state of being

    (E) a concrete image that names a historical pursuit

50. What is the function of the anecdote in paragraph 2?

    (A) It indicates that the speaker would rather write fictional stories than essays.

    (B) It illustrates the long struggle of the Negro people.

    (C) It helps keep the tone of the narrative light.

    (D) It engages the reader.

    (E) It awakens the speaker from his previous ignorance.

51. The phrase "he would not bleach his Negro soul in a flood of white Americanism" (lines 53–54) implies that

    (A) the Negro wants to discard his identity

    (B) the Negro should include his heritage in his individuality

    (C) white Americans are detrimental to the Negro identity

    (D) a Negro cannot be patriotic

    (E) Americans should balance their interests

52. The word "It" in line 48 refers to

    (A) "twoness" (line 46)   (D) "body" (line 47)

    (B) "American" (line 46)   (E) "strength" (line 47)

    (C) "Negro" (line 46)

53. What is the effect of the author's use of dialogue?

    (A) It highlights important historical sentiments.

    (B) It characterizes the speaker as tolerant.

    (C) It shows the tension between the speaker and the world.

    (D) It makes the experience between the author and the reader more intimate.

    (E) It provides comic relief.

54. The author employs all of the following EXCEPT

    (A) parallel structure   (D) allegory

    (B) emotionally-charged diction   (E) metaphor

    (C) irony

55. How does the author view "other black boys" (line 30)?

    (A) Audacious   (D) Charismatic

    (B) Capable   (E) Ingratiating

    (C) Satisfied

56. What is the "problem" to which the author refers?

    (A) Fighting in the Civil War

    (B) Southern outrages

    (C) Being an educated African American

    (D) Appealing to white audiences

    (E) Controversy between whites and blacks

57. The speaker's style can be described as

    (A) pedantic   (D) didactic

    (B) informative   (E) radical

    (C) outraged

58. What is the overall purpose of this passage?

    (A) To educate all Americans about the plight of the African American

    (B) To garner sympathy from white audiences

    (C) To ignite passions in black Americans

    (D) To show the author's deepest desires

    (E) To provide historical context for future rhetorical endeavors

STOP

This is the end of Section 1.
If time still remains, you may check your work only in this section.
Do not begin Section 2 until instructed to do so.

Section 2

Question 1   (Suggested reading time—15 minutes)
         (Suggested writing time—40 minutes)

Directions: The following prompt is based on the accompanying seven sources.

This question requires you to synthesize a variety of sources into a coherent, well-written essay. *Refer to the sources to support your position; avoid mere paraphrase or summary. Your argument should be central; the sources should support this argument.*

Remember to attribute both direct and indirect sources.

Introduction: Throughout the history of the United States, the country's presidents have delivered speeches and propaganda to Congress and the public. These presentations reflect their concerns and beliefs as they lead the country. What have these campaigns had in common, and what have been the results? What do they reflect about the focus of this country? Do these productions seem to indicate that any specific topics or themes have run throughout the history of America?

Assignment: Read carefully the following sources, all of which are passages taken from speeches and polling results of United States presidents. **Then, in an essay that synthesizes at least three of the sources for support, take a position that defends, challenges, or qualifies the claim that the concerns and beliefs of American presidents have remained basically the same throughout the history of this country.**

You may refer to the sources by their titles (Source A, Source B, etc.) or by the descriptions in parentheses.

Source A (Washington)

Source B (Roosevelt)

Source C (Truman)

Source D (Kennedy)

Source E (Reagan)

Source F (Clinton)

> ## Source A
>
> Washington, George. 1790 State of the Union Address. January 8, 1790.

. . . In resuming your consultations for the general good, you cannot but derive encouragement from the reflection that the measures of the last Session have been as satisfactory to your Constituents, as the novelty and difficulty of the work allowed you to hope. Still further to realize their expectations and to secure the blessings which a Gracious Providence has placed within our reach, will in the course of the present important Session, call for the cool and deliberate exertion of your patriotism, firmness and wisdom.

Among the many interesting objects, which will engage your attention, that of providing for the common defence will merit particular regard. To be prepared for War is one of the most effectual means of preserving peace.

A free people ought not only to be armed but disciplined; to which end a uniform and well digested plan is requisite: And their safety and interest require, that they should promote such manufactories, as tend to render them independent on others for essential, particularly for military supplies. . . .

The interests of the United States requires that our intercourse with other nations should be facilitated, by such provisions as will enable me to fulfill my duty in that respect, in the manner which circumstances may render most conducive to the public good. . . .

. . . I cannot forbear intimating to you the expediency of giving effectual encouragement as well to the introduction of new and useful inventions from abroad, as to the exertions of skill and genius in producing them at home; and of facilitating the intercourse between the distant parts of our Country by a due attention to the Post-Office and Post-Roads.

Nor am I less persuaded, that you will agree with me in opinion, that there is nothing which can better deserve your patronage than the promotion of Science and Literature. Knowledge is in every country the surest basis of public happiness. In one in which the measures of Government receive their impression so immediately from the sense of the Community as in ours it is proportionably essential. . . .

> ## Source B
>
> Roosevelt, Theodore. Inaugural Address. March 4, 1905.

My fellow-citizens,

No people on earth have more cause to be thankful than ours, and this is said reverently, in no spirit of boastfulness in our own strength, but with gratitude to the Giver of Good who has blessed us with the conditions which have enabled us to achieve so large a measure of well-being and of happiness. . . .

Much has been given us, and much will rightfully be expected from us. We have duties to others and duties to ourselves; and we can shirk neither. We have become a great nation, forced by the fact of its greatness into relations with the other nations of the earth, and we must behave as beseems a people with such responsibilities. Toward all other nations, large and small, our attitude must be one of cordial and sincere friendship. We must show not only in our words, but in our deeds, that we are earnestly desirous of securing their good will by acting toward them in a spirit of just and generous recognition of all their rights. . . .

Our relations with the other powers of the world are important; but still more important are our relations among ourselves. Such growth in wealth, in population, and in power as this nation has seen during the century and a quarter of its national life is inevitably accompanied by a like growth in the problems which are ever before every nation that rises to greatness. Power invariably means both responsibility and danger. . . .

Source C

Truman, Harry. Inaugural Address. January 20, 1949

. . . In performing the duties of my office, I need the help and prayers of every one of you. I ask for your encouragement and your support. The tasks we face are difficult, and we can accomplish them only if we work together. . . .

It may be our lot to experience, and in large measure to bring about, a major turning point in the long history of the human race. The first half of this century has been marked by unprecedented and brutal attacks on the rights of man, and by the two most frightful wars in history. The supreme need of our time is for men to learn to live together in peace and harmony.

The peoples of the earth face the future with grave uncertainty, composed almost equally of great hopes and great fears. In this time of doubt, they look to the United States as never before for good will, strength, and wise leadership. . . .

We are moving on with other nations to build an even stronger structure of international order and justice. We shall have as our partners countries which, no longer solely concerned with the problem of national survival, are now working to improve the standards of living of all their people. We are ready to undertake new projects to strengthen the free world. . . .

The United States is pre-eminent among nations in the development of industrial and scientific techniques. The material resources which we can afford to use for the assistance of other peoples are limited. But our imponderable resources in technical knowledge are constantly growing and are inexhaustible. . . .

Greater production is the key to prosperity and peace. And the key to greater production is a wider and more vigorous application of modern scientific and technical knowledge. . . .

Steadfast in our faith in the Almighty, we will advance toward a world where man's freedom is secure.

To that end we will devote our strength, our resources, and our firmness of resolve. With God's help, the future of mankind will be assured in a world of justice, harmony, and peace.

Source D

Kennedy, John F. Inaugural Address. January 20, 1961

. . . I have sworn before you and Almighty God the same solemn oath our fore-bears prescribed nearly a century and three quarters ago.

The world is very different now. For man holds in his mortal hands the power to abolish all forms of human poverty and all forms of human life. And yet the same revolutionary beliefs for which our forebears fought are still at issue around the globe—the belief that the rights of man come not from the generosity of the state but from the hand of God . . . .

Let every nation know, whether it wishes us well or ill, that we shall pay any price, bear any burden, meet any hardship, support any friend, oppose any foe to assure the survival and the success of liberty . . . .

To those old allies whose cultural and spiritual origins we share, we pledge the loyalty of faithful friends. United, there is little we cannot do in a host of cooperative ventures. Divided, there is little we can do—for we dare not meet a powerful challenge at odds and split asunder.

To those new states whom we welcome to the ranks of the free, we pledge our word that one form of colonial control shall not have passed away merely to be replaced by a far more iron tyranny. . . .

Finally, to those nations who would make themselves our adversary, we offer not a pledge but a request: that both sides begin anew the quest for peace, before the dark powers of destruction unleashed by science engulf all humanity in planned or accidental self-destruction. . . .

Let both sides seek to invoke the wonders of science instead of its terrors. Together let us explore the stars, conquer the deserts, eradicate disease, tap the ocean depths and encourage the arts and commerce . . . .

Now the trumpet summons us again—not as a call to bear arms, though arms we need—not as a call to battle, though embattled we are—but a call to bear the burden of a long twilight struggle, year in and year out, "rejoicing in hope, patient in tribulation"—a struggle against the common enemies of man: tyranny, poverty, disease and war itself.

And so, my fellow Americans: ask not what your country can do for you—ask what you can do for your country.

My fellow citizens of the world: ask not what America will do for you, but what together we can do for the freedom of man.

Finally, whether you are citizens of America or citizens of the world, ask of us here the same high standards of strength and sacrifice which we ask of you. With a good conscience our only sure reward, with history the final judge of our deeds, let us go forth to lead the land we love, asking His blessing and His help, but knowing that here on earth God's work must truly be our own.

Source E

Interview with voters at polls. *New York Times*. November 9, 1980. P. 28

Social groups and the presidential vote, 1980 and 1976

	Size	'80 Carter	'80 Reagan	'80 Anderson	'76 Carter	'76 Ford
Party						
Democratic	43	66	26	6	77	22
Independent	23	30	54	12	43	54
Republican	28	11	84	4	9	90
Ideology						
Liberal	18	57	27	11	70	26
Moderate	51	42	48	8	51	48
Conservative	31	23	71	4	29	70
Ethnicity						
Black	10	82	14	3	82	16
Hispanic	2	54	36	7	75	24
White	88	36	55	8	47	52
Sex						
Female	48	45	46	7	50	48
Male	52	37	54	7	50	48
Religion						
Protestant	46	37	56	6	44	55
White Protestant	41	31	62	6	43	57
Catholic	25	40	51	7	54	44
Jewish	5	45	39	14	64	34
Family income						
Less than US$10,000	13	50	41	6	58	40
$10,000–$14,999	15	47	42	8	55	43
$15,000–$24,999	29	38	53	7	48	50
$25,000–$50,000	24	32	58	8	36	62
Over $50,000	5	25	65	8	—	—
Occupation						
Professional or manager	39	33	56	9	41	57
Clerical, sales, white-collar	11	42	48	8	46	53
Blue-collar	17	46	47	5	57	41
Agriculture	3	29	66	3	—	—
Unemployed	3	55	35	7	65	34
Education						
Less than high school	11	50	45	3	58	41
High school graduate	28	43	51	4	54	46
Some college	28	35	55	8	51	49
College graduate	27	35	51	11	45	55

Source F

Clinton, William. Second Inaugural Address. January 20, 1997.

. . . Each and every one of us, in our own way, must assume personal responsibility not only for ourselves and our families but for our neighbors and our Nation. Our greatest responsibility is to embrace a new spirit of community for a new century. For any one of us to succeed, we must succeed as one America. The challenge of our past remains the challenge of our future: Will we be one Nation, one people, with one common destiny, or not? Will we all come together, or come apart?

. . . now we are building bonds with nations that once were our adversaries. Growing connections of commerce and culture give us a chance to lift the fortunes and spirits of people the world over. And for the very first time in all of history, more people on this planet live under democracy than dictatorship. . . .

The promise we sought in a new land, we will find again in a land of new promise. In this new land, education will be every citizen's most prized possession. Our schools will have the highest standards in the world, igniting the spark of possibility in the eyes of every girl and every boy. And the doors of higher education will be open to all. The knowledge and power of the information age will be within reach not just of the few but of every classroom, every library, every child. Parents and children will have time not only to work but to read and play together. And the plans they make at their kitchen table will be those of a better home, a better job, the certain chance to go to college. . . .

We will stand mighty for peace and freedom and maintain a strong defense against terror and destruction. Our children will sleep free from the threat of nuclear, chemical, or biological weapons. Ports and airports, farms and factories will thrive with trade and innovation and ideas. And the world's greatest democracy will lead a whole world of democracies.

Our land of new promise will be a nation that meets its obligations, a nation that balances its budget but never loses the balance of its values, a nation where our grandparents have secure retirement and health care and their grandchildren know we have made the reforms necessary to sustain those benefits for their time, a nation that fortifies the world's most productive economy even as it protects the great natural bounty of our water, air, and majestic land. And in this land of new promise, we will have reformed our politics so that the voice of the people will always speak louder than the din of narrow interests, regaining the participation and deserving the trust of all Americans. . . .

From the height of this place and the summit of this century, let us go forth. May God strengthen our hands for the good work ahead, and always, always bless our America.

CONTINUE TO QUESTION 2

Question 2 (Suggested time—40 minutes.) This question is worth one-third of the total essay score.

E.B. White was an American author and social commentator. Read the following passage from his essay, "Some Remarks on Humor," and write a persuasive essay which analyzes how White typifies humor through his use of diction, syntax and tone.

Analysts have had their go at humor, and I have read some of this interpretive literature, but without being greatly instructed. Humor can be dissected, as a frog can, but the thing dies in the process and the innards are discouraging to any but the pure scientific mind.

5   In a newsreel theater the other day I saw a picture of a man who had developed the soap bubble to a higher point than it had ever before reached. He had become the ace soap bubble blower of America, had perfected the business of blowing bubbles, refined it, doubled it, squared it, and had even worked himself up into a convenient lather. The effect was not pretty. Some of the bubbles were too big to be beautiful, and the
10 blower was always jumping into them or out of them, or playing some sort of unattractive trick with them. It was, if anything, a rather repulsive sight. Humor is a little like that: it won't stand much blowing up, and it won't stand much poking. It has a certain fragility, an evasiveness, which one had best respect. Essentially, it is a complete mystery. A human frame convulsed with laughter, and the laughter becoming hysteri-
15 cal and uncontrollable, is as far out of balance as one shaken with the hiccoughs or in the throes of a sneezing fit.

    One of the things commonly said about humorists is that they are really very sad people—clowns with a breaking heart. There is some truth in it, but it is badly stated. It would be more accurate, I think, to say that there is a deep vein of melancholy running
20 through everyone's life and that the humorist, perhaps more sensible of it than some others, compensates for it actively and positively. Humorists fatten on trouble. They have always made trouble pay. They struggle along with a good will and endure pain cheerfully, knowing how well it will serve them in the sweet by and by. You find them wrestling with foreign languages, fighting folding ironing boards and swollen drain-
25 pipes, suffering the terrible discomfort of tight boots (or as Josh Billings wittily called them, "tite" boots). They put out their sorrows profitably, in a form that is not quite fiction nor quite fact either. Beneath the sparkling surface of these dilemmas flows the strong tide of human woe.

    Practically everyone is a manic-depressive of sorts, with his up moments and his
30 down moments, and you certainly don't have to be a humorist to taste the sadness of situation and mood. But there is often a rather fine line between laughing and crying, and if a humorous piece of writing brings a person to the point where his emotional responses are untrustworthy and seem likely to break over into the opposite realm, it is because humor, like poetry, has an extra content. It plays close to the big hot fire
35 which is Truth, and sometimes the reader feels the heat.

    The world likes humor, but it treats it patronizingly. It decorates its serious artists with laurel, and its wags with Brussels sprouts. It feels that if a thing is funny it can be presumed to be something less than great, because if it were truly great it would be wholly serious. Writers know this, and those who take their literary selves with great

40 seriousness are at considerable pains never to associate their name with anything funny or flippant or nonsensical or "light." They suspect it would hurt their reputation, and they are right. Many a poet writing today signs his real name to his serious verse and a pseudonym to his comical verse, being unwilling to have the public discover him in any but a pensive and heavy moment. It is a wise precaution. (It is often a bad
45 policy too.)

When I was reading over some of the parody diaries of Franklin P. Adams, I came across this entry for April 28, 1926:

Read H. Canby's book, Better Writing, very excellent. But when he
50 says, "A sense of humor is worth gold to any writer," I disagree with him vehemently. For the writers who amass the greatest gold have, it seems to me, no sense of humor; and I think also that if they had, it would be a terrible thing for them, for it would paralyze them so that they would not write at all. For in writing, emotion is more to be treasured than a sense of humor,
55 and the two are often in conflict.

That is a sound observation. The conflict is fundamental. There constantly exists, for a certain sort of person of high emotional content, at work creatively, the danger of coming to a point where something cracks within himself or within the paragraph
60 under construction—cracks and turns into a snicker. Here, then, is the very nub of the conflict: the careful form of art, and the careless shape of life itself. What a man does with this uninvited snicker (which may closely resemble a sob, at that) decides his destiny. If he resists it, conceals it, destroys it, he may keep his architectural scheme intact and save his building, and the world will never know. If he gives in to it, he becomes
65 a humorist, and the sharp brim of the fool's cap leaves a mark forever on his brow.

CONTINUE TO QUESTION 3 >

Question 3 (Suggested time—40 minutes.) This question is worth one-third of the total essay score.

The Roman philosopher Marcus Tullius Cicero once said, "Nothing is so unbelievable that oratory cannot make it acceptable." Consider the implications of this quotation. Then, write an essay that defends, challenges, or qualifies Cicero's assertion that with persuasive commentary, any radical idea can be made tolerable. Support your argument with appropriate evidence from your reading, observation, or experience.

END OF EXAM

PRACTICE EXAM 1

AP English Language & Composition

Answer Key

Section 1

1.	**(C)**	21.	**(D)**	41.	**(E)**
2.	**(B)**	22.	**(D)**	42.	**(C)**
3.	**(E)**	23.	**(B)**	43.	**(C)**
4.	**(A)**	24.	**(E)**	44.	**(B)**
5.	**(D)**	25.	**(C)**	45.	**(A)**
6.	**(C)**	26.	**(C)**	46.	**(E)**
7.	**(B)**	27.	**(D)**	47.	**(A)**
8.	**(C)**	28.	**(E)**	48.	**(D)**
9.	**(B)**	29.	**(A)**	49.	**(B)**
10.	**(E)**	30.	**(C)**	50.	**(E)**
11.	**(D)**	31.	**(B)**	51.	**(B)**
12.	**(C)**	32.	**(D)**	52.	**(D)**
13.	**(B)**	33.	**(D)**	53.	**(C)**
14.	**(C)**	34.	**(A)**	54.	**(D)**
15.	**(A)**	35.	**(D)**	55.	**(E)**
16.	**(E)**	36.	**(A)**	56.	**(C)**
17.	**(B)**	37.	**(B)**	57.	**(D)**
18.	**(E)**	38.	**(A)**	58.	**(A)**
19.	**(A)**	39.	**(B)**		
20.	**(C)**	40.	**(D)**		

PRACTICE EXAM 1

AP English Language & Composition

Detailed Explanations of Answers

Section 1

1. **(C)** (C) is the correct answer because although it was established that the actors' free time spent with other groups may have been problematic previously, the actors would now be permitted "to use their extra time as they would" under the Group's unofficial policy. (A) is incorrect due to the fact that the Group had been worried about—rather than encouraging—their actors being involved with other acting groups. (B) is also incorrect since it had been the mention of actors involved in other acting groups prior to this unofficial policy which prompted the policy. (D) is incorrect because it is specifically mentioned in the passage that involvement in other acting groups could be noted but not held against the members of the Group. Lastly, (E) is also incorrect because it is stated that "our actors were free to use their extra time as they would."

2. **(B)** Since (B) is clearly stated in paragraph 4, this is the correct answer. There is no mention of (A), (C), (D), or (E) in the passage, despite each sounding as if it were plausible.

3. **(E)** (E) is the correct answer since each choice is stated within the first two paragraphs and are all positive aspects of the Group's members. While (A), (B), and (C) are each true, each is only one aspect of the inference, thereby making each incorrect. (D) contains two of the three aspects of the correct answer but omits the third, which causes it to be incorrect also.

4. **(A)** The characters in this piece do not represent a larger moral lesson (B), thus they are also not metaphors (C). The author is not trying to persuade (D), nor is he presenting a conflicting truth (E). The paragraph provides a story (A) to contribute to the setting of the biography.

5. **(D)** The response the character makes, "Besides, I like workers," is not rude (A), insightful (B), thoughtful (C) or unabashed (E). It is entirely irrelevant to the previous context of the conversation (D).

6. **(C)** Each example except (C) is a continued embellishment or logical progression of the previous sentence. Only in (C) does the author transition his subject, thus the tone shifts from anecdotal to focused chronology.

7. **(B)** The sentence contains alliteration (A), with the phrase, "prepared publically." It provides descriptive context of the setting (C), shows the qualities of the characters (D) and provides a feel of real life (E). It does not, however, contain the poetic strategy of caesura (B), natural pauses to show the rhythm of speech.

8. **(C)** It could be argued that some of the characters actors represent good, while others represent bad (A), however, there is no definitive evidence for either's quality. The characters actors do showcase wit, but not necessarily stupidity (B). (D) is the second best choice because serious issues are introduced at the end, but the actions of the characters actors are more humorous than trivial. There is not a warring struggle between truth and fiction (E), so the best choice is (C), a contrast between humor and seriousness.

9. **(B)** The sentence is complicated and long-winded, but it does not contain parallel syntactical structure (A) because it does not mirror the structure of previous or following sentences. It is not a series of prepositional phrases (C), nor is it a periodic sentence (D), or a sentence in which the subject comes at the conclusion. It is retrospective (E), but so is the entire work, so this sentence is not notably unique for that characteristic. The best answer is (B) because the humor and colloquial images provide an easy cohesiveness and narrative flow.

10. **(E)** This passage is mainly humorous and joking (E). It does not seek to persuade through righteousness or correct behavior (A). While it occasionally employs sarcasm (B), it is not the focused or predominant style. The passage does not use a great deal of analogous comparisons (C), nor is it particularly surprising (D) in its outcomes.

11. **(D)** The parenthetical comment is poking fun at the character-actor, so it is facetious (D). It may be misconstrued as apologetic (A) because it does its teasing of the actor in a kind manner, but it is still mocking. The sentiment does not deal with death (B). While the comment is light-hearted, it is not superficial (C) because it enriches the tone of the passage. The statement is not obsequious (E) because it mocks, not flatters.

12. **(C)** (A) is correct because the invaluable life of a child is understatedly appraised as "somewhat dear". (B) is also correct because the passage's dominant metaphor is that of parents raising their infants as food for the wealthy; here the parents are being "devoured". (D) and (E) are correct, and (C) is incorrect because

the landlords are sarcastically indicted. They have financially "eaten up" the parents and can be held responsible for the ends of their children.

13. **(B)**   While the monetary mechanics of buying and selling a child for food (C) are mentioned and scientific jargon briefly used (D), "animal husbandry," (B), is the best answer. The wives/mothers are referred to as "Breeders" and the children as "a most delicious, nourishing and wholesome Food" when cooked in ways associated with cuts of animal meats. Lines 35–40 compare ratios of human males and females to those found among domesticated animal herds. Children are described as if they were holiday turkeys, with instructions for fattening them and calculating the number of persons they will serve. Images of a dying, unstable city [urban decay, (A)], or religious rituals (E) are not found in the passage.

14. **(C)**   (C) is correct because "Popish" is a disparaging term used to describe someone or something as being of the Roman Catholic church. Although "Fish Eating" (D) and the "Irish" (E) are mentioned in the passage, they are unrelated to the term "Popish," as are "Tiny" (A) and "Unruly" (B).

15. **(A)**   The argument in these lines moves from a statement of a problem to a refutation of previously suggested solutions. Evidence to support a new remedy (the shocking revelation of the "American") is followed by this new proposal. The juxtaposition of such a frightening suggestion with such logical order shows the proposal in heightened horrific relief; therefore, (A) is correct. "Souls" is simply a synonym for "persons"; moreover, no other religious sentiments or principles follow. (D) is incorrect because the author is using statistics to introduce and clarify his idea, not to befuddle his reader. References to animal breeding (C) and first person openings (E) occur but do not have the effects given.

16. **(E)**   The speaker is calculating the number of fertile "Couples" and subtracts the 30,000 who can afford the upkeep of their children (although there cannot be "so many" because of the economic situation). The "couples" are numbered, not the "children" (A). "Number" (B) is incorrect because its own antecedent is "200,000 Couple" (line 2). "Souls" (C) is equal to the total number of persons in Ireland and not the subtracted "many." "Wives" (D) is incorrect because it is only a component of the "many" couples.

17. **(B)**   III and IV may appear correct; the author creates a satiric speaker who leads the reader to expect a plausible solution suggested by a rational, concerned citizen. The terrifying and definitively unmeasured proposal shatters these initial illusions. The author's actual appraisal of the landlords as uncaring (I), and even responsible for much of the problem of poverty, is revealed in lines 51–53 (they financially "devoured" parents and are best suited nonmetaphorically to consume their children), lines 62–63 (cottagers and farmers have beggars' status), and lines 68–69 (the landlord will learn that being good to his tenants means giving them financial assistance). The previous proposals (lines 12–14) have seemed impossible;

juxtaposed with such an improbable idea as raising children for food, they accrue new reasonableness and possibility (II).

18. **(E)** Stylistically the passage is neither philosophical (A); lyrical (B), expressing the writer's thoughts and sentiments, usually poetically; scientific (C); nor hortative (D), earnestly urging a specific course of action. It is satirical, (E), sarcastically and ironically exposing vice or folly.

19. **(A)** The best answer is (A); the animalistic connotations of "Breeders" dehumanizes the women. The speaker is so removed from these persons that no emotions toward them, such as those in choices (B) and (E) are present. The women are not given any special status over that of the men (C); they are simply singled out as the actual producers of children. The speaker does not blame or chastise the women for bearing children, (D) but the landlords for impoverishing these children.

20. **(C)** The proposal which follows these lines is likely to cause explosive reactions far beyond the understated "least Objection". It does not contain a hyperbole (A), seemingly opposite but apt terms (B), or an implied comparison (D). The phrase signals the coming of the main point of the argument rather than a distraction from it (E).

21. **(D)** Under an argument whose logical progression seems to suggest the coming of a rational proposal, these references are warning flags. While couched in non-emotional language, they the terms imply that people can be bought and sold as animals. The "knowing American" adds the concept of children as food. If the reader has missed this direction so far, letting the argument's rational layout sweep over him/her, the speaker "humbly" hammers it home. (A) and (E) are incorrect because the references are key elements of the argument, not digressions from or objections to it. Children as food of breeder mothers are not actual occurrences (B) but the speaker's "invention." The argument has not been fully introduced; therefore, these terms cannot be summarizing it (C).

22. **(D)** The statement does not prove the author is trustworthy (A), for that it would have to explain why he has the authority to make this statement. Though the sentence does show the author understands the biological growth of children, they are not his audience (B). The diction in this sentence is calculated, not emotional (C). The sentence cites logical fact, not belief (E). The best answer is (D), because it shows the author has considered the subject and turned his attention towards the facts to make an informed, thoughtful proposal.

23. **(B)** (A) and (C) show logical consideration for the shortcomings of the subject. (D) and (E) both consider logical benefits to the solution. (B) is the claim itself, not a logical deduction.

24. **(E)** The author does not call for rational thinking (A), in fact he explains in the passage how this has not worked. While he may demand immediate freedom (B),

he knows that the only way to get this freedom is to act on behalf of patriotism (E). He does not make a series of unwarranted claims (C), as most of his claims are negations of previously made arguments. The speaker may indeed be hyper-emotional (D), but he is calling for war, not equality.

25. **(C)** The sirens were mythical creatures, so allusion (C), is the only correct response. It is not a simile (A) because there is no use of *like* or *as*, not exaggeration (B), not a seemingly true statement about life (D), nor is it repeated again in the speech (E).

26. **(C)** The speaker is not addressing the British government (A); in fact he explains how this has been tried and failed. He may be addressing Democrats in the American government (B), but there is no direct evidence of this. Though he speaks for oppressed people (D), he is addressing those with the authority to make decisions. British citizens (E) are highly unlikely as the audience, and no rationale is provided for that response. In this instance, (C) is the only logical answer.

27. **(D)** The author continues speaking before his audience can reply to his questions (A). He does ask rhetorical questions (B), but that is only one aspect of his style. He does not demand answers (C), because he provides his own arguments for the questions he asks (D). He does not provide evidence alone (E), he provides arguments (D) which often include evidence.

28. **(E)** The questions in (A) and (D) are logical appeals rather than emotional ones. The metaphor in (B) provides imagery, which is arguably emotional, but there is a better selection. (C) is also a logical appeal, providing past precedent and explaining how it has failed. The diction and plea in (E) is a clear emotional appeal.

29. **(A)** Although "warlike preparations" (B) and "war and subjugation" (C) are phrases which could easily replace "they," these responses are not the direct antecedents of the word. "Kings" (D) and "last arguments" (E) are not logical choices because neither of these would be "meant for us." Navies and armies (A) are "meant for us," and is the correct answer.

30. **(C)** If the audience felt liberty was worthy of war (A) or a valuable commodity (B), the speaker would not have to make this persuasive speech. The reader may feel the audience thinks only governments can negotiate liberty (D), but if this were so, the audience would not have already tried other measures which supersede peaceful negotiations through governments (petitioning, supplication, etc.). Besides which, historically Americans had no government, as they were under British control. The audience may feel liberty is a slow process (E), but there is nothing to indicate this as they have been trying to attain it in peaceful ways. The best answer choice is (C), because the audience is hesitant to employ war tactics, and that is what the speaker is trying to persuade them to do.

31. **(B)**   Although the speaker does have a harsh and didactic tone at times, and a teaching one (A), it is not the best description of how he shifts his tone. The speaker is neither conventional nor intimate (C). He is sarcastic at times, but not specifically informative (D). He supplicates himself, rather than being haughty (E). The best choice is (B), as he pleads with his audience in the beginning, and shifts his tone to cynicism as he argues against what his audience believes.

32. **(D)**   The speaker does not use slang (A), and while he is occasionally abstract with his use of figurative language (B), it is better described as (D) idiomatic, or having a definitive style. The author's points are not at all mundane and weak (C), nor does he try to make himself seem superior to his audience (E).

33. **(D)**   When the speaker proclaims, "Give me liberty or give me death!" he makes himself a martyr, but the diction is electrifying, not morbid. Additionally, through his use of cause and effect reasoning, he employs logical rhetoric. The only correct answer is (D).

34. **(A)**   When the author asks the question in (B), he is exaggerating the consequences of inaction. In (C), he makes an inflated claim, as he does in (D). (E) is a hyperbolic, inflammatory sentiment, while (A) is merely a repetition of an earlier exclamation. This may seem to be hyperbole, as it is passionate, but the other options are far more exaggerated than this repeated call to action.

35. **(D)**   The author does not use passive voice (A); if he did, the phrase would read, "…bound hand and foot by our enemies." In this sentence the author uses emotional appeal, not ethical (B). Though he does use figurative language (C) "delusive phantom of hope," it is only a part of his style, not the best description of the sentence as a whole. The question is hyperbole, not understatement (E). The best answer is (D) because the author is mocking the beliefs of his audience when he foreshadows the negative outcomes of their decision to remain neutral.

36. **(A)**   Lamp (B), kiss (C), storm (D) and arms (E) are each only directly stated once, even if they are indirectly constructed again in the passage. The metaphor of chains (A) is repeated throughout.

37. **(B)**   The article mentions (A) the changing behavior of teenagers, (C) adolescent brain matter, (D) the use of MRIs in brain research, and (E) functional and structural changes in the brain throughout life. However, none of the topics is the main subject of the article. The main subject of the entire article is (B) research on brain development during adolescence.

38. **(A)**   The answer (A) is correct because the first paragraph states "a pruning process that occurs early in life that appears to follow the principle of 'use-it-or-lose-it:' neural connections, or synapses, that get exercised are retained, while those that don't are lost." Choices (B), (C), (D), and (E) are all part of the brain development

that the passage describes, but they do not refer specifically to the "pruning" that lines 3 and 20 address.

39. **(B)** The author is presenting the facts and implications of studies on the brain's development primarily during the teen years. The author's tone is (B) informative. Nothing in the passage is (A) humorous, (C) sarcastic, or (D) urbane. And although the author does not appear to be concealing information, the tone is more informative than (E) candid; a candid tone would be more blunt and outspoken.

40. **(D)** In answering this question, you must know the different parts of a footnote but be known, regardless of the format used. In the first footnote, Giedd, Blumenthal, Jeffries and others (indicated by "et al") are the authors. "Brain Development During Childhood and Adolescence: A Longitudinal MRI Study" is the title of the article. Depending on the format used, an article title may or may not be placed in quotation marks. Following the article title is the name of the magazine or journal, which may be italicized or underlined. Here, the journal is *Nature Neuroscience*. The volume number and the issue number come next: here, the article appears in the tenth issue of the second volume. The last part of the footnote is the page number or numbers. This particular article appears on pages 861 to 863. (D) is the only one choice that correctly describes the parts of the first footnote. *Nature Neuroscience* is the journal title, not the article title; the article title is "Brain Development During Childhood and Adolescence: A Longitudinal Study." Therefore, (A) and (E) are incorrect. The article appears on pages 861–863, instead of page 10; the number 10 refers to the issue number. So (B) is wrong. Nothing in the footnote indicates that the article is one of several articles; instead, the number 2 refers to the volume number, and the number 10 refers to the issue number. Therefore, choice (C) is incorrect.

41. **(E)** (E) is the only choice that correctly indicates the similarity between the two researchers' studies. The article says that Dr. Toga and colleagues used "4-D time-lapse animations of children's brains morphing as they grow up," but nothing indicates that Dr. Rapoport's study used such animations. Therefore, (A) is incorrect. (B) is wrong because nothing specifically says that the two researchers focused on the pruning process mentioned elsewhere in the paragraph, although one might infer that the concepts are related. Although Dr. Toga did use Dr. Rapoport's data, we do not know if Dr. Rapoport used the findings of Dr. Toga; thus, (C) is not correct. And nothing in the article indicates that either of them studied the differences between the brains of males and females; therefore, (D) is incorrect.

42. **(C)** Lines 39–44 refer to "striking growth spurts...from ages 6 to 13 in areas connecting brain regions specialized for language . . . ," which stop "sharply after age 12, coinciding with the end of a critical period for learning languages." Thus, (C) is the correct answer.

43. **(C)** The author refers to "waves" of growth to emphasize that parts of the brain grow more rapidly at some stages of development than at others. Lines 15–17 mention "a second wave of overproduction of gray matter . . . just prior to puberty."

Lines 37–38 reveal "a wave of white matter growth that begins at the front of the brain in early childhood . . . then subsides after puberty." And lines 43–44 address "a wave of brain white matter development that flows from front to back." The article does not indicate that (A) the brain contains water, (B) the brain's gray matter and white matter develop steadily, or the size of the brain's (D) gray matter or (E) white matter is limited.

44. **(B)** The purpose of a footnote is to let the reader know the original source of the information; usually, this source contains additional information about the footnoted topic. In this article, the footnote is used to indicate the source where the author found information about the UCLA 4-D study conducted by Dr. Toga and his colleagues. It is reasonable to assume that additional information is available in this source, which is an article written by Thompson, Giedd, Woods, and others. Therefore, (B) is correct. We have no way of knowing if Thompson (A) interviewed Dr. Toga or (C) worked with him. *Nature* is the title of the journal, not (D) the title of the article. And the article appeared on pages 190–3; the volume number—not the page number—is (E) 404.

45. **(A)** (A) is the best description of lines 22–32, since the statement "Researchers are not confronted with structural changes that occur much later in adolescence" is a general statement. The sentences that finish the paragraph give specific examples of those structural changes. This passage does not contain (B) a general statement followed by more general statements. It does not (C) start with specific examples that are followed by a general statement. And it does not contain technical terminology; so (D) and (E) are not correct.

46. **(E)** The author clarifies the phrase "waxes and wanes" in the following sentences, indicating that the gray matter has growth spurts in different areas of the brain at different stages of development. So (E) is the correct answer. (A) is incorrect because the term "progress" implies steady, continuous growth or development. If you chose (C), you may have read the passage too quickly: the sentence immediately following the quoted sentence indicates that the gray matter growth spurt in the frontal lobe—not the gray matter itself—predominates at a certain point in development. Although the last sentence of the paragraph indicates that the brain's white matter becomes more efficient, (C) the phrase "becomes increasingly efficient" is not an accurate substitution for the phrase "waxes and wanes" in reference to gray matter in the quoted sentence. Likewise, (D) "wishy-washy"—meaning "ineffectual or weak"—is an inappropriate description of the brain's gray matter and has nothing to do with the phrase "waxes and wanes."

47. **(A)** While all of the choices are synonyms that you might find in a dictionary or thesaurus if you looked up of the word "dynamic," the only one that fits in this context is (A) "ever-changing."

48. **(D)** The three articles cited in this passage were published in 1999 or 2000. The titles of all three articles indicate that the topics are scientific studies, and the

article itself indicates that they all focus on brain development. Therefore, (D) is an appropriate conclusion. (A) is incorrect because the footnotes tell us nothing about how the technical level of the language in the articles. (B) is not correct, since we know only that the three cited journals contain articles about brain research, and we do not know how popular the topic was during that time. And (C) is incorrect, since the footnotes tell us nothing about how much brain research was conducted prior to 1999, although paragraph 3 of the passage does indicate that research had been conducted prior to the 1999 NIMH study. And although Giedd was one of the writers of two of the articles, we have no way of knowing if he liked writing those articles with the other writers., and And, the footnotes do not tell us if any of the writers were scientists. Therefore, (E) is not correct.

49. **(B)**   While the "veil" is a symbol (A), it does represents a mask, not the anger of the Negroes. It is a metaphor (C), but has nothing to do with representing the genre, which is an essay. It is a state of being, but not a simile (D), because it does not use *like* or *as*. The veil is figurative language, so it cannot be a concrete image (E). (B) is correct because the veil becomes the direct and indirect topic of the entire work, which is the definition of a conceit.

50. **(E)**   Although this paragraph has a great deal of narrative, it is autobiographical, which by definition is not fictitious. (B) is incorrect because this example only shows the long, personal struggle of the author, not of the Negro people. Though the narrator's tone might be light at times (C), the anecdote is relatively tragic (a young white girl rejects his card). Though the anecdote may engage the reader (D), the real function of the anecdote is to awaken the author to his differences (E).

51. **(B)**   (A) is incorrect because the quotation specifically states "he would NOT bleach his Negro soul," which contradicts the implications in the first option. It may be true that white Americans are detrimental to the Negro's identity, but the author also states that he would not "Africanize America," for "America has too much to offer," indicating he does not feel whites have a negative effect on Negro identity. Like (C), (D) is also contradictory to the other statements the author makes, even if the response makes sense out of context from the rest of the passage. (E) is a rather irrelevant statement. (B) is correct because it explains the rather complex figurative language.

52. **(D)**   "It" is the "body" whose strength keeps it from being torn asunder. Though "twoness," "American," "Negro," and "strength" are each mentioned, none of them replace the word "it."

53. **(C)**   Although the dialogue does mention some historical events, "Mechanicsburg" (A), it does not show the sentimentality of history regarding blacks, only mentions that history exists. The speaker cannot be seen as tolerant (B), as he may "reduce the boiling to a simmer" later in the line. While the dialogue may make the reader feel more intimately connected to the author, (D), there is no guarantee of such, so it is not the absolute effect. The dialogue provides no comic relief (E)

because it causes the author strife. (C) is correct because it shows the divide between the author and the experience of the other speakers.

54. **(D)** The author uses parallel structure (A) throughout; "He would not…", "He would not…" is just one example. The author often employs emotionally-charged diction, (B); "without being cursed or spit upon" is one instance. The author employs imagery, (C), when he describes the "wee wooden school house," among other examples. The author also uses metaphor, (E), with reference to the "veil." It is allegory (D) that the author does not use, at least it is not evident in this excerpt.

55. **(E)** Among other descriptions, the author notes the other black boys' "taste-less sycophancy," or flattery for praise. He does not refer to them as brave (A), able (B), content (C) or particularly compelling (D). Ingratiating (E) is the only correct answer.

56. **(C)** The author recognizes he is a "problem" for white people, because they are unsure what to do with a black man with his level of education. They do not wish to show prejudice when they speak to him, yet do not feel comfortable accepting him, and this gives them feelings of guilt, making the speaker a problem for them. Fighting in the Civil War (A) may have been a problem for some people, but in this instance, the problem relates back to the speaker, not an action. In the same way, Southern outrages (B), appealing to white audiences (D), and controversy between blacks and whites (E) do not make the speaker a problem. Only (C) identifies the speaker as the problem.

57. **(D)** Though (A) might be a good choice, the author's diction is not necessarily overly concerned with perfection. Though it is informative (B), it is not the best way to describe the style. The author never shows outrage (C), nor is he radical (E). The speaker does have a cause, and does seek to educate, making (D) the best choice.

58. **(A)** The author seeks to explain the plight of African Americans (A), not get sympathy from whites (B). Though he may ignite the passions of black Americans (C), that is not his goal in this piece, nor does it seem they are his intended audience. He does highlight some of his desires (D), but again that is not his overall goal. (E) may be correct, but without further context from the whole work, there is no way to be sure that is the author's purpose in this excerpt.

Section 2

Model Student Response to Essay Question 1:

The United States of America has a firm foundation, based on the standards established by the U.S. Constitution. Since the beginning of the Presidency, it has been the responsibility of our leaders to uphold certain principles. Our Presidents' beliefs and concerns have focused on those issues, as their speeches to Congress and to the public reveal.

Faith in God, on which our nation was founded, has remained important to our Presidents. Therefore, they often thanked God for America's good fortune or prayed for God's blessing and help. Our first President, George Washington, referred to "the blessings which a Gracious Providence has placed within our reach." Roosevelt expressed "gratitude to the Giver of Good." Truman requested the prayers of his audience, and implied the importance of "faith in the Almighty" and "God's help." Likewise, Kennedy mentioned "Almighty God" as he acknowledged that his predecessors had taken the same oath. And, like the other Presidents, he asked for God's blessing and help, indicating that "here on earth God's work must truly be our own." And, like those who had led America before him, President Clinton sought God's blessing as he asked for strength.

Clearly, American Presidents have understood the importance of the country's military forces and readiness for war, as well as efforts to maintain peace. None have been eager to fight, but all have been willing to defend our freedom:. "To be prepared for War is one of the most effectual means of preserving peace" (Washington). Referring to the wars in which the United States had been involved, Truman emphasized that we must "live together in peace and harmony." Other Presidents have stressed the need to stand up to any enemy (Kennedy), and defend our country against all types of weapons and potential destruction (Clinton).

Closely related to these concerns is America's establishment of foreign relations. George Washington believed in facilitating the country's "intercourse with other nations. . . . for the public good." And as it has progressed into perhaps the greatest nation on earth, our country has needed to establish positive relationships with nations around the world (Roosevelt). Harry Truman was aware that other nations regarded the United States as a leader who was working to achieve "international order and justice." The Presidents have realized the endless potential in our country's united efforts with other nations (Kennedy), and understood the importance of joint cultural and commercial efforts (Clinton).

Also, the Presidents have consistently promoted education. Washington, Truman, and Kennedy all stressed the importance of scientific knowledge. Washington encouraged Americans to come up with new inventions, and believed knowledge results in happiness. Truman also promoted the acquisition and application of our technical knowledge. President Clinton regarded education as "every citizen's most prized possession," and believed that all Americans should have access to knowledge and education.

A look at these six Presidents' campaigns tells us that the beliefs and concerns of our nation's leaders have not changed much throughout history. They have focused on the importance of faith in God, strength in the military forces and defense, relations with foreign countries, and promotion of education. These principles have been part of the foundation of the United States throughout history.

Analysis of Student Response to Essay Question 1:

The student's response has addressed the main challenge of the question (synthesize at least three of the sources for support, and take a position that defends, challenges, or qualifies the claim that the concerns and beliefs of American presidents have remained basically the same throughout the history of this country). The first paragraph introduces the general topic of the foundation of the U.S., gradually narrowing to the specific idea of the essay. The writer has analyzed the five excerpts from presidential speeches, selecting four beliefs or concerns that appear in at least three of those speeches. One paragraph is devoted to each belief or concern. Each paragraph contains direct references to the sources. Sometimes the writer directly quotes a portion of the essay; for example, the second paragraph says, "Our first President, George Washington, referred to 'the blessings which a Gracious Providence has placed within our reach.'" At other times, the writer paraphrases the ideas in the presidents' speeches. The conclusion echoes the main ideas of the essay's body. Each source is clearly attributed. The language and development of the essay are effective, and the writer's position is supported with appropriate examples. Overall, the essay is an effective response to the prompt.

Model Student Response to Essay Question 2:

It is often said that there is a bit of truth in every joke, and that every person who employs humor as a means of defense is, in truth, insecure. In his essay, "Some Remarks on Humor," social commentator E.B. White deconstructs the nature of a humorist, and exhibits the difficult obstacles he faces in his existence. White's influential diction, varied syntax and facetious tone all construct his argument that the humorist is misunderstood in his time.

According to White, the humorist has several challenges in his career. He is often viewed by the serious crowd as unwilling to engage his emotions, the "clown with a breaking heart," and give proper respect to grave issues, which will, in turn, cause the humorous writer to be branded as nothing more than a "nonsensical" "fool," unable to produce work the world views as valuable and insightful. However, White argues that the humorist is able to succeed with integrity in the face of these challenges, as he "struggle[s] along with a good will and endure[s] pain cheerfully, knowing how well it will serve [him] in the sweet by and by." Throughout the essay, White continues to frame humorists in this sympathetic and compassionate light, all with a bit of humor himself. White makes the humorist a victim in a world of staid writers, branded with the "brim of the fool's cap," but avoids channeling pity, calling the humorist "sensible," "active," and "positive" because White feels he has a healthy and well-adjusted way of dealing with adversity. Rather than constantly exist as "heavy" and "pensive," the humorist is able to see the "fine line between laughing and crying," and capitalize on it. As a humorist himself, White chooses words that frame the conflict for humorists, but allow him to be seen as a credible writer, not "flippant," "funny," or "light."

White's sentence structure strengthens his characterization of humor, as he punctuates silly stories with understated, direct witticisms and critique. He is never "careless" or exuberant in his comedy, and rather than employ hyperbole, he uses sarcastic wit, a less embellished form of humor. White jumps from a complicated, anecdotal diatribe about the "bubble blower" to a caustic comment, "The effect was not pretty." This juxtaposition of nearly run-on, lyrical sentences with a short, dry, mocking comment shows White as seriously humorous about humor. Even those trying to be funny can take themselves too seriously, like the bubble blower, but White is able to analyze humor through his sentences without leaving it "dissected" like "a frog" or "fatten[ed] on trouble." White uses parallel structure throughout his essay to cement his notion that humor can be refined. He constantly stems his sentences with pronouns followed by verbs, "They have…", "They struggle…", "They put…", "It pays…", "It decorates…", "It feels…." White characterizes humorists and humor as misunderstood victims, and White is their champion as he couches their plights with compassionate, parallel and sophisticated structure.

White's tone maintains a nature of facetiousness, because it helps to give his piece the flair of humor, even though his subject is somewhat sober; after all, he is analyzing the treatment a person gets in this life for choosing a path of humor. White is nearly satirical throughout his essay, though he maintains an air of sincerity. He has taken it upon himself to be the hero for misunderstood humorists throughout the world, because even though the world "likes humor," it treats the humorist "patronizingly." White employs humor, yet in analyzing it, manages to remain free of any of the "Brussels sprouts" given to the "wags" because the essayist is its own exempt breed of humorist. To maintain his facetious tone, White uses parenthetical asides, "(which may closely resemble a sob, at that)," and maybe, "(…an unwise decision, at that)" to jab at the critics of humorists. This dual awareness allows White to avoid being "'paralyze[d]'" in his career for his humor, because he assumes the position of humorous critic, effectively making himself somber and funny.

In order to be a funny humorous writer and recognized positively professionally, an author has to approach humor and "dissect" it. E.B. White manages to do this without killing "the thing… in the process" because he keeps his writing tongue in cheek, prominent and amusing. Through his use of facetious tone, varied syntax and influential diction, White manages to paint the humorist in a sympathetic yet powerful light. Perhaps if humorists had more champions like White, comedians like Dane Cook would be more respected and considered valuable members of the literary world.

Analysis of Student Response to Essay Question 2:

This essay has tackled the main requirements of the prompt (analyze how White typifies humor through diction, syntax and tone), and has constructed a stance – that White feels humorists are misunderstood, and champions them through his presentation. The essay continues to support its claim throughout, using evidence from the text to support its arguments. It is clearly focused and persuasive, not just a summary of the work itself. The essay contains a strong introduction and conclusion, and one body paragraph dedicated to the analysis of each literary feature required by the prompt. The essay uses an appropriate vocabulary, and shows sophisticated understanding of the arguments, subtleties and implications of the given piece. Overall, this is an effective and persuasive response to the prompt.

Model Student Response to Essay Question 3:

By his impassioned and persuasive speech to the Virginia Convention, Patrick Henry convinced the American people to go to war with Britain, although their militaries were outnumbered by the thousands, simply by his impassioned and persuasive speech to the Virginia Convention. Martin Luther King's "I Have a Dream" Speech has been noted as one of the most influential oratories in the continued struggle for civil rights, and Jonathan's Swift's "A Modest Proposal" stood as one of the most preposterous solutions that inevitably helped change the fate of Ireland. Indeed, passionate speeches and rhetorical essays can change even the stodgiest people in the world.

When America was still a collection of colonies under the iron-fisted rule of the English Government, there was little reason to hope for a revolution. Britain's resources trumped the reserves of the colonies, and the American people had no organization or centralized force. However, Patrick Henry changed the minds of the colonists when he addressed the Virginia Convention. His powerful words, energy, ardor and rhetorical appeal convinced the colonists to organize and fight for freedom. He may have been considered radical, even crazy by his peers, but his beliefs and linguistic style brought won them over to his way of thinking. It was his use of language and presence, his confidence that managed to change the world. Patrick Henry made the inconceivable conceivable, and if it were not for his courageous and disruptive oratory, most people in America might now be speaking with a British accent.

Similarly, Martin Luther King is still quoted in high schools and television programs everywhere because of his famous "I Have a Dream" oratory. In a time when the American population was struggling against the backlash of Jim Crow laws, and the painful integration after *Brown v. the Board of Education,* Martin Luther King delivered a speech that inspired and united Americans. He brought hope to a divided country and helped ease the struggle between blacks and whites. Martin Luther King's rhetorical work is a masterpiece, and his delivery bolstered the impact. Indeed, de facto segregation may still be a factor in today's world, but King helped to ensure that de jure segregation was eliminated from the hearts and minds of the American people in the 1960s.

Jonathan Swift faced a similar set of circumstances as Patrick Henry, violent and abusive control over Ireland from Britain's government. Instead of rallying his people into war, he encouraged them to take stock of their foul behavior towards each other, and examine options among themselves to remain a peaceful and productive nation. His satirical essay, "A Modest Proposal," suggested the Irish become cannibals and eat the overpopulated and poor infants in Ireland, which is ironic given his actual agenda. Disturbingly radical, this essay caught the attention of the Irish citizens, and sparked debate among them. Shortly after Swift's scathing social commentary, Ireland once again began to ascend into profit and self-control. If Swift had not presented this controversial and articulate reproach, the fate of the Irish may have remained downtrodden and dismal.

It is clear that Cicero was correct in his assertion that, "Nothing is so unbelievable that oratory cannot make it acceptable." Swift, King and Henry are each excellent examples in their own right of this sentiment. There is a reason that the arts and publications are first to go when one country takes over another. These are the things that incite people to action.

Analysis of Student Response to Essay Question 3:

This essay has chosen three appropriate examples to support the quotation given in the prompt. While the writer does not give direct quotations from any of the pieces, this is acceptable because he or she would not have the sources to reference during the exam. It is occasionally vague (this essay would likely score a 7), particularly in its conclusion, but it nonetheless maintains adequate analysis and response to the prompt. The student writer has a clear understanding of the implications of the task, and maintains a persuasive stance. The language is knowledgeable and pertinent.

END OF PRACTICE TEST 1

PRACTICE EXAM 2

AP English Language & Composition

PRACTICE EXAM 2

AP English Language & Composition

Section 1

TIME: 60 Minutes
57 Questions

(Answer sheets appear in the back of this book.)

DIRECTIONS: This test consists of selections from literary works and questions on their use of language. After reading each passage, choose the best answer to each question and blacken the corresponding oval on the answer sheet.

Questions 1–10 are based on the following passage. Read the passage carefully and answer the accompanying questions.

Sawyer shouted at her when she entered the kitchen, but she just turned her back and reached for her apron. There was no entry now. No crack or crevice available. She had taken pains to keep them out, but knew full well that at any moment they could rock her, rip her from her moorings, send the birds
5   twittering back into her hair. Drain her mother's milk, they had already done. Divided her back into plant life—that too. Driven her fat-bellied into the woods—they had done that. All news of them was rot. They buttered Halle's face; gave Paul D iron to eat; crisped Sixo; hanged her own mother. She didn't want any more news about whitefolks; didn't want to know what Ella knew
10 and John and Stamp Paid, about the world done up the way whitefolks loved it. All news of them should have stopped with the birds in her hair.

Once, long ago, she was soft, trusting. She trusted Mrs. Garner and her husband too. She knotted the earrings into her underskirt to take along, not so much to wear but to hold. Earrings that made her believe she could discrimi-
15 nate among them. That for every schoolteacher there would be an Amy; that for every pupil there was a Garner, or Bodwin, or even a sheriff, whose touch

at her elbow was gentle and who looked away when she nursed. But she had come to believe every one of Baby Suggs' last words and buried all recollection of them and luck. Paul D dug it up, gave her back her body, kissed her divided

20 back, stirred her memory and brought her more news: of clabber, of iron, of roosters' smiling, but when he heard *her* news, he counted her feet and didn't even say goodbye.

"Don't talk to me, Mr. Sawyer. Don't say nothing to me this morning."

"What? What? What? You talking back to me?"

25 "I'm telling you don't say nothing to me."

"You better get them pies made."

Sethe touched the fruit and picked up the paring knife.

When pie juice hit the bottom of the oven and hissed, Sethe was well into the potato salad. Sawyer came in and said, "Not too sweet. You make it too

30 sweet they don't eat it."

"Make it the way I always did."

"Yeah. Too sweet."

None of the sausages came back. The cook had a way with them and Sawyer's Restaurant never had leftover sausage. If Sethe wanted any, she put them

35 aside soon as they were ready. But there was some passable stew. Problem was, all her pies were sold too. Only rice pudding left and half a pan of gingerbread that didn't come out right. Had she been paying attention instead of daydreaming all morning, she wouldn't be picking around looking for her dinner like a crab. She couldn't read clock time very well, but she knew when the hands

40 were closed in prayer at the top of the face she was through for the day. She got a metal-top jar, filled it with stew and wrapped the gingerbread in butcher paper. These she dropped in her outer skirt pockets and began washing up. None of it was anything like what the cook and the two waiters walked off with. Mr. Sawyer included midday dinner in the terms of the job—along with

45 $3.40 a week—and she made him understand from the beginning she would take her dinner home. But matches, sometimes a bit of kerosene, a little salt, butter too—these things she took also, once in a while, and felt ashamed because she could afford to buy them; she just didn't want the embarrassment of waiting out back of Phelps' store with the others till every white in Ohio

50 was served before the keeper turned to the cluster of Negro faces looking through a hole in his back door. She was ashamed, too, because it was stealing and Sixo's argument on the subject amused her but didn't change the way she felt; just as it didn't change schoolteacher's mind.

1. In lines 4–5, the words "send the birds twittering back into her hair" provide an example of

   (A) alliteration

   (B) simile

   (C) onomatopoeia

   (D) metaphor

   (E) hyperbole

2. The passage suggests

   (A) Sawyer is Sethe's husband

   (B) the Garners stole Sethe's earrings

   (C) Sethe was not intelligent

   (D) the others waiting at the back of Phelps' store were whites

   (E) Sethe has a sense of pride

3. To which of the following people does "she" refer in the sentence, "Once, long ago, she was soft, trusting?"

   (A) Mrs. Garner

   (B) Mrs. Sawyer

   (C) Sethe

   (D) Ella

   (E) Bodwin

4. What might be the purpose of the author's first paragraph?

   (A) To show how whites mistreated Sethe

   (B) To list the atrocities committed upon her friends

   (C) To create sympathy for Sethe

   (D) To demonstrate her fragile state of mind at this point

   (E) To reinforce Seethe's lack of memory

5. "Clabber" (paragraph 2) probably means

   (A) speak incessantly

   (B) positive emotional experiences

   (C) engage in love making

   (D) thickened or curdled sour milk

   (E) beat in a brawl

6. In line 2 the sentences "There was no entry now. There was no crack or crevice available" indicate all of the following EXCEPT

    (A) how the speaker uses figurative language to illustrate her fortitude

    (B) that the speaker is not afraid of Sawyer's threats

    (C) how Sawyer could not get to her since the doors were all locked and closed

    (D) how Sethe has had to do all she can to keep focused on her task

    (E) that if she is not careful that she will once again be deeply hurt

7. By stating, "and she made him understand from the beginning she would take her dinner home," the reader understands that the "she" is understood to be a person who is

    (A) pedantic   (D) ambivalent

    (B) timorous   (E) pertinacious

    (C) reverent

8. In the last sentence of the passage, the sentence ends with the following statement, "because *it* was stealing and Sixo's argument on the subject amused her but didn't change the way she felt;" to what does the *it* refer to in the passage?

    (A) filling the metal-top jar with stew

    (B) wrapping the gingerbread in butcher paper

    (C) looking for dinner like a crab

    (D) looking for a hole in his back door

    (E) taking matches and other items that she could afford

9. All of the following are present in the second paragraph of the passage EXCEPT

    (A) an objective tone   (D) repetition

    (B) parallel structure   (E) a typical narrative opening

    (C) metaphor

10. Choose the reason why it was a problem that "all her pies were sold, too."

    (A) Sawyer told Sethe to save a pie for him

    (B) Sawyer needed pies for families at night

    (C) Sethe did not make the pies sweet enough for their guests

    (D) Sethe had no pies to share through the hole in the back door

    (E) Sethe had no pie to take home for herself

Questions 11–18 are based on the following passage. Read the passage carefully and answer the accompanying questions.

"Are you ill, Edward?" she said, rising immediately.

"I felt some uneasiness in a reclining posture. I will sit here for a time." She threw wood on the fire, wrapped herself up, and said, "You would like me to read to you?"

5   "You would oblige me greatly by doing so, Dorothea," said Mr. Casaubon, with a shade more meekness than usual in his polite manner. "I am wakeful: my mind is remarkably lucid."

"I fear that the excitement may be too great for you," said Dorothea, remembering Lydgate's cautions.

10   "No, I am not conscious of undue excitement. Thought is easy." Dorothea dared not insist, and she read for an hour or more on the same plan as she had done in the evening, but getting over the pages with more quickness. Mr. Casaubon's mind was more alert, and he seemed to anticipate what was coming after a very slight verbal indication, saying, "That will do—mark that"

15   or "Pass on to the next head—I omit the second excursus on Crete." Dorothea was amazed to think of the bird-like speed with which his mind was surveying the ground where it had been creeping for years. At last he said—

"Close the book now, my dear. We will resume our work to-morrow. I have deferred it too long, and would gladly see it completed. But you observe that

20   the principle on which my selection is made, is to give adequate, and not disproportionate illustration to each of the theses enumerated in my introduction, as at present sketched. You have perceived that distinctly, Dorothea?"

"Yes," said Dorothea, rather tremulously. She felt sick at heart.

"And now I think that I can take some repose," said Mr. Casaubon. He lay

25   down again and begged her to put out the lights. When she had lain down too, and there was a darkness only broken by a dull glow on the hearth, he said—

"Before I sleep, I have a request to make, Dorothea."

"What is it?" said Dorothea, with a dread in her mind.

"It is that you will let me know, deliberately, whether, in case of my death,

30   you will carry out my wishes: whether you will avoid doing what I should deprecate, and apply yourself to do what I should desire."

Dorothea was not taken by surprise: many incidents had been leading her to the conjecture of some intention on her husband's part which might make a new yoke for her. She did not answer immediately.

35   "You refuse?" said Mr. Casaubon, with more edge in his tone.

"No, I do not yet refuse," said Dorothea, in a clear voice, the need of freedom asserting itself within her, "but it is too solemn—I think it is not right—to make a promise when I am ignorant what it will bind me to. Whatever affection prompted I would do without promising."

40   "But you would use your own judgment: I ask you to obey mine; you refuse."

"No, dear, no!" said Dorothea, beseechingly, crushed by opposing fears. "But may I wait and reflect a little while? I desire with my whole soul to do what will comfort you; but I cannot give any pledge suddenly—still less a pledge to
45   do I know not what."

    "You cannot then confide in the nature of my wishes?"

    "Grant me till to-morrow," said Dorothea beseechingly.

    "Till to-morrow then," said Mr. Casaubon.

11.   "Excursus" in the fifth paragraph probably means

    (A)   excuses

    (B)   appendix or germane digression

    (C)   illustration

    (D)   map

    (E)   allusion

12.   In paragraph six, the author is inferring

    (A)   Mr. Casaubon doubted Dorothea's ability to finish the work

    (B)   Dorothea had already expressed no desire to help him

    (C)   Mr. Casaubon feared he would not be able to complete his work alone

    (D)   Dorothea was Mr. Casaubon's teacher

    (E)   Mr. Casaubon and Dorothea were partners in this scholarly work

13.   Mr. Casaubon's statement, "Before I sleep, I have a request to make, Dorothea," is an example of

    (A)   double entendre   (D)   figure of speech

    (B)   metaphor   (E)   elegy

    (C)   simile

14. Mr. Casaubon's question to Dorothea, "You cannot then confide in the nature of my wishes?" implies

   (A) he thinks her a liar

   (B) he feels trapped

   (C) he wants her to promise blindly

   (D) he has had past experience with disobedience

   (E) Dorothea has always questioned his orders

15. By writing "Dorothea was not taken by surprise…," the author is telling us

   (A) she was unaware that she would be expected to make this promise

   (B) she knew Mr. Casaubon well

   (C) she had not had to take orders from him before

   (D) she was unintelligent

   (E) she didn't understand her role in this relationship

16. The line "many incidents had been leading her to the conjecture of some intention on her husband's part which might make a new yoke for her" helps the reader to understand that the writer is implying that

   (A) Dorothea is led to believe that her husband has a happy surprise in store for her

   (B) Dorothea feels that another burden will weigh her down

   (C) Dorothea is remembering Lydgate's cautions

   (D) Dorothea is afraid of Mr. Casaubon

   (E) Mr. Casaubon gives his wife free rein in their marriage

17. The following sentence, "Dorothea was amazed to think of the bird-like speed with which his mind was surveying the ground where it had been creeping for years," utilizes which literary technique?

   (A) simile   (D) juxtaposition

   (B) personification   (E) imagery

   (C) allusion

18.   The tone of the passage can best be described as

(A)   scathingly bitter   (D)   pretentious

(B)   wistfully observant   (E)   ambiguous

(C)   aggressively judgmental

Questions 19-35 are based on the following passage. Read the passage carefully and answer the accompanying questions.

"Is this the end?
O Life, as futile, then, as frail!
What hope of answer or redress?"

A cloudy day: do you know what that is in a town of iron-works? The sky sank down before dawn, muddy, flat, immoveable. The air is thick, clammy with the breath of crowded human beings. It stifles me. I open the window, and, looking out, can scarcely see through the rain the grocer's shop opposite,
5   where a crowd of drunken Irishmen are puffing Lynchburg tobacco in their pipes. I can detect the scent through all the foul smells ranging loose in the air.

The idiosyncrasy of this town is smoke. It rolls sullenly in slow folds from the great chimneys of the iron-foundries, and settles down in black, slimy pools on the muddy streets. Smoke on the wharves, smoke on the dingy boats,
10   on the yellow river,—clinging in a coating of greasy soot to the house-front, the two faded poplars, the faces of the passersby. The long train of mules, dragging masses of pig-iron through the narrow street, have a foul vapor hanging to their reeking sides. Here, inside, is a little broken figure of an angel pointing upward from the mantel-shelf; but even its wings are covered with
15   smoke, clotted and black. Smoke everywhere! A dirty canary chirps desolately in a cage beside me. Its dream of green fields and sunshine is a very old dream,—almost worn out, I think.

From the back-window I can see a narrow brick-yard sloping down to the river-side, strewed with rain-butts and tubs. The river, dull and tawny-colored,
20   (*la belle rivière!*) drags itself sluggishly along, tired of the heavy weight of boats and coal-barges. What wonder? When I was a child, I used to fancy a look of weary, dumb appeal upon the face of the negro-like river slavishly bearing its burden day after day. Something of the same idle notion comes to me to-day, when from the street-window I look on the slow stream of human life creeping
25   past, night and morning, to the great mills. Masses of men, with dull, besotted

faces bent to the ground, sharpened here and there by pain or cunning; skin and muscle and flesh begrimed with smoke and ashes; stooping all night over boiling caldrons of metal, laired by day in dens of drunkenness and infamy; breathing from infancy to death an air saturated with fog and grease and soot,
30 vileness for soul and body. What do you make of a case like that, amateur psychologist? You call it an altogether serious thing to be alive: to these men it is a drunken jest, a joke,—horrible to angels perhaps, to them commonplace enough. My fancy about the river was an idle one: it is no type of such a life. What if it be stagnant and slimy here? It knows that beyond there waits for it
35 odorous sunlight,—quaint old gardens, dusky with soft, green foliage of apple-trees, and flushing crimson with roses,—air, and fields, and mountains. The future of the Welsh puddler passing just now is not so pleasant. To be stowed away, after his grimy work is done, in a hole in the muddy graveyard, and after that,—*not* air, nor green fields, nor curious roses.

40 Can you see how foggy the day is? As I stand here, idly tapping the window-pane, and looking out through the rain at the dirty back-yard and the coalboats below, fragments of an old story float up before me,—a story of this old house into which I happened to come to-day. You may think it is a tiresome story enough, as foggy as the day, sharpened by no sudden
45 flashes of pain or pleasure.—I know: only the outline of a dull life, that long since, with thousands of dull lives like its own, was vainly lived and lost: thousands of them,—massed, vile, slimy lives, like those of the torpid lizards in yonder stagnant water-butt.—Lost? There is a curious point for you to settle, my friend, who study psychology in a lazy, *dilettante* way.
50 Stop a moment. I am going to be honest. This is what I want you to do. I want you to hide your disgust, take no heed to your clean clothes, and come right down with me,—here, into the thickest of the fog and mud and foul effluvia. I want you to hear this story. There is a secret down here, in this nightmare fog, that has lain dumb for centuries: I want to make it
55 a real thing to you. You, Egoist, Pantheist, or Arminian, busy in making straight paths for your feet on the hills, do not see it clearly,—this terrible question which men here have gone mad and died trying to answer. I dare not put this secret into words. I told you it was dumb. These men, going by with drunken faces and brains full of unawakened power, do not ask
60 it of Society or of God. Their lives ask it; their deaths ask it. There is no reply. I will tell you plainly that I have a great hope; and I bring it to you

to be tested. It is this: that this terrible dumb question is its own reply; that it is not the sentence of death we think it, but, from the very extremity of its darkness, the most solemn prophecy which the world has known
65 of the Hope to come. I dare make my meaning no clearer, but will only tell my story. It will, perhaps, seem to you as foul and dark as this thick vapor about us, and as pregnant with death; but if your eyes are free as mine are to look deeper, no perfume-tinted dawn will be so fair with promise of the day that shall surely come.

19. What is the function of the epigraph that opens the passage?

    (A) It makes it clear that the passage which follows is a retrospective of the speaker's life.

    (B) It establishes a mood of despair and hopelessness.

    (C) It lends authority to the speaker's work by quoting another writer.

    (D) It sets the scene as that of a pre-apocalyptic society.

    (E) It comments critically upon the speaker's work.

20. The opening sentence of the passage (line 1) does all of the following EXCEPT

    (A) draw the reader into the passage

    (B) directly address the reader

    (C) challenge the reader's knowledge and experience

    (D) reveal to the reader the speaker's lack of knowledge about her subject matter

    (E) imply that the reader belongs to a different world than that being described here

21. It can be inferred that "Lynchburg tobacco" (line 5) is

    (A) the preferred brand of Irishmen

    (B) detrimental to its smokers' health

    (C) a particularly inferior brand

    (D) obtainable at the "grocer's shop"

    (E) a scent pleasing to the speaker

22. The sentence "Smoke...passersby" (lines 9–11) contains which of the following?

    (A) An ellipsis   (D) Alliteration

    (B) A metaphor   (E) Abstract imagery

    (C) Metonymy

23. Which of the following best describes what the "little broken figure of an angel" (line 13) represents?

    (A) The poverty that extends even into the homes of the inhabitants of the ironworks town

    (B) The irreverence that prevails in the speaker's home

    (C) The smoke that invades every aspect of ironworks town life

    (D) The grime of ironworks town life that weighs down even dreams of an afterlife

    (E) The sincere piety of the speaker

24. The aside "(*la belle rivière*)" (line 20) can best be interpreted as

    (A) an ironical description

    (B) a nostalgic memory

    (C) a pedantic display of the speaker's education

    (D) a humorous comment

    (E) a redundant characterization

25. A "dirty canary" (line 15) with its "dream of green fields and sunshine" (line 16) and the river that "drags itself sluggishly along, tired of the heavy weight of boats and coal-barges" (lines 20–21) are examples of

    (A) metaphor   (D) hyperbole

    (B) personification   (E) assonance

    (C) oxymoron

26. The expository technique of the third paragraph (lines 18–39) is best described as

    (A) cause and effect   (D) question and answer

    (B) chronological order   (E) comparison/contrast

    (C) classification

27. The relationship between the rivers and men (paragraph 3)

    I.   crosses the characteristics of water and humans

    II. comparatively implies that the town's workers are slaves

    III. gives superior status to the river

    IV. dehumanizes the worker

    (A) I only

    (B) II and III only

    (C) III only

    (D) II, III, and IV only

    (E) I, II, III, and IV

28. The speaker assumes that the reader's attitude toward the ironworks laborer is one of

    (A) sympathy

    (B) defensiveness

    (C) clinical observation

    (D) antipathy

    (E) ignorance

29. A "Welsh puddler" (line 37) is most probably

    (A) a grave digger

    (B) an ironworks employee

    (C) a hand on a coal barge

    (D) a street cleaner

    (E) a bartender

30. In line 36, the phrase "air, and fields, and mountains" parallels, yet contrasts with

    (A) "fog and grease and soot" (line 29)

    (B) "skin and muscle and flesh" (lines 26–27)

    (C) "soul and body" (line 30)

    (D) "*not* air, nor green fields, nor curious roses" (line 39)

    (E) "quaint old gardens, dusky with soft, green foliage of apple-trees, and flushing crimson with roses" (lines 35–36)

31. The antecedent of "it" (line 54) is

    (A) "this nightmare fog" (line 54)

    (B) "this story" (line 53)

    (C) the "foul effluvia" (line 53)

    (D) the "secret down here" (line 53)

    (E) "this terrible question" (line 56)

32. Considering the passage as a whole, the "terrible question which men here have gone mad and died trying to answer" (lines 56–57) can best be identified as:

    (A) How can the life of the ironworks town laborer be bettered?

    (B) What is the meaning of life?

    (C) How can the pollution from the ironworks be lessened?

    (D) What is the responsibility of the upper to the lower classes?

    (E) Why are the workers Western Europeans?

33. The speaker's characterization of the reader as "Egoist, Pantheist, or Arminian, busy in making straight paths for [his/her] feet on the hills, [does] not see it clearly" (lines 55–56) implies that

    (A) the reader, absorbed in ordering his/her own life according to various doctrines, cannot fully comprehend the struggle for meaning in life

    (B) the reader is a landowner making civic improvements without regard to the concerns of ironworks town inhabitants

    (C) the reader seeks meaning in a materialistic existence

    (D) the reader, relying on psychology and its terminology, would scientifically order life

    (E) as a foreigner, the reader is only briefly and dispassionately trekking through the ironworks town

34. It can be inferred that the speaker believes that

    (A) human existence is pointless

    (B) social reform is imminent

    (C) afterlife is the ultimate hope

    (D) men live more desperate lives than women

    (E) educated persons experience life differently than factory workers

35. The speaker's story is most probably

    (A) a bitter life lived without redress

    (B) an example of a terrible life ending with an anticipated unearthly reward

    (C) a retelling of his/her own life in the ironworks town

    (D) a futuristic tale of life to come in the ironworks town

    (E) a fantasy transporting the pampered reader into the ironworks employee's role

Questions 36–48 are based on the following passage. Read the passage carefully before choosing your answers.

I then inquired for the person that belonged to the petticoat; and, to my great surprise, was directed to a very beautiful young damsel, with so pretty a face and shape, that I bid her come out of the crowd, and seated her upon a little crock at my left hand. "My pretty maid," said I, "do you own yourself to
5 have been the inhabitant of the garment before us?" The girl I found had good sense, and told me with a smile, "That notwithstanding it was her own petti- coat, she should be very glad to see an example made of it; and that she wore it for no other reason, but that she had a mind to look as big and burly as other persons of her quality; that she had kept out of it as long as she could, and till
10 she began to appear little in the eyes of all her acquaintance; that if she laid it aside, people would think she was not made like other women." I always give great allowances to the fair sex upon account of the fashion, and therefore was not displeased with the defense of the pretty criminal. I then ordered the vest, which stood before us to be drawn up by a pulley to the top of my great hall,
15 and afterwards to be spread open by the engine it was placed upon, in such a manner, that it formed a very splendid and ample canopy over our heads, and covered the whole court of judicature with a kind of silken rotunda, in its form not unlike the cupola of St. Paul's. I entered upon the whole cause with great satisfaction, as I sat under the shadow of it.

20 The counsel for the petticoat was now called in, and ordered to produce what they had to say against the popular cry which was raised against it. They answered the objections with great strength and solidity of argument, and expa- tiated in very florid harangues, which they did not fail to set off and furbelow (if I may be allowed the metaphor) with many periodical sentences and turns
25 of oratory. The chief arguments for their client were taken, first, from the great benefit that might arise to our woolen manufactory from this invention, which was calculated as follows: the common petticoat has not above four yards in the circumference; whereas this over our heads had more in the semidiameter; so that by allowing it twenty-four yards in the circumference, the five millions
30 of woolen petticoats, which (according to Sir William Petty) supposing what ought to be supposed in a well-governed state, that all petticoats are make of that stuff, would amount to thirty millions of those of the ancient mode. A prodigious improvement of the woolen trade! and what could not fail to sink the power of France in a few years.

35   To introduce the second argument, they begged leave to read a petition
of the rope-makers, wherein it was represented, that the demand for cords,
and the price of them, were much risen since this fashion came up. At this, all
the company who were present lifted up their eyes into the vault; and I must
confess, we did discover many traces of cordage which were interwoven in the
40 stiffening of the drapery.

A third argument was rounded upon a petition of the Greenland trade,
which likewise represented the great consumption of whalebone which would
be occasioned by the present fashion, and the benefit which would thereby
accrue to that branch of the British trade.

45   To conclude, they gently touched upon the weight and unwieldiness of the
garment, which they insinuated might be of great use to preserve the honor of
families.

These arguments would have wrought very much upon me (as I then told
the company in a long and elaborate discourse), had I not considered the great
50 and additional expense which such fashions would bring upon fathers and
husbands; and therefore by no means to be thought of till some years after a
peace. I further urged, that it would be a prejudice to the ladies themselves,
who could never expect to have any money in the pocket, if they laid out so
much on the petticoat. To this I added, the great temptation it might give to
55 virgins, of acting in security like married women, and by that means give a
check to matrimony, an institution always encouraged by wise societies.

36. The argument takes the form of

   (A) a question and answer session

   (B) a trial

   (C) a confession

   (D) a sermon

   (E) a debate

37. The girl "began to appear little in the eyes of all her acquaintance" (line 10)

   (A) in girth and social standing

   (B) in size and wealth

   (C) in body and mind

   (D) in waist and undergarment

   (E) in weight and education

38. The girl's statement in lines 6–11 can best be interpreted as

    (A) the actions of a slave to fashion

    (B) the scheme of a social climber

    (C) the tricks of an underweight woman

    (D) the response of a sensible woman pressured by social dictates

    (E) the rantings of a condemned woman

39. The "vest" of line 13 is

    (A) a garment   (D) a jacket

    (B) a petticoat   (E) a robe

    (C) an umbrella

40. All of the following are present in the sentence in lines 13–18 EXCEPT

    (A) hyperbole   (D) metaphor

    (B) simile   (E) humor

    (C) oxymoron

41. The description of the argument of the counsel for the petticoat (lines 21–25) parallels

    (A) the petticoat itself

    (B) the formality of the inquiry

    (C) the complexity of the woolen industry

    (D) the "power of France" (line 34)

    (E) the good sense of the owner of the petticoat

42. The observation that the production of large petticoats "could not fail to sink the power of France in a few years" (line 34) is

    (A) an understatement of the might of fashion

    (B) a hyperbolic statement

    (C) a declaration of war

    (D) an economic statistic

    (E) an egotistical boast

43. The "petition of the Greenland trade" (line 41) was most likely issued from

    (A) petticoat makers   (D) whalers

    (B) carvers   (E) shipowners

    (C) merchants

44. Why would petticoats, such as the one being examined in the passage, "be of great use to preserve the honor of families" (lines 46–47)?

    (A) Ladies would be able to dress as fashion demands women of their station should.

    (B) Families would exhibit their wealth through their clothing.

    (C) A bulky petticoat could not be easily removed during illicit love affairs.

    (D) The size of the petticoat would prevent young ladies from being kidnapped.

    (E) Demeaning small places could not be entered by ladies wearing large petticoats.

45. The final point of the speaker's judgment against the petticoat (lines 54–56)

    (A) assents to the concluding point of the counsel's argument

    (B) turns the concluding point of the counsel's argument against itself

    (C) opposes the concluding point of the counsel's argument

    (D) is not linked to the concluding point of the counsel's argument

    (E) is weakened by the concluding point of the counsel's argument

46. Who/what can best be identified as the passage's criminal?

    (A) The girl who owned the petticoat

    (B) Society

    (C) Fashion

    (D) "Persons of her quality" (line 9)

    (E) The petticoat

47. Both the defense of the petticoat and the speaker's reply are primarily structured as

    (A) appeals to authority   (D) patriotic arguments

    (B) appeals to emotion   (E) ethical appeals

    (C) economic appeals

48. The style of the passage taken as a whole can best be described as

(A) gently satiric   (D) colloquially informal

(B) bitterly ironic   (E) pedantically formal

(C) wryly humorous

Questions 49–57 are based on the following passage. Read the passage carefully before you choose your answers. This passage is a portion of "On the Importance of Being Ernst Mayr: 'Darwin's apostle' died at the age of 100" by Axel Meyer. This tribute appeared in the PLoS Biology journal on April 5, 2006.

Born on July 5, 1904, in Kempten in southern Germany, Ernst Mayr passed away peacefully at the Methuselah-like age of 100 on February 3, 2005, in Bedford near Cambridge, Massachusetts. Mayr was, by the accounts of his Harvard colleagues the late Stephen Jay Gould and Edward O. Wilson, not

5 only the greatest evolutionary biologist of the 20th century, but even its greatest biologist overall. . . . Ernst Mayr has been called "Darwin's apostle" or the "Darwin of the 20th century" for promoting and dispersing Darwin's hypotheses throughout the past century. . . .

Ernst Mayr had many fundamental insights into evolutionary biology,

10 and almost every topic of importance in evolution was advanced by his ideas. Perhaps his most widely known contribution is to the current notion of what constitutes a species. Darwin did not think that species were real in the philosophical sense, but rather that they were the result of the human predilection to perceive discontinuity among continuously varying individuals. Most biolo-

15 gists nowadays disagree with Darwin's view of species, largely because of Mayr's "biological species concept." Together with [population geneticist] Dobzhansky, Mayr developed this definition of species "as groups of interbreeding populations in nature, unable to exchange genes with other such groups living in the same area."[1,2] Barriers to gene flow between species—termed reproductive

20 isolating mechanisms—keep biological species distinct through processes such as species-specific mate choice and hybrid sterility. Although there are theoretical and operational problems with the biological species concept (e.g., it does not apply to asexually reproducing organisms such as bacteria), it is still, by far,

---

[1.] T. Dobzhansky, *Genetics and the Origin of Species* (New York: Columbia University Press, 1937), p. 364

[2.] E. Mayr, *Systematics and the Origin of Species* (New York: Columbia University Press, 1942) p. 334

the most widely used species concept among the 20 or so competing defini-
25 tions that have been proposed in the past several decades. Students of biology
all over the world have memorized Mayr's definition of species for more than
half a century.

. . . Mayr's understanding of the biogeographic distributions of bird species,
overlaid with extensive knowledge about variation in morphology, led him to
30 develop concepts about the geographic mechanisms of speciation—cornerstones for those studying speciation today. The geographic separation of populations, such as by rivers or valleys, he argued, prohibits homogenizing gene
flow between them. If such isolated (termed allopatric) populations accumu-
late mutations over time, this might lead to the divergence of such populations
35 from each other, and reproductive isolation might arise as a simple byproduct
of these separate evolutionary histories. Mayr staunchly defended this idea during sometimes heated debates and further developed it and other hypotheses
regarding geographic mechanisms of speciation over many decades (outlined
in depth in the 797 pages of *Animal Species and Evolution*[3]) . . . .

40 Clearly, Ernst Mayr felt very strongly that he had something of importance
to say to the world. . . . Although Ernst Mayr lived only about a tenth of the
969 years that Methuselah is purported to have lived, he still accomplished
much more than one might expect to get done, even in 100 years. . . . On the
occasion of his 100th birthday Mayr published an article in Science[4] looking
45 back over eight decades of research in evolution that he closed with the following words: "The new research has one most encouraging message for the active
evolutionist: it is that evolutionary biology is an endless frontier and there is
still plenty to be discovered. I only regret that I won't be present to enjoy these
future developments."

49. The purpose of footnotes 1 and 2 is to inform the reader that the quotation
in lines 16–19

(A) was Mayr's own original creation, copied by Dobzhansky

(B) was used by both Mayr and Dobzhansky in their books on the origin of
species

(C) Mayr needed Dobzhansky's help in developing this definition

---

[3.] E. Mayr, *Animal Species and Evolution*. (Cambridge, Massachusetts: Belknap Press, 1963),
p. 797

[4.] E. Mayr, *"Happy Birthday: 80 Years of Watching the Evolutionary Scenery."* Science 305,
46–47 (2004).

(D) was Dobzhansky's own original creation, copied by Mayr

(E) was the definition that students memorized for many years

50. In line 33, the pronoun "them" refers to

(A) gene flow

(B) rivers or valleys

(C) separation

(D) mutations

(E) populations

51. Based on the information in line 39 and footnote 3, which of the following statements is accurate?

(A) Mayr's explanation of animal species and evolution appears on page 797 of his book.

(B) The author of the book *Animal Species and Evolution* quotes Mayr on page 797.

(C) An outline of Mayr's hypotheses appears in the book *Animal Species and Evolution*.

(D) Mayr wrote a 797-page book titled *Animal Species and Evolution*.

(E) In 1942, the Columbia University Press wrote a book about Mayr's theories on animal species and evolution.

52. Which of the following accurately describes the author's tone as he describes Mayr and his work?

(A) Envy

(B) Gratitude

(C) Admiration

(D) Disgust

(E) Cynicism

53. This article compares Mayr to

(A) Darwin and Dobzhansky

(B) Darwin and Methuselah

(C) Dobzhansky and Methuselah

(D) Wilson and Gould

(E) Wilson and Darwin

54. The structure of lines 11–16 can best be described as

(A) moving from general to specific

(B) moving from specific to general

(C) moving from general to general

    (D)   moving from specific to specific

    (E)   a presentation of conflicting ideas

55.   A look at the footnotes tells the reader that

    (A)   both Dobzhansky and Mayr wrote about Mayr's life

    (B)   Dobzhansky had a longer writing career than Mayr did

    (C)   Dobzhansky relied heavily on the works of Mayr regarding evolutionary biology

    (D)   Mayr's writing career lasted at least sixty years

    (E)   Mayr often liked to write about himself

56.   The passage's purpose can be characterized as

    (A)   expository   (D)   judicial

    (B)   analytical   (E)   exhortative

    (C)   eulogistic

57.   The quote taken from Mayr's *Science* article (lines 46–49) implies that

    (A)   Mayr believed evolutionary biology had unveiled many intriguing mysteries

    (B)   Mayr believed that evolutionary biologists will continue making new discoveries

    (C)   advances in evolutionary biology were likely to end with Mayr's death

    (D)   Mayr was worried that he would die soon

    (E)   Mayr had made tremendous contributions to the field of evolutionary biology

STOP

This is the end of Section 1.
If time still remains, you may check your work only in this section.
Do not begin Section 2 until instructed to do so.

Section 2

TOTAL TIME – 2 hours 15 minutes

Question 1 (Spend 15 minutes reading the materials. Suggested writing time—40 minutes. This question is worth one-third of the total essay score.)

Directions: The following prompt is based on the accompanying six sources.

This question requires you to synthesize a variety of sources into a coherent, well-written essay. Refer to the sources to support your position; avoid mere paraphrase or summary. Your argument should be central; the sources should support this argument.

Remember to attribute both direct and indirect sources.

Introduction: As technology has advanced, the curricula in American schools have changed. Schools are increasingly using technology as a means of educating students today. Not only are schools teaching computer skills, but also including the use of such technology as video games and iPods as part of normal class work. What is the effect of this changing approach to education? Is it an improvement over traditional education, or is it a compromise?

Assignment: Read the following sources (including any introductory information) carefully. **Then, in an essay that synthesizes at least three of the sources for support, take a position that defends, challenges, or qualifies the claim that schools that are embracing the new technological approach to education are effectively teaching students the skills they need in today's world.**

You may refer to the sources by their titles (Source A, Source B, etc.) or by the descriptions in parentheses.

Source A (Empire High School)

Source B (U. S. Department of Education)

Source C (Cartoon)

Source D (Johnson)

Source E (Miller)

Source A

"Arizona High School Chooses Laptops Over Textbooks." *VOANews.com*. Voice of America, 20 Oct. 2005. Web. 15 Oct. 2010.

The following passage is excerpted from an article about a new educational approach adopted by Empire High School in Vail, Arizona.

A new high school opened in Vail, Arizona, this past July with all the resources you would expect to find in classrooms these days—except textbooks. Instead, every student received an Apple laptop computer . . . making Empire High School a pioneer in the growing use of technology in American education.

. . . a committee visited classrooms that were making partial use of laptops, and came away with two distinct impressions. "One was that students in schools where laptops were being used were clearly more engaged," Mr. Baker says. "And the other impression was that we felt we could do more with laptops. Because we had the opportunity here of opening a new school, we could make them an integral part of what we do, and actually change the way we do things. And we sort of forced that issue by not buying any textbooks."

Teachers helped plan the school's wireless curriculum, often experimenting with different ideas in classrooms where they taught before. . . .

Michael Frank teaches a first year biology course, where students use their laptops to access instructions for their lab work, organize data, and graph the results. . . . "[Students] will be putting together all the results from this experiment in a Power Point presentation for the class later. . . . And I know I can just give them an address for a web site that has information and they can go look at it there. A lot of times with science, we use it because you can get immediate access to the most recent information. You don't have to wait 5 or 6 years for it to get into a textbook. So there's much more access to just a huge amount of data about things."

. . . There was a surprise once classes got underway as well. . . . "We thought the kids would be better at computing than they actually are. Being able to drive your X-box or your iPod is not the same thing as being able to take a computer, use it, create a document, save it with a file name, put it in a particular location and retrieve it. And that has been a real challenge."

But administrators say the system is working well overall, and students seem to agree. . . .

Calvin Baker also stresses that he is not trying to make Empire High a technology school. And he says quality education still has to be about things like hard work, self-discipline and outstanding teaching—with laptops becoming a natural part of the classroom, just as they have become a natural part of workplaces across America.

Source B

"Archived: Educational Technology Fact Sheet." *Ed.Gov*. U.S. Department of Education, 29 Mar. 2006. Web. 15 Oct. 2010.

The following information is excerpted from the Department of Education's "Educational Fact Sheet" regarding the availability of technology to students in the United States. Today's technology allows distance learning courses; in these courses, students work on their own from home or another off-site location, communicating with teachers and other students by using such technology as e-mail, video-conferencing, and instant messaging.

Statistics:

- In 2003, the ratio of students to computers in all public schools was 4.4 to 1.

- 48 states included technology standards for students in 2004–2005.

- In 2003, 8 percent of public schools lent laptop computers to students. . . .

- Schools in rural areas (12 percent) were more likely than city schools (5 percent) and urban fringe schools (7 percent) to lend laptops.

- In 2003, 10 percent of public schools provided a handheld computer to students or teachers.

- 16 states had at least one cyber charter school operating in 2004–2005.

- 22 states had established virtual schools in 2004–2005.

- 56 percent of 2- and 4-year degree-granting institutions offer distance education courses, with 90 percent of public institutions offering distance education courses. . . .

Distance Learning

- 36% of school districts and 9% of all public schools have students enrolled in distance education courses.

- There were an estimated 328,000 enrollments in distance education courses by K-12 students during the 2001–2002 school year.

- 68% of the enrollments were in high school with an additional 29% in combined or ungraded schools.

- 45,300 enrollments in distance education were Advanced Placement or college-level courses.

- A greater proportion of rural area districts had students enrolled in distance education courses than did urban and suburban districts.

- 42% of districts that have students enrolled in distance-education courses are high poverty districts.

- When small districts offer distance learning, they are more likely to involve a greater proportion of schools.

- 80% of public school districts offering online courses said that offering courses not available at their schools is one of the most important reasons for having distance education.

- 50% of public school districts offering online courses cited distance learning as very important in making Advanced Placement or college-level courses available to all students.

- 92% of districts enrolled in online distance education courses had students access online courses from school.

- 24% of districts with students accessing online courses from home provided or paid for a computer for all students, while an additional 8% did so for some students.

Friendship Through Education

- Using the Internet to connect students in the U.S. and Arab nations to develop mutual understandings of one another's cultures.

Source C

Rosandich, Dan. "EDUCATION CARTOONS." *Danscartoons.com*. Web. 16 Oct. 2010.

"What a school day! The computers broke down and we had to LISTEN!"

Source D

Johnson, Doug. "School Media Services for the "Net Generation" Part One." *Doug Johnson Website*. 1 Jan. 2007. Web. 15 Oct. 2010.

This passage is excerpted from an article by Doug Johnson who has been director of media and technology for the Mankato (Minnesota) Public Schools since 1991.

. . . kids expect fast communication responses, tune out when things aren't interesting, and may be more visually than verbally literate. For them, technology is a tool for learning on any topic they choose. (Are you reading anything you don't already know from the media or from personal observation?)

. . . Our current crop of students believes "teachers are vital," "computers can't replace humans," and motivation is critical in learning. They like group activities, believing building social skills is a part of schooling. They identify with their parents' values. And they are achievement oriented, feeling it is "cool to be smart." And although they are fascinated with new technologies, their knowledge of them is often "shallow."

(Who actually maintains the computers in your home or school?)

Finally, the studies point to how this generation learns—or likes to learn. Our current crop of students with their hypertext minds like inductive discovery rather than being told what they should know. In other words, they want to learn by doing rather than simply listening or reading. They enjoy working in teams, on "things that matter," often informally, and not just during school hours. And given their quick response requirements, they need to be encouraged to reflect.

It is my firm belief that schools will be more productive if educators acknowledge the unique attributes and preferences of the Net Generation and adapt educational environments to suit students instead of trying to change their basic natures. So what are some implications for NG (Net Generation) library media centers?

To a large degree, media centers may be the most NG-oriented places in schools. . . . Given their preference to work in groups, the NG media center should provide spaces for collaboration on school projects and socialization. It should contain the tools necessary for the production of information, not just its consumption—computers with the processing power and software to edit digital movies and photographs, scanners, and high-quality printers and projection devices—and, of course, assistance in the use of these tools.

. . . It should have comfy chairs, and be a friendly atmosphere, low-stress, safe, and forgiving—and yes, in high schools, an in-house coffee shop. Spaces for story times, puppetry, plays, and games along with computer stations with age-appropriate software and Web sites are just as important in elementary schools. If the "room" is not a wonderful place to be, students and teachers will stay on the Internet or in the classroom. Period. (And given the rise in online schools, is there a lesson here for classrooms as well?)

Source E

Miller, Ed, and Joan Almon. "Child Advocates Challenge Current Ed Tech Standards" (press release). Alliance for Childhood. 30 Sept. 2004. Retrieved 21 Jan. 2011 at *http://drupal6.allianceforchildhood.org/computer_press_release*. Reprinted by permission.

The following passage has been excerpted from a press release from the Alliance for Childhood, a non-profit organization concerned with healthy child development.

The high-tech, screen-centered life style of today's children—at home and at school—is a health hazard and the polar opposite of the education they need to take part in making ethical choices in a high-tech democracy, according to a new report released today by the Alliance for Childhood.

Tech Tonic: Towards a New Literacy of Technology challenges education standards and industry assertions that all teachers and children, from preschool up, should use computers in the classroom to develop technology literacy. That expensive agenda ignores evidence that high-tech classrooms have done little if anything to improve student achievement, the report says.

The report strongly criticizes the extensive financial and political connections between education officials and school technology vendors. It urges citizens to wake up to the increasing influence of corporations in policymaking for public education.

"The lack of evidence or an expert consensus that computers will improve student achievement—despite years of efforts by high-tech companies and government agencies to demonstrate otherwise—is itself compelling evidence of the need for change," *Tech Tonic* states. "It's time to scrap…national, state, and local policies that require all students and all teachers to use computers in every grade, and that eliminate even the possibility of alternatives."

At the same time, the Alliance suggests, high-tech childhood is making children sick—promoting a sedentary life at a time when childhood obesity is at epidemic levels

Today's children will inherit social and ecological crises that involve tough moral choices and awesome technological power, *Tech Tonic* warns. To confront problems like the proliferation of devastating weapons and global warming, children will need all the "wisdom, compassion, courage, and creative energy" they can muster, it adds. Blind faith in technology will not suffice.

"A new approach to technology literacy, calibrated for the 21st century, requires us to help children develop the habits of mind, heart, and action that can, over time, mature into the adult capacities for moral reflection, ethical restraint, and compassionate service," the report states.

The Alliance for Childhood is a nonprofit partnership of educators, researchers, health professionals, and other advocates for children, based in Maryland. *Tech Tonic* is a follow-up to the Alliance's widely noted 2000 report *Fool's Gold*. In *Tech Tonic* the Alliance proposes a new definition of technology literacy as "the mature capacity to participate creatively, critically, and responsibly in making technological choices that serve democracy, ecological sustainability, and a just society."

Tech Tonic proposes seven reforms in education and family life. These will free children from a passive attachment to screen-based entertainment and teach them about their "technological heritage" in a new way, rooted in the study and practice of technology "as social ethics in action" and in a renewed respect for nature.

The seven reforms:

- Make human relationships and a commitment to strong communities a top priority at home and school.

- Color childhood green to refocus education on children's relationships with the rest of the living world.

- Foster creativity every day, with time for the arts and play.

- Put community-based research and action at the heart of the science and technology curriculum.

- Declare one day a week an electronic entertainment-free zone.

- End marketing aimed at children.

- Shift spending from unproven high-tech products in the classroom to children's unmet basic needs.

"To expect our teachers, our schools, and our nation to strive to educate all of our children, leaving none behind, is a worthy goal," *Tech Tonic* says. "To insist that they must at the same time spend huge amounts of money and time trying to integrate unproven classroom technologies into their teaching, across the curriculum with preschoolers on up, is an unwise and costly diversion from that goal. It comes at the expense of our neediest children and schools, for whom the goal is most distant."

The report proposes 10 guiding principles for the new technology literacy and offers examples of each. It also includes suggestions for educators, parents, and other citizens to develop their own technology literacy, with a similar emphasis on social ethics in action.

"Today's children will face complex and daunting choices, in a future of biotechnology, robotics, and microchips, for which we are doing very little to prepare them," says Joan Almon, head of the Alliance. "We immerse them in a virtual, high-tech world and expect them to navigate the information superhighway with little guidance and few boundaries. It is time for a new definition of technology literacy that supports educational and family habits that are healthy both for children and for the survival of the Earth."

"It is within the context of relationships that children learn best," adds Dr. Marilyn Benoit, past president of the American Academy of Child and Adolescent Psychiatry and vice president of the Alliance Board of Trustees. "As we shift more towards the impersonal use of high technology as a major tool for teaching young children, we will lose that critical context of interactive relationship that so reinforces early learning."

CONTINUE TO QUESTION 2 >

Question 2 (Suggested time—40 minutes. This question is worth one-third of the total essay score.)

In the classic American novel *The Grapes of Wrath (1939)*, John Steinbeck relates the struggles of midwestern farmers during the Great Depression. In this excerpt, Steinbeck digresses from his story of the Joad family to show the determination of a turtle. Read the following passage carefully and write an essay that analyzes how Steinbeck uses rhetorical strategies to display the perseverance of the turtle.

The sun lay on the grass and warmed it, and in the shade under the grass the insects moved, ants and ant lions to set traps for them, grasshoppers to jump into the air and flick their yellow wings for a second, sow bugs like little armadillos, plodding restlessly on many tender feet. And over the grass at the roadside a land turtle crawled, turning aside for nothing, dragging his high-domed shell over the grass. His hard legs and yellow-nailed feet threshed slowly through the grass, not really walking but boosting and dragging his shell along. The barley beards slid off his shell, and the clover burrs fell on him and rolled to the ground. His horny beak was partly open, and his fierce, humorous eyes, under brows like fingernails, stared straight ahead. He came over the grass leaving a beaten trail behind him, and the hill, which was the highway embankment, reared up ahead of him. For a moment he stopped, his head held high. He blinked and looked down. At last he started to climb the embankment. Front clawed feet reached forward but did not touch.

The hind feet kicked his shell along, and it scraped on the grass, and on the gravel. As the embankment grew steeper and steeper, the more frantic were the efforts of the land turtle. Pushing hind legs strained and slipped, boosting the shell along, and the horny head protruded as far as the neck could

stretch. Little by little the shell slid up the embankment until at last a parapet cut straight across its line of march, the shoulder of the road, a concrete wall four inched high. As though they worked independently the hind legs pushed the shell against the wall.

The head upraised and peered over the wall to the broad smooth plain of cement. Now the hands, braced on top of the wall, strained and lifted, and the shell came slowly up and rested its front end on the wall.

For a moment the turtle rested. A red ant ran into the shell, into the soft skin inside the shell and suddenly head and legs snapped in, and the armored tail clamped in sideways. The red ant was crushed between body and legs. And one head of wild oats was clamped into the shell by a front leg. For a long moment the turtle lay still, and then the neck crept out and the old humorous frowning eyes looked about and the legs and tail came out. The back legs went to work, straining like elephant legs, and the shell tipped to an angle so that the front legs could not reach the level cement plain. But higher and higher the hind legs boosted it, until at last the center of balance was reached, the front tipped down, the front legs scratched at the pavement, and it was up. But the head of wild oats was held by its stem around the front legs.

CONTINUE TO QUESTION 3 ▷

Question 3 (Suggested time—40 minutes.) This question is worth one-third of the total essay score.

In 1983, the D.A.R.E. (Drug Abuse Resistance Education) program, a school-based substance abuse prevention program began in a nationwide effort to "teach students good decision-making skills to help them lead safe and healthy lives."

Supporters argue that D.A.R.E. effectively helps millions of kids find alternatives to drug abuse in ways beyond what schools and families can provide. Proponents contend that kids and parents like the program, and that it fosters valuable relationships between police, family, and schools.

Critics argue that scientific evidence shows no significant difference between future drug use in kids who have "graduated" from the costly D.A.R.E. program and those who have not. They contend that the program is misleading and can actually increase drug use by students.

Think about the effectiveness of this program. Then, write an essay that defends, challenges, or qualifies the claim that the D.A.R.E. program is an effective method of preventing teenage drug abuse. Use specific, appropriate evidence to develop your position.

Source: ProCon.org. "D.A.R.E. Home." DARE.ProCon.org. ProCon.org, 5 Oct. 2010. Web. 14 Oct. 2010.

END OF EXAM

PRACTICE EXAM 2

AP English Language & Composition

Answer Key

Section 1

1.	**(D)**	20.	**(D)**	39.	**(B)**
2.	**(E)**	21.	**(C)**	40.	**(C)**
3.	**(C)**	22.	**(A)**	41.	**(A)**
4.	**(D)**	23.	**(D)**	42.	**(B)**
5.	**(D)**	24.	**(A)**	43.	**(D)**
6.	**(C)**	25.	**(B)**	44.	**(C)**
7.	**(E)**	26.	**(E)**	45.	**(B)**
8.	**(E)**	27.	**(E)**	46.	**(E)**
9.	**(A)**	28.	**(C)**	47.	**(C)**
10.	**(E)**	29.	**(B)**	48.	**(C)**
11.	**(B)**	30.	**(D)**	49.	**(B)**
12.	**(D)**	31.	**(D)**	50.	**(E)**
13.	**(A)**	32.	**(B)**	51.	**(D)**
14.	**(C)**	33.	**(A)**	52.	**(C)**
15.	**(B)**	34.	**(C)**	53.	**(B)**
16.	**(B)**	35.	**(B)**	54.	**(A)**
17.	**(B)**	36.	**(B)**	55.	**(D)**
18.	**(E)**	37.	**(A)**	56.	**(C)**
19.	**(B)**	38.	**(D)**	57.	**(B)**

PRACTICE EXAM 2
AP English Language & Composition

Detailed Explanations of Answers

Section 1

1.   **(D)**   (D) is the correct answer since this figure of speech is applied to the idea that others could make Sethe become mentally unstable, the birds representing other people and their twittering representing her mental unease from what others have done to her. (A) is incorrect since the initial sounds of most of the words are not the same. Nor is (B) the answer because no two things are being compared in the phrase. Likewise, (C) is wrong due to the lack of the words' pronunciation contributing in any way to their meaning. Finally, (E) is not acceptable; there is neither exaggeration nor extravagance in the phrase.

2.   **(E)**   (E) is the correct answer; in paragraph 11, it states, "…she just didn't want the embarrassment of waiting out back of Phelps' store with the others till every white in Ohio was served before the keeper turned to the cluster of Negro faces looking through a hole in his back door." (A) cannot be correct; Sawyer is not Sethe's husband, but her employer, as it is made clear in sentence, "Mr. Sawyer included midday dinner in the terms of the job…." Since Sethe remembers the Garners among those who treated her well, "…whose touch at her elbow was gentle and who looked away when she nursed," rather than poorly, as in stealing from her, (B) is incorrect. (C) is also not the answer since Sethe figures out the time without being able to read the clock. We already know that those waiting at the back of Phelps' store are not white—but Negro—so (D) is not true, either.

3.   **(C)**   (A) and (E) are both incorrect since each was included among the people being trusted rather than being the one who was doing the trusting as explained in (B) of Item No. 2. (B) is incorrect because it is "Mr.," not "Mrs.," Sawyer who is mentioned. (D) is another incorrect answer since Ella is only mentioned in passing. Therefore, (C) is the correct answer by a process of elimination.

4.   **(D)**   While Sethe's mistreatment by whites is included in the passage, this mistreatment is a part of a list of people who were mistreated, so both (A) which refers to only Sethe and (B) which refers only to her friends are incorrect. (C) may have worked, except for the unemotional statements of these facts; sympathy is an emotional reaction. The passage is a string of Sethe's memories, which makes (E) an incorrect answer. (D) is the correct answer since the metaphors refer to Sethe's mind being carefully held together despite her past experience.

5.   **(D)**   (A) and (E) are incorrect since the word "clabber" comes after the preposition "of." This positioning means that the following word is a noun (the object of the preposition), not the verbs offered in these two choices. Both (B) and (C) are incorrect since each is considered a positive act which does not belong in a negative paragraph such as this one. Therefore, (D) is the correct answer.

6.   **(C)**   (C) is the correct answer since Sethe does not literally lock the doors. Answer (A) is not the correct answer since Sethe shows her strength.

7.   **(E)**   Sethe is clearly not trying to be overly proud and pretentious which would be (A); she is neither afraid (B) nor is she deeply respectful (C) or ambivalent (D); she is definitely one who makes her own decisions. (E) shows this specific persistence in her nature in demanding food for her dinner.

8.   **(E)**   Answers (E) clearly reflects the fact that she knows it was stealing despite what she is told. Answers (A), (B), (C), and (D) are details that do not answer the question.

9.   **(A)**   Answers (B), (C), (D), and (E) are all present in paragraph 2. However, the paragraph reads in a judgmental tone; therefore, it is not objective and the correct answer is (A).

10.   **(E)**   Answers (A), (B), (C), and (D) do not answer the question of why it is a problem that there are no pies left. Now she has no food to eat for herself. Therefore the correct answer is (E).

11.   **(B)**   While (A) is grammatically correct, logically it makes no sense. (C), (D), and (E) may be rejected on grammatical terms; the word *on* after "excursus" would have to be *of* for (C) and (D) and *to* for (E) in order for these nouns to be used. Therefore, (B) is the correct answer.

12.   **(C)**   The correct answer is (C) since Dorothea begins the passage inquiring about Mr. Casaubon's health and he acknowledges not feeling well. She wonders if the excitement of her reading to him would be too exciting for him. In addition, Dorothea wonders at the rush in completing the work she has been helping him with, as well as his clarifying for her just what it is they are doing. These same facts point out that (A), (B), (D), and (E) are not true.

13. **(A)**   Since (B) and (C) are comparisons and none is made in this statement, neither is the correct answer. (D) is used to produce mental images, not ordinarily thought of when reading the word and also is incorrect. (E) is employed after someone has died. Therefore, (A) is the correct answer; "sleep" is meant both as a night's rest and death.

14. **(C)**   (C) is the correct answer since he will not tell her specifically what it is he wants her to promise. (A), (B), (D), and (E) may be true, but cannot be validated from the passage; therefore, they are all incorrect answers.

15. **(B)**   The key word is *not*; therefore (A), (C), and (E) are all incorrect since they imply a lack of knowledge about Mr. Casaubon on Dorothea's part. (D) is also incorrect since her reading to him and his request that she work to help him quickly complete the project demonstrates her intelligence. The correct answer is (B).

16. **(B)**   The line that reads "many incidents lead..." shows the reader that Dorothea is used to the figurative and literal burdens that her husband places on her and that she is unwilling to yet discover his newest request. Her hesitation quickly shows that (A) and (E) are wrong; (C) and (D) cannot be proven.

17. **(B)**   (B) is the correct answer because this line gives a personal trait to an inanimate object. A mind does not survey the ground where it has been creeping is clearly not (A), (C), (D), or (E).

18. **(E)**   (E) is the correct answer because the speaker is worried about Mr. Casaubon's reactions and how he will adjust to her and to how she reacts to him. She is not bitter (A), wistfully observant (B), or aggressively judgmental (C); if anything, she is a bit passive and withdrawn, but she is not (D) pretentious.

19. **(B)**   The epigraph describes life as "futile" and "frail" and altogether hopeless, creating an aura of despair (B). (A) is incorrect because it misreads "end" (line A) as "death" rather than the highest attainable standard of living. Because the source of the quoted epigraph is unclear, it carries no particular weight (C). (D) would also misread "end" as "the end of the world"; furthermore, there is no indication in the passage which follows that this society is awaiting annihilation. Taking the passage as a whole, the reader can infer that the despairing statement of the epigraph is in agreement with, rather than contrary to (E), the speaker's attitudes.

20. **(D)**   The speaker brings the reader into the passage (A) by directly asking him/her "do you know..."(B). And, by immediately providing the answer makes it clear that the reader could not possibly have firsthand knowledge [(C) and (E)] of life in an ironworks. (D) is incorrect because it misinterprets the intent of the question; the speaker's swift and detailed response indicates that the information is not actually sought from the audience.

21. **(C)**   The speaker implies that Lynchburg tobacco is inferior (C) by having it smoked by men who are loitering, drunken, and, as a result of these states, assumably poor. The smoking of this tobacco by this group does not imply that all Irishmen smoke it or even that these particular men prefer it to other brands (A). There is no suggestion of the tobacco's effect upon its smokers (B). One cannot assume that the smokers bought their tobacco at the grocer's shop simply because they are loitering outside it (D). Rather than being pleasing, the scent of the tobacco must be particularly noxious to be distinguishable "through all the foul smells ranging loose in the air" (line 6) (E).

22. **(A)**   The sentence omits several easily understood words (A), such as a verb in the main clause ("smoke [lies] on the… X") and the preposition *to* (preceding "the two faded poplars" and "the faces"). There is no comparison being implied (B) or descriptive substitution of a part for a whole [(C), metonymy]. Alliteration (D) is incorrect because there is no repetition of initial consonants. The imagery of this sentence is decidedly concrete, making (E) incorrect.

23. **(D)**   "Pointing upward" (line 14), the angel symbolizes heavenly afterlife; such hope, however, is "broken" and dirtied by the ironworks town life (D). Although the angel is broken, it does not indicate that its owner lives a life of deprivation (A). The soot that covers the angel is atmospheric rather than an intentional dishonoring (B); the statue's spot on the mantle may even be a place of honor. The smoke (C) does not need to be symbolically portrayed—it is literally described as omnipresent. Display of an angel figurine is not an indication of religious fervor (E). In addition, it is unclear if the house and its contents are the speaker's own.

24. **(A)**   The "dull and tawny-colored" (line 19) river is mockingly described as its opposite, a beautiful river (A). The beautiful river cannot possibly be a wistful, yearning memory (B) since the speaker later describes the river of her childhood as tired and overburdened. Neither here, nor elsewhere in the passage, is the speaker seeking arrogantly to display "book learning" (C); in fact, the speaker is sharing knowledge from life experience. The comment is not amusing (D)—it is bitterly mocking. The river is first described as dirty and slow; a second depiction of it as beautiful cannot possibly be repetitious (E).

25. **(B)**   Both descriptions attribute human characteristics, dreaming and weariness, to an animal or inanimate object [(B), personification]. "Metaphor" (A) is incorrect because there is no comparison being made in these specific phrases. There is no joining of seemingly opposite terms, making "oxymoron" (C) incorrect. Neither phrase is overly exaggerated [(D), hyperbole]. "Assonance" (E), repetition of vowel sounds in words with differing initial consonants, is not present here.

26. **(E)** This paragraph compares and contrasts (E) the river and the ironworks laborer, both "working" slavishly, but one bearing hope of a better future. The paragraph does not present a series of actions or occurrences and their consequences (A). The narration is not chronological (B) because the speaker moves from present

to past to present to future. There is no ordering of terms or things by groups or classes (C). (D) misinterprets the questions in lines 30–31 and 34: they are rhetorical, and the speaker expects no answers.

27. **(E)**   The river is given the human sensation of weariness (line 20), and man is dehumanized by being given the river's status of "stream…creeping past" (lines 24–25) (I, II). The speaker implies that the workers are slaves (III) by describing the river as "negro-like…slavishly bearing its burden day after day" (lines 22–23) and subsequently noting that "something of the same idle notion comes to [him/her] today" when viewing the routine of the worker. The river ultimately has the higher status (IV) because it will pass on to a better "life," whereas the laborer will simply go slavishly on until his death (lines 37–39).

28. **(C)**   The speaker anticipates the reader's reaction to be what an "altogether serious thing to be alive" (line 31), a coldly detached remark (C). This projected response is not one of shared feelings (A) or contempt (D). There is no sign that the speaker considers the reader to be fending off an anticipated attack (B). The reader seems to have some understanding of the seriousness of the laborer's situation, making (E) incorrect.

29. **(B)**   By analogy, "Welsh puddler" is one out of the "masses of men" who labor in the ironworks (line 25). The river is compared to the human masses, and then it is contrasted with an individual member. (A) relies upon a misreading of lines 36–39; the grave is the puddler's end, not his place of occupation. (C), (D), and (E) all misinterpret puddler as having to do with liquid.

30. **(D)**   The phrases in line 36 and in (D) are parallel in structure, being set off by dashes and organized as a series of three; the former phrase, however, is an expected destination while the latter is the opposite of an ultimate end point. Although they are tripartite in structure, (A) and (B) are not contextually related to the phrase in line 36. (C) and (E) do not have the tripartite structure necessary for parallelism.

31. **(D)**   The antecedent of "it" can be found by dropping the descriptive subordinate clauses and joining the independent clauses in lines 52–54: "there is a secret down here… I want to make it a real thing to you." The "nightmare fog" (A) is part of a prepositional phrase that describes the secret's location and not the thing that is to be made real. This "story" (B) reveals the secret. While the reader may not have yet experienced it firsthand, "foul effluvia" (C) is already a real thing. The "terrible question" (E) is the secret, but it follows "it" and thus cannot be its antecedent.

32. **(B)**   The very lives and deaths of the workers (lines 57–59) are lives so terrible and hopeless and deaths so unremarkable that they ask, "What is the point of existence?" (B). In order for (A) to be correct, there would have to be suggestions for concrete reform, rather than abstract promises "of the day that shall surely come" (lines 66–67). Pollution (C) is indeed a problem, but it is a backdrop to the problems of the workers. While it is implied that the reader is of higher socioeconomic status

than the workers, there is no blame given or responsibility attributed for the condition of the workers (D). The workers are variously described as Irish and Welsh, but the question of their ethnicity is irrelevant (E).

33. **(A)**   Egoism, Pantheism, and Arminianism are, respectively, self-worship, nature worship, and a theology opposed to predestination. They are all systems of belief; by using such a system, the reader seeks to make his/her own way through life without seeing "it" (the "secret"/"question," inferentially the meaning of life) (A). (B) mistakenly takes the concept of making paths literally. (C) is incorrect because there is no indication that the reader considers physical possessions to be the key to life. Harkening back to the speaker's comment of "amateur psychologist" (lines 30–31) (D) misinterprets "Egoism" as the scientific jargon of Freudianism. (E) confuses "Arminian" with *Armenian* and also interprets "paths" as literal places for walks.

34. **(C)**   The speaker states that the question answers itself and is "the most solemn prophecy…of the Hope to come" (lines 62–63); in addition, the story to be told "will be so fair with promise of the day that shall surely come" (lines 66–67). These phrases indicate that there is a reason for human life [ruling out (A)], and their religious connotations imply that this reason is a "life" after human toil (C). The predicted relief is described in vague and religious terms, not in socioeconomic language (B). Although only the terrible lives of men are described, the omission of women does not imply that they fare better (D). The reader, inferentially more educated than the worker, is "busy in making straight paths for his/her feet" (lines 54–55): he/she too is looking for a rationale for life, and by projecting [his/her] interest in the story about to be told, the speaker implies that afterlife will fulfill this goal (E).

35. **(B)**   The speaker describes the projected story as "the outline of a dull life, that long since…vainly lived and lost" (lines 45–46); its conclusion in the past rules out (C), (D), and (E). (A) is incorrect because a hard life without remedy holds none of the hope the speaker foretells. Lines 64–68 imply that the story will be dark but will end with promise of otherworldly redress (B).

36. **(B)**   The argument is structured as "a trial" (B), with a defendant (the girl/petticoat) seated at a judge's left hand and counselors presenting arguments and petitions. While questions are asked and answered (A), the aforementioned persons and activities make "trial" a better answer. There is no admission of sin or error, making "confession" (C) incorrect. The argument is not a discourse on a religious or moral topic [sermon (D)]. Although the argument in front of the judge can be described as debating, the official term is a "trial." Therefore, (E) is incorrect.

37. **(A)**   Without the voluminous petticoat mandated by fashion, the girl would not be physically "big and burly as other persons of her quality" (lines 8–9) or, by implication, as "large" in social standing. (B), (C), and (E) are partially correct because they name the first element of physical size. Their second elements, however, are incorrect: the girl's "quality" (line 9) depends more on social than monetary status (B), and her mental abilities [(C) and (E)] would not be indicated by her underwear.

(D) includes only the literal interpretation of "little," making the girl small because she lacks the proper underwear.

38. **(D)** The young lady dislikes the petticoat and had put off wearing one until pressured by her slipping social reputation to don one (D). Her reluctance to immediately wear the garment indicates that she is not a slave to fashion (A). A social climber (B) would be so concerned about her reputation that she would quickly do what the ladies "of quality" do. (C) takes "little" (line 10) literally, assuming that the girl is actually physically undersized. The girl has yet to be blamed [versus being condemned, (E)], and in fact the judge seems pleased by her defense.

39. **(B)** A "vest" is "a garment" (A); "petticoat" (B) is a better answer, however, as it is the item being discussed, and its "big and burly" size matches the canopy-like description. There is no mention of any other article of clothing [(D) and (E)]. The vest is opened like "an umbrella" (C), but the displayed article is the focus of the passage, and thus the petticoat.

40. **(C)** "Oxymoron" (C) is not present because this description of the petticoat does not contain a pairing of seemingly contradictory terms. The description of the petticoat is exaggerated (A) as forming a canopy over a "great hall" (line 14). Through a "simile" (B), its form is "not unlike [equaling 'like'] the cupola of St. Paul's" (line 18). Metaphorically (D) it is called a "canopy" and a "silken rotunda" (line 17). It is amusing (E) to think of a woman wearing an undergarment big enough to overspread a large room.

41. **(A)** The argument is described as great, solid, and heavily ornamented, "furbelowed…with many periodical sentences and turns of oratory," (lines 24–25), like the petticoat (A) that spreads over the room. The argument is elaborate and decorated, but the ridiculous subject matter destroys any formality (B). The woolen industry would grow larger, but not necessarily more elaborate (C), with the production of such large petticoats. The "power of France" (D) would lessen, not grow and become more detailed. The statement which characterizes the girl's good sense (lines 5–11) is straightforward and plain, lacking elaborate devices or syntax (E).

42. **(B)** This remark grossly overstates (B) the effect that large petticoats would have on a rival economy. It exaggerates, rather than understates (A) the impact of fashion upon the larger world. While the downfall of France is predicted as a side effect, the passage is concerned with the defense of the petticoat and not a direct economic attack (D). The statement may be a boast, but it is not self-aggrandizing (E) its speaker, the counselor.

43. **(D)** The "Greenland trade" supports large petticoats because of the great amount of whalebone used therein; consequently, the members of this trade must be "whalers" (D). "Petticoat makers" (A) would use whalebone, but would be more concerned with consumption of their garments than the materials for making them. "Carvers" (B), "merchants" (C), and "shipowners" (E) could deal in whalebone

(or other goods). (D) is the best answer because whalers would be specifically and directly affected by the use of whalebone.

44. **(C)** The counsel can only insinuate (line 47) and not directly describe how the family's honor may be sullied; the petticoat must, consequently, prevent some extremely delicate matter, such as an adulterous or premarital affair (C). Dressing fashionably (A) and expensively (B) may preserve a family's social status, but not their honor. There is no information in the passage to suggest that dishonor results from being kidnapped (D) or from entering small rooms (E).

45. **(B)** The speaker's final point is linked to the counsel's [making (D) incorrect]: it asserts that the petticoat would remove any fear that a woman would be molested. The counsel would use this assertion in favor of wearing the petticoat, the speaker against (being secure from male assault makes seeking marriage for security unlikely). The speaker's point both assents to (A) and opposes (C) the counsel's; (B) is a better answer, however, because the speaker uses this point to make the opposite conclusion. The speaker's point is strengthened, rather than weakened (E), by being able to use the counsel's own ammunition against it.

46. **(E)** Although the speaker refers to the girl (A) as the "pretty criminal" (line 13), "the petticoat" (E) is the best choice for the criminal because it is the object whose merits are being debated. "Society" (B), "fashion" (C), and "persons of her quality" (D) are not being indicted; in fact, the speaker gives "great allowances to the fair sex upon account of the fashion" (line 12) and by inference the persons who dictate the styles.

47. **(C)** Both counsel and speaker concentrate on the large petticoat's effect upon the economy (C): boosting industry with increased consumption of raw materials or draining family fortunes. The counsel's argument seems logical (A), yet it ignores the expense and impracticality of the huge petticoat and raises it from mere underwear to economic savior. Neither argument appeals primarily to emotions (B) such as fear, love, or anger. An appeal to patriotism (D) occurs in the counsel's arguments, but not in the speaker's. There is no appeal to moral duty (E) in either argument.

48. **(C)** The style of the passage can best be described as wryly humorous because the speaker is making fun of the use of various undergarments. Answers (A) and (B) are not correct because the speaker is neither bitter nor satirical. (E) is incorrect because the speaker is not trying to impress the reader with his pompous language. (D) is wrong because it is not using a type of dialect.

49. **(B)** The fact that both sources are cited tells that the reader this quote appears in both sources. One source is by Dobzhansky and one is by Mayr; each has the words "the origin of species" in the title. Therefore, (B) is the correct answer. The passage specifically says "together with Dobzhansky, Mayr developed this definition"; it does not say that the definition is (A) Mayr's or (D) Dobzhansky's own creation. And although it does say that the two men developed the definition together, nowhere

does it say that (C) Mayr needed Dobzhansky's help. The question specifically asks about the purpose of footnotes 1 and 2. These footnotes have nothing to do with the fact that "students of biology . . . memorized Mayr's definition of species for more than half a century," which appears at the end of the paragraph; therefore, (E) is incorrect.

50. **(E)** This question requires close reading of the sentence in lines 31–33 carefully. (E) is the only logical choice: geographic separation prohibits gene flow between populations—not through (B) rivers or valleys or through (D) mutations. It does not make sense to say "gene flow through (A) gene flow" or "through (C) separation." *Note*, if you are confused about the antecedent of the pronoun "them," you should try to replace the pronoun with each answer choice and determine which one makes the most sense.

51. **(D)** Even if the reader is not familiar with the footnote style used in this paper, line 39 refers to "the 797 pages of *Animal Species and Evolution*"; therefore, (D) is correct. Another clue to the correct answer is that in a footnote, a number followed by the abbreviation *p.* indicates how many pages are in the source. In contrast, the abbreviation *p.* or *pp.* followed by a number indicates the page(s) on which the cited information appears in the source. Here, "797 p." indicates that the book contains 797 pages. It does not indicate (A) where Mayr's explanation of animal species and evolution appears. Actually, the entire book is about animal species and evolution, as the title indicates. (B) makes little sense, because Mayr is the author of the book. (C) is not correct; the passage does use the word "outlined" in referring to the book; however, the phrase "outlined in depth" means that the principles of Mayr's ideas were explained in detail. And Mayr—not the Columbia University Press (E)—is the author of the book. The Columbia University Press is the publishing company.

52. **(C)** References to Mayr as "the greatest evolutionary biologist of the 20th century," "greatest biologist overall," "Darwin's apostle," and "Darwin of the 20th century" convey the author's admiration, so does the comment that "he accomplished much more than one might expect to get done, even in 100 years." The passage contains no evidence that the author feels envy (A), gratitude (B), disgust (D), or cynicism (E) toward Mayr.

53. **(B)** The first paragraph states, "Ernst Mayr has been called 'Darwin's apostle' or the 'Darwin of the 20th century'" because of his work in evolutionary biology. And, lines 2 and 42 compare Mayr to Methuselah because of his longevity (long life), so (B) is the correct choice. The article does not compare Mayr to Dobzhansky; therefore, (A) and (C) are incorrect. It does not compare him to Wilson or Gould; these two men were his colleagues who praised him; thus, (D) and (E) are wrong.

54. **(A)** The sentence that starts with line 9 offers the general idea that "Mayr had many fundamental insights in to evolutionary biology." The next sentence becomes a little more specific, presenting "his most widely known contribution." The next sentence is more specific, explaining the specific "notion" mentioned in the preceding

statement. Therefore, the structure can be described as (A) moving from general to specific. It does not move from specific to general (B), from general to general (C), or from specific to specific (D). And, the answer is not (E), a presentation of conflicting ideas.

55. **(D)** Three of the sources cited in the footnotes are by Mayr. The earliest was published in 1942, and the latest was published in 2004—a span of 62 years. So without any information other than these three footnotes, it is reasonable to assume that Mayr's writing career lasted at least sixty years. Only the first footnote cites a work by Dobzhansky, and nothing implies that this work discussed Mayr's life. Likewise, the second and third footnotes do not cite works that appear to be about Mayr's life; thus, (A) is not a reasonable choice. A look at the footnotes tells us only that Dobzhansky wrote one book—not how long his writing career was; so (B) is incorrect. And although footnote 1 tells us that Dobzhansky wrote about the origin of the species, just as Mayr did, it does not tell us whether or not (C) he relied on Mayr's works. Footnote 4 reveals that Mayr wrote at least one article about himself, but we have no way of knowing if (E) he often wrote about himself or if he liked doing so.

56. **(C)** The passage is eulogistic (C), praising a man who recently died. It is not expository (A), since it does not set forth a meaning or purpose. It is not analytical (A), since it does not break down and discuss component parts. It is not judicial (D), since it does not argue a case. And it is not exhortative (E), since it does not try to persuade the reader to act.

57. **(B)** The passage quotes Mayr as referring to evolutionary biology as "an endless frontier" with "still plenty to be discovered," implying that he believed that evolutionary biologists would continue making new discoveries (B). (A) and (E) are not correct; note that the question focuses specifically on Mayr's comments quoted in lines 46–49. Although Mayr may have believed evolutionary biology had unveiled many intriguing mysteries, nothing in the quote indicated this belief; thus, (A) is incorrect. Likewise, although Mayr did make tremendous contributions to the field of evolutionary biology, nothing in lines 46–49 relates to that fact; thus, (E) is not the correct choice. Mayr was 100 years old when he made these comments. And although Mayr expressed his regret that he would not be present to enjoy the future accomplishments of active evolutionists, nothing in his statement implies that he was worried that he would die soon (D).

Section 2

Model Student Response to Essay Question 1:

Technology has become an important part of our lives in today's world. One can hardly get through a day without encountering computers, video games, cell phones, iPods, and many other forms of technology. So it is not surprising that such technology can be found in our schools as they seek to prepare students for today's world.

Although technology is prevalent in all areas of modern society, there is more to life than manipulating a mouse and a keyboard. And at the college level, using an iPod to listen to a lecture may be convenient, but it cheats the student out of face-to-face interactions with the professor and with fellow students. As Miller points out, children have a "passive attachment to screen-based entertainment." And although Source B may encourage friendships via the Internet, one can learn so much more with face-to-face friendships. As Source D points out, humans and social skills are important and necessary in our schools.

Clearly, technology should not replace human interaction at school or anywhere else. However, it definitely has a place in today's education. Empire High School in Arizona successfully uses computers instead of textbooks in every classroom and every subject (Source A). Because of technological advances, education is no longer physically confined to a classroom or even a building. The many students who are enrolled in distance learning courses (Source B) may complete courses without ever actually meeting their instructors or classmates.

Schools are responsible for preparing students for the world of work, and it is difficult to be a productive worker today without possessing certain skills. Although students are familiar with gaming technology, many do not have the skills to complete basic word processing and presentation tasks (Source A). Utilizing technology in classes other than computer labs helps students gain real-world computer skills. Also, an inviting school media center that offers adequate technology can encourage teamwork among students (Source D). As Source B points out, computers are becoming just as important in the classroom as they are in the workplace.

Careful examination of the issue reveals that technology in the schools can be both detrimental and beneficial. Computers, iPods, and video games as educational tools may encourage the individual to become isolated from others. However, these devices obviously have entered the educational world and the workplace, and they are not likely to go away. So it is the responsibility of the individual—young or old—not to use technology as a substitute for interaction with teachers and peers. And it is the school's responsibility to allow time and activities to encourage students to develop their imagination and creativity, to make sure students develop adequate technology skills, and to focus on enhancing students' learning experiences and preparation for work and for life in the 21st century.

Analysis of Student Response to Essay Question 1:

The student's response effectively addresses the challenge of the question (synthesize at least three of the sources for support and take a position that defends, challenges, or qualifies the claim that schools who are embracing the new technological approach to education are effectively teaching students the skills they need in today's world). The first paragraph introduces the general topic of technology in today's world, gradually narrowing to the specific idea of the essay. In this essay, the writer has chosen to show both positive and negative effects of the use of technology in schools. The writer synthesizes—combines the sources with an opinion to form a cohesive argument—rather than simply paraphrasing or quoting the sources. Each source is clearly attributed. The second paragraph focuses on the negative aspects of schools' use of technology as an educational tool, citing specific examples from the sources. For example, the writer cites: "As Mitch Resnick points out, children use their imagination and learn as they create things with blocks and make pictures with finger paints (Source A)." The next two paragraphs cite sources to help support the positive aspects of technology in the classroom—for example, "an inviting school media center that offers adequate technology can encourage teamwork among students (Source E)." The conclusion echoes the main ideas of the essay's body. The essay's language and development are effective, and the writer's position is supported with well-chosen examples. Overall, this is an effective response to the prompt.

Model Student Response to Essay Question 2:

When one thinks of a turtle, determination and perseverance are not the first words to come to mind. Steinbeck perhaps was thinking of Aesop's fable of the tortoise and the hare. In this excerpt from *The Grapes of Wrath*, the speaker uses syntax and diction to show the fortitude of this seemingly insignificant creature in the face of various obstacles.

The first paragraph opens with a scene of great activity. All of the insects are busy trying to reach their destination. In the midst of all this movement, the lone turtle begins his struggle. The turtle is dragging his shell while "barley beards slid off his shell, and the clover burrs fell on him and rolled to the ground." Steinbeck uses the passive voice to show the turtle's inability to control his surroundings. The speaker's choice of "hard legs" and "yellow-nailed feet" reveal that this is not his first encounter with difficulty. Struggles are common in his life.

As he plods along, he assesses the situation. Short sentences like "For a moment he stopped, his head held high" emphasize the turtle's determination to continue his journey. The passage continues with one obstacle after another coming into his path. The "embankment grew steeper and steeper" but the turtle's efforts increase to a "frantic" level. Through all of the difficulty, the turtle keeps working. The speaker uses participial phrases such as "pushing hind legs," "boosting the shell," and "braced on top of the wall" to emphasize the ongoing struggle of the turtle.

Steinbeck also uses vivid adjectives to describe this persistent turtle. He doesn't just "stare straight ahead," but "his fierce, humorous eyes, under brows like fingernails stare straight ahead." The turtle appears as an old warrior whose seen many a battle and lives to fight another day. He eyes are fierce in that they will stare down anything that gets in the way. The eyes are also humorous as if to say that the turtle knows that he will reach his destination no matter what blocks his path. By the end of the passage the eyes are still "humorous" yet now are "frowning" due to the futile attempt of the red ant to impede his progress.

Finally, the turtle's strong will leads him to success as he makes his last move to climb the concrete wall. Again Steinbeck uses the participial phrase in combination with a simile as the turtle cautiously continues. His legs, "straining like elephant legs," reveal the force with which he moves to reach his goal.

Although the turtle is successful, Steinbeck is careful to caution the audience that "the head of wild oats was held by its stem around the front legs." This last detail begins with the word "but" letting the reader know that the turtle has another battle ahead of him. The speaker's use of sentence structure, word choice, and figurative language all work together to portray the determination of one little turtle.

Analysis of Student Response to Essay Question 2:

The student's response effectively analyzes the methods Steinbeck uses to show the determination of the turtle. The essay is organized and utilizes mature style and advanced vocabulary such as "fortitude." The analysis is insightful and thoughtful. In the first paragraph, the student focuses on the diction and syntax that reveals the turtle's perseverance. The essay refers to the text both directly and indirectly to support the thesis. The student moves beyond mere summary of devices and focuses on how Steinbeck uses language and the effect of his language on the overall passage. The discussion of the participial phrases is especially apt in showing the movement of the turtle over the embankment. The student effortlessly weaves the quotes into the analysis and in so doing provides seamless transitions from one idea to the next. The closing effectively reiterates the thesis without needless repetition. Overall, the style and in-depth analysis represent an upper-level essay response.

Model Student Response to Essay Question 3:

For close to thirty years, the DARE program has been seeking to teach children the skills needed in making good, responsible decisions. While the program's goals are lofty, they are not feasible. The DARE program is not an effective method of preventing teenage drug abuse.

According to critics, a cost-benefit analysis of DARE "shows no significant difference between future drug use in kids who have 'graduated'" from the program. The program has been around long enough to produce results. Keeping DARE in schools just because "kids and parents like the program" is not a responsible decision. If officials see that this program is not working, then they should rethink their motives. One resource education always needs is more money. It's time for those who hold to tradition to let go of the nostalgia they feel for an ineffective program. The money used to fund DARE could be better spent on integrating more technology, hiring more teachers, or building more schools.

In addition to the costs, this program has not been shown to decrease drug use among teenagers. In fact, DARE introduces drugs to elementary and middle school children at a time when they may not even be thinking of using these substances. Parents should be the ones held responsible for teaching their children decision-making skills in all areas, not just drugs. Because each child is unique, the parents are best equipped to know when the conversation about drugs should take place. The "Just Say No" campaigns have been around longer than DARE, do not rely on community resources, and teach kids to avoid drugs altogether.

While proponents of the DARE program argue that it "fosters valuable relationships between police, family, and schools," I believe these relationships would exist without DARE. Most schools have at least one school resource officer (SRO) to assist with campus security. Even with an increased police presence, students are still dealing and doing drugs on high school campuses. Everyday, I have to cross through crowds of students smoking in the student parking lot. Although I've reported this behavior to the administration, the smoking hasn't stopped. The students just find another location to smoke. If a student is found to be intoxicated or under the influence of a drug, the administrator will usually send the student home with no other consequence. As long as a student is not in possession of the illegal substance, the SRO has no recourse in pursuing the incident. While students should not be so afraid of a policeman that they wouldn't approach one if in need of assistance, programs like DARE teach students to lose the healthy respect they should have for police officers. Children should not view police officers, parents, teachers, and principals as friends, like many do.

Oftentimes, letting go of a fondly-remembered tradition is difficult. Adults need to recognize that the DARE program is not fulfilling its promises to children, schools, and communities. It's time for parents to take the responsibility of drug education away from DARE.

Analysis of Student Response to Essay Question 3:

This essay takes the unusual position against the DARE program. While most students would write in support of the popular program, this student's essay stands out by taking the negative position. The student presents a succinct thesis making clear the focus of the essay. The evidence is organized effectively with clear transitions between the proponents of the DARE program and the critics. In addition, the student uses a logos appeal in presenting the negative aspects of DARE by providing counter arguments to the proponent's claims. For example, the student writes in the fourth paragraph, "While proponents of the DARE program argue that it 'fosters valuable relationships between police, family, and schools,' I believe these relationships would exist without DARE." While most of the examples come from personal experience, the student presents the evidence with logic and in-depth details. Overall, the essay presents an effective argument supported by sufficient evidence while using a mature prose style.

END OF PRACTICE TEST 2

PRACTICE EXAM 3

AP English Language & Composition

PRACTICE EXAM 3

AP English Language & Composition

Section 1

TIME: 60 Minutes
52 Questions

(Answer sheets appear in the back of this book.)

DIRECTIONS: This section of the test consists of selections from literary works and questions on their use of language. After reading each passage, choose the best answer to each question and blacken the corresponding oval on the answer sheet.

Questions 1–10 are based on the following passage. Read the passage carefully before choosing your answers.

The following letter was published in The Freedmen's Book, *a collection of African American writings complied by the abolitionist Lydia Marie Child in 1865. The letter is a response to a slave owner who has written to his former slave at the war's end, asking him to return to work in Tennessee.*

To my old Master, Colonel P.H Anderson, Big Spring, Tennessee.

Sir. I got your letter, and was glad to find that you had not forgotten Jourdan, and that you wanted me to come back and live with you again, promising to do better for me than anybody else can. I have often felt uneasy
5 about you. I thought the Yankees would have hung you long before this, for harbouring Rebs they found at your house. I suppose they never heard about your going to Colonel Martin's to kill the Union soldier that was left by his company in their stable. Although you shot at me twice before I left you, I did not hear of your being hurt, and am glad you are still living.
10 It would do me good to go back to the dear old home again, and see Miss Mary and Miss Martha and Allen, Ester, Green, and Lee. Give my love to them all, and tell them I hope we will meet in the better world, if not in

this. I would have gone back to see you all when I was working in Nashville
Hospital, but one of the neighbors told me that Henry intended to shoot
me if he ever got a chance.

I want to know particularly what the good chance is you propose to give
me. I am doing tolerably well here. I get twenty-five dollars a month, with
victuals and clothing; have a comfortable home for Mandy,—the folks call her
Mrs. Anderson, —and the children—Milly, Jane, and Grundy—go to school
and are learning well....we are kindly treated. Sometimes we overhear others
saying, "Them colored people were slaves" down in Tennessee. The children
feel hurt when they hear such remarks; but I tell them it was no disgrace in
Tennessee to belong to Colonel Anderson. Many darkeys would have been
proud, as I used to be, to call you master. Now if you will write and say what
wages you will give me, I will be better able to decide whether it would be to
my advantage to move back again.

As to my freedom, which you say I can have, there is nothing to be
gained on that score, as I got my free papers in 1864 from the Provost-
Marshall-General of the Department of Nashville. Mandy says she would
be afraid to go back without some proof that you were disposed to treat us
justly and kindly; and we have concluded to test your sincerity by asking
you to send us our wages for the time we served you. This will make us
forget and forgive old scores, and rely on your justice and friendship in the
future. I served you faithfully for thirty-two years, and Mandy twenty years.
At twenty-five dollars a month for me, and two dollars a week for Mandy,
our earnings would amount to eleven thousand six hundred and eighty dollars. Add to this the interest for the time our wages have been kept back, and
deduct what you paid for our clothing, and three doctors visits for me, and
pulling a tooth for Mandy, and the balance will show what justice we are
entitled. Please send the money by Adam's Express, in the care of V. Winters,
Esq., Dayton, Ohio. If you fail to pay us for faithful labors in the past, we
can have little faith in your promises in the future. We trust the good Maker
has opened your eyes to the wrongs which you and your fathers have done
to me and my fathers, in making us toil for you for generations without
recompense....Surely there will be a day of reckoning for those who defraud
the laborer of his hire.

In answering this letter, please state if there would be any safety for my Milly
and Jane, who are now grown up, and both good-looking girls. You know how

50 it was with poor Matilda and Catherine. I would rather stay here and starve—
and die, if it came to that—than have my girls brought to shame by the violence and wickedness of their young masters. You will also please state that if
there has been any schools opened for the colored children in your neighbor-
hood. The great desire of my life now is to give my children an education, and
have them form virtuous habits.

55 Say howdy to George Carter, and thank him for taking the pistol from you
when you were shooting at me.

From your old servant,
Jourdan Anderson

1. In paragraph 3 the line, "If you fail to pay us for faithful labors in the
past, we can have little faith in your promises in the future..," is an example
of a(n)

   (A) oxymoron   (D) metaphor

   (B) subordinate clause   (E) antithesis

   (C) parallelism

2. In paragraph 4, what is inferred about Matilda and Catherine?

   (A) they were sold by Colonel P. H. Anderson

   (B) Colonel P. H. Anderson's sons raped them

   (C) Colonel P. H. Anderson did not feed them and clothe them

   (D) Colonel P. H. Anderson's sons killed them

   (E) Colonel P. H. Anderson raped them when he was younger

3. Jourdan Anderson uses all of the following rhetorical techniques to convince
Colonel P. H. Anderson of his "sincere" desire to return to work for him
EXCEPT

   (A) irony   (D) logos

   (B) anecdote   (E) apostrophe

   (C) allusion

4. In paragraph 1 the sentence, "I have often felt uneasy about you" (line 4–5), is an example of which rhetorical device?

    (A) metaphor   (D) hyperbole

    (B) understatement   (E) euphemism

    (C) ethos

5. Jourdan Anderson's attitude toward his old master is best described as

    (A) reverential and laudatory

    (B) pedantic and didactic

    (C) candid and colloquial

    (D) clinical and moralistic

    (E) condescending and sardonic

6. In paragraph 2, "the folks here call her Mrs. Anderson" (line 18–19) implies which of the following?

    (A) Jourdan Anderson's wife was not married to him when he worked for Colonel P. H. Anderson.

    (B) Slaves were not called by their names at Colonel P. H. Anderson's plantation.

    (C) She is respected where she now lives, unlike when she worked for Colonel P. H. Anderson.

    (D) slaves only used their first names on a plantation.

    (E) Slaves were not allowed to use a title such as "Mrs." on a plantation.

7. The speaker's primary purpose in writing a response to Colonel P. H. Anderson is to

    (A) work for him again and see his old friends

    (B) forgive Colonel P. H. Anderson and make amends

    (C) collect his wages from working for Colonel P. H. Anderson in the past

    (D) seek restitution for wrongs committed against him

    (E) assert ironically how ludicrous Colonel P. H. Anderson's offer is

8.   Since Colonel P. H. Anderson wrote to Jourdan Anderson first, all of the fol-
     lowing can be inferred by the Colonel's letter and the resulting response from
     his former slave EXCEPT

     (A)   Colonel P. H. Anderson believed that he is offering Jourdan Anderson a
           good opportunity

     (B)   Colonel P. H. Anderson did not feel that he has wronged Jourdan
           Anderson at all

     (C)   Colonel P. H. Anderson believed that payment for his services in the
           future erases all of his past debts

     (D)   Colonel P. H. Anderson offered to pay Jourdan Anderson all the money
           he owed him, so he asked his former slave to send him the bill for services
           rendered

     (E)   Colonel P. H. Anderson did not apologize to his former slave for the
           wrongs from his past in this letter to his former slave

9.   "We trust the good Maker has opened your eyes to the wrongs ...."
     (line 42–43) is an example of which rhetorical strategy?

     (A)   Biblical allusion

     (B)   antithesis

     (C)   anecdote

     (D)   metaphor

     (E)   hypothetical example

10. Paragraph 5 is a short sentence: "Say howdy to George Carter, and thank him
     for taking the pistol from you when you were shooting at me." What is this
     paragraph's function?

     (A)   a repetition of views previously established

     (B)   a diatribe against Colonel P. H. Anderson

     (C)   an authorial judgment on how Colonel P. H. Anderson treated him

     (D)   a controversial conclusion to a benign letter

     (E)   a satirical remark to show why Jourdan Anderson would never trust his
           old master

Questions 11–24 are based on the following passage. Read the passage carefully before choosing your answers.

Unjust laws exist: shall we be content to obey them, or shall we endeavor to amend them, and obey them until we have succeeded, or shall we transgress them at once? Men generally, under such a government as this, think that they ought to wait until they have persuaded the majority to alter them. They think

5   that, if they should resist, the remedy would be worse than the evil. But it is the fault of the government itself that the remedy *is* worse than the evil. *It* makes it worse. Why is it not more apt to anticipate and provide for reform? Why does it not cherish its wise minority? Why does it cry and resist before it is hurt? Why does it not encourage its citizens to be on the alert to point out

10   its faults, and *do* better than it would have them? Why does it always crucify Christ, and excommunicate Copernicus and Luther, and pronounce Washington and Franklin rebels?

If the injustice is part of the necessary friction of the machine of government, let it go, let it go: perchance it will wear smooth—certainly the machine will

15   wear out. If the injustice has a spring, or a pulley, or a rope, or a crank, exclusively for itself, then perhaps you may consider whether the remedy will not be worse than the evil; but if it is of such a nature that it requires you to be the agent of injustice to another, then, I say, break the law. Let your life be a counter-friction to stop the machine. What I have to do is to see, at any rate,

20   that I do not lend myself to the wrong which I condemn.

Under a government which imprisons any unjustly, the true place for a just man is also a prison. The proper place today, the only place which Massachusetts has provided for her freer and less desponding spirits, is in her prisons, to be put out and locked out of the State by her own act, as they have already put

25   themselves out by their principles. It is there that the fugitive slave, and the Mexican prisoner on parole, and the Indian come to plead the wrongs of his race should find them; on that separate, but more free and honorable, ground, where the State places those who are not *with* her, but *against* her—the only house in a slave State in which a free man can abide with honor. If any think

30   that their influence would be lost there, and their voices no longer afflict the ear of the State, that they would not be as an enemy within its walls, they do not know by how much more eloquently and effectively he can combat injustice who has experienced a little in his own person. Cast your whole vote, not a strip of paper merely, but your whole influence. A minority is powerless while

35   it conforms to the majority; it is not even a minority then; but it is irresistible

when it clogs by its whole weight. If the alternative is to keep all just men in prison, or give up war and slavery, the State will not hesitate which to choose. If a thousand men were not to pay their tax-bills this year, that would not be a violent and bloody measure, as it would be to pay them, and enable the State
40   to commit violence and shed innocent blood. This is, in fact, the definition of a peaceable revolution, if any such is possible. If the tax-gatherer, or any other public officer, asks me, as one has done, 'But what shall I do?' my answer is, 'If you really wish to do anything, resign your office.' When the subject has refused allegiance, and the officer has resigned his office, then the revolution
45   is accomplished. But even suppose blood should flow. Is there not a sort of blood shed when the conscience is wounded? Through this wound a man's real manhood and immortality flow out, and he bleeds to an everlasting death. I see this blood flowing now.

11.   In paragraph 2, the author refers to "the machine of government" (line 13). How does this metaphor characterize the government as the author uses it?

    (A)   Efficient and reliable   (D)   Reparable and industrious

    (B)   Noisy and polluting   (E)   Labor-saving and cost-effective

    (C)   Single-minded and unfeeling

12.   The opening paragraph poses a series of questions. What is the author's purpose?

    (A)   He states the topics, to be covered in the essay, as questions

    (B)   He expects government officials to provide the reasons he seeks

    (C)   He is satirically posing the questions to those with whom he disagrees

    (D)   He is rhetorically stating what the government does and should not

    (E)   He wants to polarize his readers between those who agree with him and those who do not

13.   In the passage, one goal of the speaker is to

    (A)   evoke the moral responsibility of the reader

    (B)   encourage an armed rebellion

    (C)   attract persecuted minorities to Massachusetts

    (D)   promote a political party

    (E)   reduce the tax burden

14. The passage contains all of the following EXCEPT

   (A) proposal for a peaceful protest

   (B) historical reference to other governments

   (C) criticism of specific persons

   (D) justification of bloodshed

   (E) unanswered questions

15. Which location is the "there" referring to in line 25?

   (A) Massachusetts   (D) a Church

   (B) the prison   (E) the grave

   (C) a Legislative building

16. Lines 34-36 are best restated as

   (A) a minority must maintain a difference from the majority, so it can disable the majority

   (B) a minority is an important part of the majority; without the minority, the majority would collapse under its own weight

   (C) a majority exists only by actively contrasting the minority and it is unconquerable when it acts in unison

   (D) a minority remaining in silence brings injustice upon itself; the minority could stand against with its voice and unified action

   (E) a minority that complies to the will of the majority ceases to exist, but a minority that fully commits itself is unconquerable

17. According to the passage, what should the tax-gatherer do?

   (A) Steal the state's funds   (D) Expect gunshots for greetings

   (B) Submit counterfeit money   (E) Be cautious of a surprise attack

   (C) Quit his job

18. In lines 5-10, what is the antecedent of "it" and "its"?

   (A) Fault of the government   (D) Deceit of the government

   (B) Evil of the government   (E) Assistance from the government

   (C) the governors

19.   Contrast lines 19-20 with lines 21-22.

   (A)   In lines 19-20, the author is content not to participate in injustice; but in lines 21-22, the existence of an injustice compels the author to give up his freedom in protest.

   (B)   Lines 19-20 imply the author needs only react to what he sees; but lines 21-22 imply the author must react to all he knows.

   (C)   Lines 19-20 advise neither a borrower nor a lender be; but lines 21-22 advise one to give up one's freedom for a man unjustly imprisoned.

   (D)   In lines 19-20, the author implies it is enough to condemn injustice; but in lines 21-22, the author says the only place for an honest man under a dishonest government is prison.

   (E)   Lines 19-20 advise a man to circumvent the wrongs of his state; but lines 21-22 advise him to meet them at every sacrifice to himself.

20.   What does "cast your whole vote" (line 33) mean?

   (A)   Vote in every election, even the most local

   (B)   Vote for the same party in every election

   (C)   Run for office

   (D)   Do everything possible to influence lawmaking

   (E)   Vote with a conscience

21.   It can be inferred from lines 22-25 that

   (A)   the author has been unjustly imprisoned

   (B)   the author has a loved one who is unjustly imprisoned

   (C)   the author is either in prison or not in Massachusetts

   (D)   Massachusetts' prisons are overcrowded

   (E)   Massachusetts has banished citizens that the author feels are principled

22.   What change in tone would occur if, in the series of questions in the first paragraph, "it" were replaced with the word *they*?

   (A)   The paragraph would lose some of its impact

   (B)   The paragraph would be less condemning and more of a general complaint

   (C)   The paragraph would no longer lump all governments, past and present, into a convenient whipping post

   (D)   The paragraph would be more accusatory, showing greater dissent

   (E)   The paragraph would be more condescending, chastising a multitude instead of a single entity

23.　Identify the stages of the discussion through the passage.

(A)　Question, answer, enact　　(D)　Criticize, suggest, inspire

(B)　Goad, insult, attack　　(E)　Argue, reason, propose

(C)　Taunt, imply, condemn

24.　Which idea can be inferred from lines 36-37?

(A)　The state is a democracy

(B)　"All just men" will act simultaneously

(C)　The prisons will not be large enough

(D)　The women will not bail out the men

(E)　"All just men" are a significant number

Questions 25–38 are based on the following passage. Read the passage carefully before choosing your answers.

　　If ye be thus resolved, as it were injury to think ye were not, I know not what should withhold me from presenting ye with a fit instance wherein to show both that love of truth which ye eminently profess and that uprightness of your judgment which is not wont to be partial to yourselves by judging over
5　again that order which ye have ordained *to regulate printing. That no book, pamphlet, or paper shall be henceforth printed, unless the same be first approved and licensed by such,* or at least one of such as shall be thereto appointed. I warn that this will be primely to the discouragement of all learning and the stop of truth, not only by disexercising and blunting our abilities in what we know
10　already, but by hindering and cropping the discovery that might be yet further made both in religious and civil wisdom.

　　I deny not, but that it is of greatest concernment in the church and commonwealth to have a vigilant eye how books demean themselves, as well as men; and thereafter to confine, imprison and do sharpest justice on them as
15　malefactors: for books are not absolutely dead things but do contain a potency of life in them to be active as that soul whose progeny they are; nay, they do preserve as in a vial the purest efficacy and extraction of that living intellect that bred them. I know they are as lively and as vigorously productive as those fabulous dragon's teeth and being sown up and down, may chance to
20　spring up armed men. And yet on the other hand unless wariness be used, as good almost kill a man as kill a good book; who kills a man kills a reasonable

creature, God's image; but he who destroys a good book, kills reason itself, kills the image of God, as it were in the eye. Many a man lives a burden to the earth; but a good book is the precious life-blood of a master-spirit, embalmed
25 and treasured up on purpose to a life beyond life. 'Tis true, no age can restore a life, whereof perhaps there is no great loss; and revolutions of ages do not oft recover the loss of a rejected truth, for the want of which whole nations fare far worse. We should be wary therefore what persecution we raise against the living labours of public men, how we spill the seasoned life of man preserved
30 and stored up in books; since we see a kind of homocide may be thus committed, sometimes a martyrdom, and if it extend to the whole impression, a kind of massacre, whereof the execution ends not in the slaying of an elemental life but strikes at that ethereal and fifth essence, the breath of reason itself, slays an immortality rather than a life.
35 Hear this revelation of the Apostle of Thessalonians: 'To the pure all things are pure,' not only meats and drinks, but all kind of knowledge whether of good or evil; the knowledge cannot defile, nor consequently the books, if the will and conscience be not defiled. For books are as meats and viands are, some of good, some of evil substance, and yet God in that unapocryphal vision, said
40 without exception, 'Rise Peter, kill and eat,' leaving the choice to each man's discretion. Wholesome meats to a vitiated stomach differ little or nothing from unwholesome, and best books to a naughty mind are not unapplyable to occasions of evil. Bad meats will scarce breed good nourishment in the healthiest concoction; but herein the difference is of bad books, that they to a discreet
45 and judicious reader serve in many respects to discover, to confute, to forewarn and to illustrate.

25. Which of the following is the antecedent of "them" in line 18?

(A) Souls   (D) Books

(B) Authors   (E) Children

(C) Lives

26. The passage reads most like which of the following?

(A) A letter   (D) A rebuttal

(B) A lesson   (E) A sermon

(C) A conversation

27. The author likens "killing" a book to killing a man. In what way(s) does the author imply that the former is worse?

    I.   Books live longer than men.

    II. Books, as objects, are free of sin.

    III. Many men don't deserve to live.

    (A) I and III only   (D) III only

    (B) I and II only   (E) II only

    (C) II and III only

28. How does the author use "Rise Peter, kill and eat" to argue that printing should not be regulated?

    (A) Just as Peter should strike down his own food, each man should destroy evil books.

    (B) Just as God let Peter choose what meat to eat, men should be able to choose freely what to read.

    (C) Just as Peter eats what he himself kills, men should read whatever books they find.

    (D) Just as men need to hunt for edible food, the human mind needs the quest for truth and wisdom.

    (E) Just as hunting has physical dangers, reading should have perils for the mind and soul.

29. The passage compares books to all of the following EXCEPT

    (A) the image of God   (D) reason

    (B) armed men   (E) a vial of living intellect

    (C) a vault

30. According to the passage, the regulation of printing will

    (A) result in a ban on books

    (B) create a black market of books

    (C) discourage scientific discovery

    (D) suppress the word of God

    (E) inhibit the distribution of knowledge

31. The author's tone in the passage's opening (lines 1-5) is

    (A) scolding   (D) pleading

    (B) sarcastic   (E) agreeing

    (C) respectful

32. In paragraph 2, beginning with "Many a man" and ending with "rather than a life," there is a shift from

    (A) agreement to warning   (D) acknowledgment to justification

    (B) agreement to disagreement   (E) concern to wariness

    (C) acknowledgment to denial

33. What is the author's position on censorship?

    (A) He is against it in every form.

    (B) It should only apply to blasphemous texts.

    (C) It should be determined by the church, not the state.

    (D) It should occur after the book exists, not before the book is first circulated.

    (E) It is a necessary evil.

34. The sentence beginning "And yet on the other hand" (lines 20-23) serves primarily to

    (A) flatter the government officials being addressed

    (B) introduce the author's departure from agreeing with them

    (C) contradict the preceding part of the paragraph

    (D) start an unrelated topic

    (E) introduce the first metaphor

35. The author's argument would be more influential to a wider audience if he were to

    (A) quote prominent publishers

    (B) include graphs and illustrations

    (C) use puns and satire

    (D) use historic examples instead of religious ones

    (E) eliminate the transparently flattering introduction

36. The author's attitude toward the power of books in lines 24-25 is

    (A) envy

    (B) apathy

    (C) reverence

    (D) respect

    (E) hatred

37. What is the author's purpose in the repetition of the closing lines of the passage, ending with "to discover, to confute, to forewarn, and to illustrate"?

    (A) The author is emphasizing that reading is not man's only pastime.

    (B) The author points out that there are more ways to learn than from books.

    (C) The author is emphasizing that readers are more socially active in general.

    (D) The author points out that reading is not passive, that men read and react according to their natures.

    (E) The author is emphasizing that all knowledge, good and evil, expands the experiences of men.

38. The passage's longest sustained metaphor is that of books as

    (A) men

    (B) dragon's teeth

    (C) meat

    (D) mummies

    (E) reason itself

Questions 39–52 are based on the following passage. Read the passage carefully before choosing your answers.

Prohibition was the world's first enactment, written by the finger of God in the Garden of Eden to keep the way of life, to preserve the innocence and character of man. But under the cover of the first night, "in the cool of the day," there crept into the Garden a brewer by the name of Beelzebub, who
5 told the first man that God was a liar; that he could sin and not die; that the prohibition law upon the tree of life was an infringement upon his personal liberty and that the law had no right to dictate what a man should eat or drink or wear. The devil induced Adam to go into rebellion against the law of God in the name of personal liberty, and from that hour dates the fall of man.
10 We are hearing something of that same argument in this campaign against the serpent drink, and not only on the part of the enemy. There are many good men who look upon prohibition as an assault upon the personal liberty of the citizen; but it seems to us they do not keep clear the issues involved in this fight. They are not personal at all.

15   Personal liberty is a matter of personal choice, of personal right to eat or
to drink. No prohibitory law ever adopted or proposed attempts to interfere
with that right. It does not seek to compel a man to abstain; it does not say
that he ought not, must not, or dare not drink. It passes only upon the social
right of trade, traffic and sale. Whether a man drinks or abstains is entirely
20   his own affair, so long as he does not poison himself, compel society to cure
him, support him when he is unable to take care of himself, lock him up
when he is dangerous to be at large, bury him at the public expense when
he is a corpse, or interfere with the personal liberty of others when he is
exercising his own.

25   Men do not properly discriminate between a personal right and a social
act. Personal liberty relates to private conduct. If a man signs the temperance
pledge he surrenders his personal liberty or personal privilege to drink; when
he votes dry—to prohibit liquor traffic—it has nothing to do with the question of personal liberty.

30   You have a personal right to eat putrid meat; I have no right to sell it. If
your hog dies a natural death, or with the cholera, you have a personal right
to grind it up into a sausage and eat it, but you have no right to offer it for
public sale. A man has a personal right to corn his dead mule and serve it on
his own table. You have as good a right to eat your cat as I have my chicken, or
35   your dog as I have my pig. The Chinese in New York have a dog feast at their
New Year's celebration and the police have never interfered with their personal
right. But if you opened a meat market and skinned dogs and cats or exposed
horse sausage for public sale, the meat inspector would confiscate the entire
supply, close up the place as a public nuisance and arrest you for selling what
40   you had a personal right to eat.

To abstain is a personal act; to market, traffic and trade is a social act,
limited by the social effect of the thing sold and the place where it is kept for
sale. This distinction between total abstinence, which relates to personal liberty
or personal conduct, and prohibition, which relates to social conduct and the
45   State, is perfectly clear. The one is the act of the individual; the other is the act
of the State.

Total abstinence is the voluntary act of one man; it recognizes the right of
choice of personal liberty. Prohibition is the act of the community, the State,
the majority, which is the State, and is a matter of public policy, to conserve
50   social and civic liberty by denying to an immoral and dangerous traffic the
right of public sale.

39. Which of the following does the author use as a synonym for "the majority"?

    (A) The right   (D) The State

    (B) The God-fearing populace (E) Men

    (C) Society

40. What does the author believe about "personal rights"?

    (A) Personal rights must be agreed upon by society

    (B) Personal rights are confined to the privacy of the home

    (C) Personal rights are a fiction—societies have only personal privileges

    (D) Personal rights are forfeit when abused

    (E) Personal rights do not justify all social acts

41. What means of argument is used in paragraph 5?

    (A) A series of distinct metaphors

    (B) A sustained metaphor

    (C) Repetitious legal examples

    (D) Satirical pseudo-legal examples

    (E) Point-by-point counter-examples

42. The sentence beginning, "You have a personal right...." (line 30), is distinct from others in its paragraph in that it serves primarily to

    (A) distinguish between personal rights and public acts

    (B) associate liquor with putrid meat

    (C) emphasize the difference between reader and author

    (D) associate the author with the Prohibition movement

    (E) mirandize the reader

43. The author's tone in paragraph 2 can best be described as

    (A) annoyed   (D) impatient

    (B) corrective   (E) somber

    (C) condescending

44. Which of the following is described as "immoral" (line 50)?

   (A) Right   (D) Traffic

   (B) Sale   (E) Liberty

   (C) Public

45. What contradiction exists between paragraph 1 and paragraph 5?

   (A) Paragraph 1 uses religious/literary examples, while paragraph 5 uses legal examples

   (B) Paragraph 1 takes liberties with its source to make an example, but paragraph 5 does not

   (C) Paragraph 1 assumes the reader is a Christian, while paragraph 5 assumes the reader is a lawyer

   (D) Paragraph 1 associates prohibition with eating, while paragraph 5 associates it with sale

   (E) Paragraph 1 is about fruit, while paragraph 5 is about meat

46. The author uses all of the following to refer to Satan EXCEPT

   (A) Beelzebub   (D) the enemy

   (B) a liar   (E) a brewer

   (C) the devil

47. What is the purpose of the sentence beginning "Whether a man drinks" (lines 19–23)?

   (A) To ridicule drinkers for comic effect

   (B) To exaggerate the evils of alcohol and so demean the opposition's credibility

   (C) To demonstrate that even a personal liberty can become a social concern

   (D) To explain the pervasiveness of personal liberties

   (E) To argue that personal liberties are inherently a social burden

48. According to the passage, the purpose of prohibition is to

   (A) conserve social and civic liberty

   (B) limit hazardous personal liberties

   (C) deny public sale to immoral and dangerous traffic

   (D) enforce the will of God on weak men

   (E) eliminate the profit from liquor consumption

49. In paragraph 1, the author implies that

    (A)   Satan is a lawyer   (D)   the fruit is analogous to alcohol

    (B)   Satan was correct   (E)   Eden is abstinent

    (C)   the Eden story is historic fact

50. Which of the following does the passage say is the distinction between total abstinence and prohibition?

    I.   One relates to personal conduct; the other relates to social conduct

    II.   One is the act of the individual; the other is the act of the State

    III.   One recognizes personal liberty; the other is a matter of public policy

    (A)   I and II only   (D)   I, II and III

    (B)   I and III only   (E)   II only

    (C)   II and III only

51. In context, the word "dry" (line 28) is best interpreted as having which of the following meanings?

    (A)   To be sober

    (B)   To have signed a temperance pledge

    (C)   To not offer alcohol

    (D)   To outlaw the sale of alcohol

    (E)   To thirst for alcohol

52. What do the closing lines beginning with "Total abstinence" and ending with "public sale" imply about the speaker?

    (A)   His principal concern is the safety of the public.

    (B)   He has a strong belief in God.

    (C)   He believes laws should uphold morality.

    (D)   He wants drinkers to brew their own intoxicants.

    (E)   He maintains the majority is always right.

STOP

This is the end of Section 1.
If time still remains, you may check your work only in this section.
Do not begin Section 2 until instructed to do so.

Section 2

TOTAL TIME – 2 hours 15 minutes

Question 1 (Spend 15 minutes reading the materials. Suggested writing time—40 minutes. This question is worth one-third of the total essay score.)

Directions: The following prompt is based on the accompanying six sources.

This question requires you to synthesize a variety of sources into a coherent, well-written essay. Refer to the sources to support your position; avoid mere paraphrase or summary. Your argument should be central; the sources should support this argument.

Remember to attribute both direct and indirect sources.

Introduction: Obviously, a parent is an important part of a child's life. But in what ways does a parent influence a child, and how does that influence affect the child? What aspects of life does that influence impact?

Assignment: Read the following sources (including any introductory information) carefully. Then, in an essay that synthesizes at least three of the sources for support, take a position that defends, challenges, or qualifies the claim that a parent influences the physical and emotional development of a child.

You may refer to the sources by their titles (Source A, Source B, etc.) or by the descriptions in parentheses.

> Source A (Maslow)
>
> Source B (National Institute of Mental Health)
>
> Source C (Eisenberg)
>
> Source D (Hastings)
>
> Source E (Cartoon)
>
> Source F (Child Stats)
>
> Source G (President Bush)

Source A

Maslow, Abraham. "A Theory of Human Motivation." *Psychological Review* 50.4 (1943): 370-96. *Motional-literacy-education.com*. Mark Zimmerman, 2002. Web. 13 Oct. 2010.

The following passage is excerpted from a book by Abraham Maslow, a classical psychologist who was best known for his research on human needs.

[An] indication of the child's need for safety is his preference for some kind of undisrupted routine or rhythm. He seems to want a predictable, orderly world. For instance, injustice, unfairness, or inconsistency in the parents seems to make a child feel anxious and unsafe. This attitude may be not so much because of the injustice *per se* or any particular pains involved, but rather because this treatment threatens to make the world look unreliable, or unsafe, or unpredictable. Young children seem to thrive better under a system which has at least a skeletal outline of rigidity, in which there is a schedule of a kind, some sort of routine, something that can be counted upon, not only for the present but also far into the future. Perhaps one could express this more accurately by saying that the child needs an organized world rather than an unorganized or unstructured one.

The central role of the parents and the normal family setup are indisputable. Quarreling, physical assault, separation, divorce or death within the family may be particularly terrifying. Also parental outbursts of rage or threats of punishment directed to the child, calling him names, speaking to him harshly, shaking him, handling him roughly, or actual physical punishment sometimes elicit such total panic and terror in the child that we must assume more is involved than the physical pain alone. While it is true that in some children this terror may represent also a fear of loss of parental love, it can also occur in completely rejected children, who seem to cling to the hating parents more for sheer safety and protection than because of hope of love.

Source B

"Child and Adolescent Violence Research at the NIH." *NIMH · Home*. 2000. Web. 16 Oct. 2010. <http://www.nimh.nih.gov>.

The following passage is excerpted from a National Institute of Mental Health overview that summarizes research into the causes, diagnosis, prevention, and treatment of child and adolescent violence.

The research on risk for aggressive, antisocial, and violent behavior includes multiple aspects and stages of life, beginning with interactions in the family. Such forces as weak bonding, ineffective parenting (poor monitoring, ineffective, excessively harsh, or inconsistent discipline, inadequate supervision), exposure to violence in the home, and a climate that supports aggression and violence puts children at risk for being violent later in life . . . .

. . . When antisocial behavior emerges later in childhood or adolescence, it is suspected that genetic factors contribute less, and such youths tend to engage in delinquent behavior primarily because of peer influences and lapses in parenting. The nature of the child's social environment regulates the degree to which heritable early predisposition results in later antisocial behavior. Highly adaptive parenting is likely to help children who may have a predisposition to antisocial behavior . . . .

Research has demonstrated that youths who engage in high levels of antisocial behavior are much more likely than other youths to have a biological parent who also engages in antisocial behavior. This association is believed to reflect both the genetic transmission of predisposing temperament and the maladaptive parenting of antisocial parents.

The importance of some aspects of parenting may vary at different ages. For example, inadequate supervision apparently plays a stronger role in late childhood and adolescence than in early childhood. There is evidence from many studies that parental use of physical punishment may play a direct role in the development of antisocial behavior in their children. In longitudinal studies, higher levels of parental supervision during childhood have been found to predict less antisocial behavior during adolescence. Other researchers have observed that parents often do not define antisocial behavior as something that should be discouraged, including such acts as youths bullying or hitting other children or engaging in "minor" delinquent acts such as shoplifting.

Research examining the mental health outcomes of child abuse and neglect has demonstrated that childhood victimization places children at increased risk for delinquency, adult criminality, and violent criminal behavior. Findings from early research on trauma suggest that traumatic stress can result in failure of systems essential to a person's management of stress response, arousal, memory, and personal identity that can affect functioning long after acute exposure to the trauma has ended. One might expect that the consequences of trauma can be even more profound and long lasting when they influence the physiology, behavior, and mental life of a developing child or adolescent.

Source C

Eisenberg, Leon. "What's Happening to American Families? ERIC Digest." *ERICDigests. org.* 1991. Web. 16 Oct. 2010.

The following passage is excerpted from an article that focuses on changes in the structure and role of the American family.

Few issues vex Americans more than what has happened to the role of the family in caring for children. Almost one in four of the nation's youngsters under 18 lives with only one parent, almost always the mother. If the youngster is black, the ratio rises to one in two. The divorce ratio has tripled and the percentage of out-of-wedlock births among teenage women has doubled over the past 15 years.

Caring for infants is not just a dilemma for female-headed households. Whether or not the family is intact, more than half of all mothers with a preschool child are in the labor force, 50 percent more than the proportion employed out of the home a decade ago. The Labor Department reports that the number of women holding two or more jobs has increased five-fold since 1970.

What we need, we hear on all sides, is a return to the good old days when parents were responsible for their kids and kids obeyed their parents. We long for a return to an age when fundamental values were shared by all. If there WAS such an age, can we go back to it? No one doubts that today's family is harassed and overburdened. The question is: could what seemed to work then work now?

In the aftermath of the Industrial Revolution, the American family has been stripped of two of its traditional social functions: serving as a unit for economic production and as a school for the vocational training of children. The first function has been usurped by commercial firms, the second by the state. Two functions remain: first, the physical and emotional gratification of the family's adult members, and second, the socialization of the children into community mores and the promotion of their development. . . .

. . . economist Victor Fuchs has calculated that between 1960 and 1986, the opportunity for children to spend time with parents declined by 10 hours per week for the average white child, and 12 hours for the black child. The principal reason is the increase in the proportion of mothers holding paid jobs; not far behind is the increase in one-parent households. Fathers in intact families could offset the loss in hours of mothering by doing more fathering; there is little evidence that they do so. . . .

Parents of the past learned by modeling themselves not only on their parents, but on uncles, aunts, and grandparents at home or nearby. As they grew up, they learned how to care for younger siblings because they were expected to. The isolated nuclear family and the sharp sequestration of age groups in today's society combine to deprive today's children of these experiences.

. . . As society continues to evolve, so will the family. As the family changes, we will need to continue to monitor the state of our children.

Source D

Hastings, P. D., K. E. McShane, R. Parker, and F. Ladha. "Parents' Influence on Kids' Behavior: Not Much: Cognitive Daily." Journal of Genetic Psychology 168.2 (2007): 177-200. ScienceBlogs. Dan Munger, 20 May 2008. Web. 16 Oct. 2010.

The following is an excerpt from research findings indicating the influence or lack thereof that parents have on their children.

How do you raise "good kids"? It's one of the questions that plagues parents even before their kids are born. Although everyone's child can't be above average, we all want our kids to be nice to others, to "get along" in the world. But kids don't necessarily cooperate. How do we keep them from becoming delinquents, convicts, or worse?

Unfortunately a lot of the research suggests that parents don't actually have much influence on their kids' behavior – peers, other environmental factors, and genetics seem to have a larger impact. Yet as parents, we can't simply throw up our hands and give up. We exert whatever small influence we do have, and hope it doesn't backfire.

Some studies have suggested that mothers have a disproportionate influence on kids, and that an authoritative parenting style leads to the best results (more prosocial children, who get along with others better). But according to a research team led by Paul Hastings, many of these studies are flawed because they don't measure masculine prosocial behaviors – the actions more likely to be seen in boys than girls. Girls, they say, tend to be more helpful, sympathetic, and passionate, while boys are more friendly, engaged, and assertive (without being aggressive). All these behaviors are really prosocial.

Hastings and his colleagues had the parents of 133 two- to five-year-olds read several stories about interactions between children and asked how they would respond to the situation if their child had been involved in the situation. The parents also filled in a survey to determine how authoritative their parenting style was.

From five to nine months later, the children themselves were observed playing in a group. After playing for 40 minutes, the experimenter gave them a new toy drum and observed how well they interacted with the new toy. Did they take turns? Did they make sure everyone had a chance to play? In addition, the kids' preschool teachers answered a questionnaire about each child's prosocial behavior.

Was there a relationship between the parents' earlier responses and the children's behavior later?

Giving behaviors are those stereotypically considered feminine: giving a toy to another child, accepting an invitation to play, and offering a different activity. "Attributions" corresponds to parents stating that prosocial behaviors were part of their child's disposition. For mothers, there was a significant positive correlation between attribution and girls' later giving behavior. Mothers who discussed positive behavior with their sons had sons who later exhibited giving. Finally, mothers' indirect praise of their daughters (to teachers, for example) was also correlated significantly with later giving behavior. None of the fathers' strategies correlated significantly with giving.

"Your father kicked in the screen and threw the set out the window. He feels violence on TV is a bad influence."

Source F

"America's Children: Key National Indicators of Well-Being." *Childstats.gov.* 2000. Web. 16 Oct. 2010.

The following information is excerpted from a publication that addresses the relationship between a mother's level of education and a child's proficiency upon entry to kindergarten.

As children enter kindergarten for the first time, they demonstrate a diverse range of cognitive knowledge, social skills, and approaches to learning. This indicator highlights their proficiency in several key skills needed to develop the ability to read. How well children read eventually affects how they learn and ultimately influences their chances for school success. Social skills and positive approaches to learning are also related to success in school and are equally important at this age. The depth and breadth of children's knowledge and skills are related to both developmental and experiential factors. These include child characteristics such as age, gender, and cognitive and sensory limitations and characteristics of the child's home environment and preschool experience. Mother's education is the background variable that is consistently related to children's knowledge and skills.

> ## Source G
>
> White House. *Parents' Day Presidential Proclamation.* 25 July 2003. Web. 16 Oct. 2010.

The following is excerpted from a press release issued in July 2003 by the White House for President George W. Bush.

Children are a daily reminder of the blessings and responsibilities of life and a source of joy, pride, and fulfillment. Parents, stepparents, adoptive parents, and foster parents have the important responsibility of providing for, protecting, nurturing, teaching, and loving their children. On Parents' Day, we honor America's mothers and fathers and celebrate the values that bind families from one generation to the next and help define us as a Nation.

As a child's first teachers, parents are the most influential and effective instructors in a child's life. Through their words, actions, and sacrifices, parents are living examples for children. Young boys and girls watch their parents closely and imitate their behavior. Parents play a critical role in instilling responsibility, integrity, and other life lessons that shape the lives of America's future leaders.

My Administration is committed to supporting our Nation's families. We are working with faith-based and community organizations to promote healthy marriages, responsible parenting, and education. And we are committed to fully funding and supporting the Promoting Safe and Stable Families Program, which helps strengthen family bonds, promote adoption, and provide help for vulnerable children across our country.

Volunteer service is one way parents can spend time with their children while encouraging them to learn the value of helping others. . . . Parenting is one of the most rewarding and challenging endeavors in life. On this special day, we recognize the hard work and compassion of America's parents and celebrate the mothers and fathers who are positive role models for their children. I encourage parents to spend more time reading, talking, and volunteering with their children. I also urge parents to share the joys and wisdom of parenthood with new families in their communities and those planning families for the future.

NOW, THEREFORE, I, GEORGE W. BUSH, President of the United States of America, by virtue of the authority vested in me by the Constitution and laws of the United States and consistent with Public Law 103-362, as amended, do hereby proclaim Sunday, July 27, 2003, as Parents' Day. I encourage all Americans to express their respect and appreciation to parents everywhere for their contributions to their children, families, communities, and our Nation. I also call upon citizens to observe this day with appropriate programs, ceremonies, and activities.

IN WITNESS WHEREOF, I have hereunto set my hand this twenty-fifth day of July, in the year of our Lord two thousand three, and of the Independence of the United States of America the two hundred and twenty-eighth.

CONTINUE TO QUESTION 2

Question 2 (Suggested time — 40 minutes. This question counts one-third of the total essay section score.)

The following passage comes from the 1845 autobiography *Narrative of the Life of Frederick Douglass, an American Slave*. Read the passage carefully. Then write an essay in which you analyze the rhetorical strategies that Douglass uses to convey his conflicting attitudes toward his current position as a slave.

If at any one time of my life more than another, I was made to drink the bitterest dregs of slavery, that time was during the first six months of my stay with Mr. Covey. We were worked in all weathers. It was never too hot or too cold; it could never rain, blow, hail, or snow, too hard for us to work in the field. Work, work, work, was scarcely more the order of the day than of the night. The longest days were too short for him, and the shortest nights too long for him. I was somewhat unmanageable when I first went there, but a few months of this discipline tamed me. I was broken in body, soul, and spirit. My natural elasticity was crushed, my intellect languished, the disposition to read departed, the cheerful spark that lingered about my eye died; the dark night of slavery closed in upon me; and behold a man transformed into a brute!...

Our house stood within a few rods of the Chesapeake Bay, whose broad bosom was ever white with sails from every quarter of the habitable globe. Those beautiful vessels, robed in purest white, so delightful to the eye of freemen, were to me so many shrouded ghosts, to terrify and torment me with thoughts of my wretched condition. I have often, in the deep stillness of a summer's Sabbath, stood all alone upon the lofty banks of that noble bay, and traced, with saddened heart and tearful eye, the countless number of sails moving off to the mighty ocean. The sight of these always affected me powerfully. My thoughts would compel utterance; and there, with no audience by the Almighty, I would pour out my soul's complaint, in my rude way, with an apostrophe to the moving multitude of ships: —

"You are loosed from your moorings, and are free; I am fast in my chains, and am a slave! You move merrily before the gentle gale, and I sadly before the bloody whip! You are freedom's swift-winged angels, that fly round the world; I am confined in bands of Iron! O that I were free!

O, that I were on one of your gallant decks, and under your protecting wing! Alas! Betwixt me and you, the turbid waters roll. Go on, go on. O that I could also go! Could I but swim! If I could fly! O, why was I born a man, of whom to make a brute! The glad ship is gone; she hides in the dim distance. I am left in the hottest hell of unending slavery. O God, save me! God deliver me! Let me be free! Is there any God? Why am I a slave? I will run away, I will not stand it. Get caught, or get clear, I'll try it. I had as well die with ague as the fever. I have only one life to lose. I had as well be killed running as die standing. Only think of it; one hundred miles straight north, and I am free! Try it? Yes! God helping me, I will. It cannot be that I shall live and die a slave. I will take to the water. This very bay shall bear me into freedom. The steamboats steered in a north-east course from North Point. I will do the same; and when I get to head of the bay, I will turn my canoe adrift, and walk straight through Delaware into Pennsylvania. When I get there, I shall not be required to have a pass; I can travel without being disturbed. Let but the first opportunity offer, and, come what will, I am off. Meanwhile, I will try to bear up under the yoke. I am not the only slave in the world. Why should I fret? I can bear as much as any of them. Besides, I am but a boy and all boys are bound to some one. It may be that my misery in slavery will only increase my happiness when I get free. There is a better day coming."

Thus I used to think, and thus I used to speak to myself; goaded almost to madness at one moment, and at the next reconciling myself to my wretched lot.

CONTINUE TO QUESTION 3 >

Question 3 (Suggested time—40 minutes. This question is one third of the total essay score.)

British author C.S. Lewis once said that, "Friendship is unnecessary, like philosophy, like art... It has no survival value; rather it is one of those things that give value to survival."

Think about his assertion. Then write an essay that defends, refutes, or qualifies Lewis's claim about the value of friendship. Use specific, appropriate evidence to develop your position.

END OF EXAM

PRACTICE EXAM 3

AP English Language & Composition

Answer Key

Section 1

1. **(C)**	19. **(A)**	37. **(D)**
2. **(B)**	20. **(D)**	38. **(A)**
3. **(E)**	21. **(C)**	39. **(D)**
4. **(B)**	22. **(B)**	40. **(E)**
5. **(E)**	23. **(D)**	41. **(C)**
6. **(C)**	24. **(E)**	42. **(B)**
7. **(E)**	25. **(D)**	43. **(B)**
8. **(D)**	26. **(E)**	44. **(D)**
9. **(A)**	27. **(A)**	45. **(D)**
10. **(E)**	28. **(B)**	46. **(B)**
11. **(C)**	29. **(C)**	47. **(C)**
12. **(D)**	30. **(E)**	48. **(A)**
13. **(A)**	31. **(C)**	49. **(D)**
14. **(C)**	32. **(A)**	50. **(D)**
15. **(B)**	33. **(D)**	51. **(D)**
16. **(E)**	34. **(B)**	52. **(C)**
17. **(C)**	35. **(D)**	
18. **(E)**	36. **(C)**	

PRACTICE EXAM 3

AP English Language & Composition

Detailed Explanations of Answers

Section 1

1.   **(C)**   The answer is parallelism (C) since the first part of the sentence, "fail to pay us for faithful labors in the past/little faith in your promises in the future," clearly has the same structure, although using different context to clearly convey to the reader that the speaker cannot believe in his old master. (B) is not correct because it is not an incomplete sentence; therefore, it is not a subordinate clause. (A) is not correct because it not a device that is a pair of opposites, which is the same reason that answer (E) is not correct. It is clearly not comparing two completely different objects without using comparison words, so answer (D) is also not correct.

2.   **(B)**   The answer is (B) because the text reads that the "girls were brought to shame by the violence and wickedness of their young masters." This statement suggests that Colonel Anderson's young sons took advantage of Jourdan Anderson's daughters; this horrible crime is made clearer because Jourdan Anderson states that he would rather die that have something happen to his other children. It is not clear if they survived the attacks or not; therefore answer (D) is not correct. Answers (A), (C) and (E) are not proven at all.

3.   **(E)**   The answer is (E) because Jourdan Anderson does not address an inanimate object or one that is considered dead in his letter to Colonel Anderson. Answer (A) is not correct; throughout the letter, he is very sarcastic and uses a delightful educated irony that may trick the reader into thinking otherwise. Anderson tells anecdotes (B) to prove why he was a good worker to Colonel Anderson, so (B) is not correct. Also, also Jourdan Anderson uses facts or logos to demonstrate a type of sarcastic good will for his old employer; therefore, (D) is not correct as well. He does demonstrate allusion when he received his free papers from the Provost-Marshall.

4.   **(B)**   Answer (B) is understatement because a person feels extremely uneasy (or the opposite of hyperbole) if a person is expressing his thoughts about a person who tried to kill him. It is the opposite of hyperbole, so answer (D) is not correct. He is not comparing

two unlike things without using comparison words so it is not a metaphor. The reader does not feel ethically compelled to do anything. Answer (E) is not correct because it is not a nicer way to say something.

5.   **(E)**   Jourdan Anderson is both condescending and sardonic toward his old master. However, he is so polite and seemingly respectful that the careful reader may miss this. Jourdan Anderson continually brings up how poorly he was treated, how he did not receive proper treatment and the outlandish proposition that his old master may pay him are huge indicators that in no way, shape or form does Jourdan Anderson spare a kind thought for his old master. So the answer could not be (B), pedantic and didactic, since he is not overly pompous nor is he instructive; the answer could not be candid and colloquial (C) because he is not too relaxed in his speech. His formal tone was evident as one read his letter. The answers cannot be reverential and laudatory (A); since he definitely not praising Colonel Anderson and the answer is not (D); they do not show Jourdan Anderson as being moralistic or clinical.

6.   **(C)**   It is clear that Jourdan Anderson's wife was not treated respectfully in the days of the Colonel. This polite form of address proves this fact. Answer (A), (B), and (D) are not proven.

7.   **(E)**   Colonel Anderson wants to again inflict his obviously wrong sense of rightness on his old slave. Jourdon must know that he has to clearly and poignantly bring up all (or some) of the debts that Colonel Anderson did not take care of while he worked for him.

8.   **(D)**   Colonel Anderson did not offer at all to pay for the money owed. The letter reads as though of course he must pay, but he does not. All of the other answers are, in fact, true.

9.   **(A)**   Saying the words "the Good Maker" makes it clear that this is a biblical allusion. The reader understands that the Lord himself will make sure that Jourdan Anderson's former employer will finally understand all of the wrongs that he has committed in his past. There is no evidence of two opposing viewpoints for the answer to be an antithesis (B), it is not a short story so it is not an anecdote (C), and in choice (D) the example is not figuratively comparing two unlike things without using comparison words, and a hypothetical example (E) is wrong—it is not logical and it does not describe an imaginary or a fictitious situation.

10. **(E)**   The writer wants to clearly show and prove the irony and contempt that Jourdan Anderson does, in fact, feel for his old boss. The rest of the answers are vague assertions.

11. **(C)**   The author suggests that "injustice is part of the necessary friction" of government, implying that government does not react to the injustices it encounters. This gives the impression of a lack of awareness and concern. The idea that your life should "be a counter-friction to stop the machine" implies that the machine cannot be operated, that it is going about its purpose and can only be sabotaged. For these reasons,

the answer is (C) "single-minded and unfeeling." The passage says nothing favorable about the "machine," eliminating (A) "efficient and reliable" and (E) "labor-saving." The author finds the government as efficient as being lost but making great time. The passage also is not optimistic about the "machine," as notable in the "let your life be a counter-friction" quotation; so (D) "reparable" is incorrect. Nowhere does the author complain literally about machines; so (B) "noisy and polluting" is also incorrect.

12.   **(D)**   A quick scan of these questions will tell you that these are not "topics to be covered in the essay"; so (A) is incorrect. Also, one will note that these are the legitimate concerns of the author, so "He is satirically posing the questions of those he disagrees with" (C) is incorrect. At no point in the essay does the author antagonize his reading audience; so "He wants to polarize his readers…" (E) is incorrect. The idea of (B), that the author "expects…the reasons," seems possible at first with the beginning questions, but the last question, "Why does it always crucify Christ,…pronounce Washington and Franklin rebels?" obviously is accosting different governments of different centuries. These questions of the author do not function truly as questions—they have no addressee and expect no answers. The author is complaining about the traditional abuses of government, even "good" government. "He is rhetorically stating what the government does and should not" (D) is the correct answer.

13.   **(A)**   The speaker's primary goal is to address the injustices of the state so they may be undone. He would obviously prefer a simple tax revolt; so "encourage an armed revolution" (B) is incorrect. However, this is a means, not an end; so "reduce the tax burden" (E) is incorrect also. The author never refers to the taxes as weighty or unfair, only misused. He would certainly not "attract persecuted minorities to Massachusetts" (C), because Massachusetts supposedly "imprisons unjustly." The author cannot be said to "promote a political party" (D), because his proposal of a tax revolt would not exchange a single elected official for another person. The author seeks to "evoke the moral responsibility of the reader" (A), as in "Under a government which imprisons any unjustly, the true place for a just man is also a prison."

14.   **(C)**   The passage suggests that men not pay their taxes, which is "a proposal of peaceful protest" (A). The passage refers to the governments of Christ, Copernicus, and Washington, which are "historical references to other governments" (B). The passage states, "But even suppose blood should flow. Is there not a sort of bloodshed when the conscience is wounded?" or "justification for bloodshed" (D). The passage opens with a series of rhetorical questions, which are "unanswered questions" (E). By elimination, the answer is "criticism of specific persons" (C), which never occurs in the passage.

15.   **(B)**   The passage reads "…in her prisons…It is there that…," so the correct answer is (B) "prison." The same paragraph refers to "Massachusetts, (A)" but at best you would have to say "Massachusetts prisons" to capture the same meaning. Neither "legislative building," (C) "church," (D) nor "the grave," (E) occurs in the paragraph to be potential antecedents.

16.   **(E)**   The lines being paraphrased are "A minority is powerless while it conforms to the majority; it is not even a minority then; but it is irresistible when it clogs by its whole weight" (A). "A minority…so it can disable the majority"

is an inaccurate paraphrase because the minority should clog the "machine" of government, not assault the majority. "A minority is an important part of the majority..." (B) is obviously wrong. The minority is an important part of the people, but, by definition, not any part of the majority. "A majority exists..." (C) is incorrect because it transposes "minority" and "majority." "A minority...brings injustice upon itself" (D) is incorrect because lines 34-36 say nothing of the kind. The answer is "A minority that complies to the will of the majority ceases to exist, but a minority that fully commits itself to impeding the unjust action of the majority is unconquerable" (E), because it accurately hits all the points of the original.

17. **(C)** The author says to the tax-gatherer "if you really wish to do anything, resign your office," which is (C), "quit his job." The author never suggests "steal the state's funds" (A) or "submit counterfeit money" (B). Nor does the author threaten the officer, as "expect gunshots for greetings" (D) and "be cautious of a surprise attack" (E) suggest.

18. **(E)** (C), "the governors," can be eliminated because it is plural, while "it" and "its" need a singular antecedent. Line 10 refers to "its citizens," which allows us to eliminate (A) "fault of...," (B) "evil of...," and (D) "deceit of..." because, while governments can have citizens, the same cannot be said of faults, evils, and deceits. It is important to note the author's distinction between "the government" and "government." The use of the word "the" implies the "specification of a specific one or example," while its conspicuous absence implies a generalization. If you heard someone say, "The man is prone to violence," you would respond, "Lock him up" or "Get him help"; but if that person had said, "Man is prone to violence," you would respond, "Is it the culture or the species?" The paragraph refers to the different governments of Christ, Copernicus, and Washington as if they were one or as if he were stating a general truth. Therefore, "its" meaning is best captured by (E), "assistance from the government."

19. **(A)** The question asks to contrast "What I have to do is to see, at any rate, that I do not lend myself to the wrong which I condemn" with "Under a government which imprisons any unjustly, the true place for a just man is also a prison." "...only react to what he sees..." (B) takes "to see" from the original in the too literal sense of vision when the author meant "to see" as in "to make sure." Similarly, "...neither borrower nor lender be..." (C) takes "lend" too literally when the author used "lend myself" to mean "aid." "...it is enough to condemn justice..." (D) is incorrect because, in the original, the author insists that beyond condemning injustice, he must not assist its function. "... advise a man to circumvent the wrongs of his state..." (E) is incorrect because the author nowhere advises avoidance of problems—he always advises protesting to them, whether by strike or opposition. "In lines 19-20, the author is content not to participate in injustice; but in lines 21-22, the existence of an injustice compels the author to give up his freedom in protest." (A) accurately paraphrases the conflict of the original lines.

20. **(D)** The entire sentence referred to in this question is "Cast your whole vote, not a strip of paper merely, but your whole influence." The key word is "influence," which helps to identify (D), "do everything you can to influence

lawmaking" as the correct answer. "Vote in every election…" (A) does not convey the "whole influence" of a person, and neither does (B), "vote…across the board," or (E), "vote…your conscience." "Run for office" (C) suggests one's whole influence is given, but nowhere does the passage imply that the author is suggesting everyone run for office.

21. **(C)** While "the author has been unjustly imprisoned" (A) or "the author has a loved one…imprisoned" (B) are conceivable, they are not inferred by lines 22-25. Nowhere is it suggested that "Massachusetts' prisons are overcrowded" (D). When the passage says the state "put out and locked out" some citizens, it is metaphorically referring to imprisonment (note line 23 "in her prisons"), not the banishment suggested by (E), "…banished citizens…" While one may argue that imprisonment is a form of banishment, the correct answer must reflect most precisely what the passage's lines imply. These lines say the principled men in Massachusetts should be in prison; thus, the answer is (C), "the author is either in prison or not in Massachusetts."

22. **(B)** The change from *it* to *they* would not significantly alter the strength of the argument, so "…lose impact" (A) is incorrect. Another problem with (A) is a problem for (C), "…no longer lump all governments…"; while these choices refer to changes that may or may not be accurate, they are not "changes in tone" as the question requires. "…More accusatory…" (D) and "…more condescending…" (E) claim changes in tone, but these changes do not occur with the stated substitution. The correct answer is (B), "…less condemning and more of a general complaint: by not lumping the governments into one, as (C) mentioned, the accusation becomes buckshot, covering several targets instead of a single strike at a single entity.

23. **(D)** Because the questions of the opening paragraph are never answered, "question, answer, enact" (A) is incorrect. Because the opening paragraph does not intend to address the government, it cannot be said to prod anyone or anything into action; so "goad, insult, attack" (B) is incorrect. Similarly, (C), "taunt, imply, condemn," is incorrect because the government must be addressed to be taunted. "Argue, reason, propose" (E) is a reasonable answer; but (D) is better and correct because the opening of the passage is best described as criticizing. Also, the passage does more than merely "suggest" and "propose." It follows through to "inspire" action.

24. **(E)** These lines do not necessarily assume "the State is a democracy" (A) because any government gets its power from the tolerance of the people. While (B), "…all…act simultaneously," would be the best means of enacting the author's proposal, it would not be necessary to its success. To say that "the prisons won't be large enough" (C) is to assume the government has little imagination concerning where to put people and how else to punish them. "The women will not bail out the men" (D) ignores the option of prisoners to refuse bail. The assumption behind lines 36-37 is "all just men are a significant number" (E) of which the government will need to take notice. "All just men" is best in quotation marks because it is, as the author defines them, implicitly "those who agree with me."

25. **(D)** The clause begins at line 15 with "for books are...," and so "books" (D) is the correct answer. Books are bred by "authors"; so, (B) is not the correct option. "Souls" (A), lives (C) and "children" (E) do not occur in the sentence as plurals, so these choices cannot be the antecedent of "them."

26. **(E)** The passage lacks the personal tone of both "a letter" (A) and "a conversation" (C). The author is reacting to an event "ye have ordained" (line 5) but not in a point by point way like one would react to an argument in the form of "a rebuttal" (D). The religious nature of the discussion makes the passage most like "a sermon" (E). Because a sermon is a form of "a lesson" (B), that answer seems correct, but (E) is more detailed and more accurate.

27. **(A)** The passage says in lines 23-25, "Many a man lives a burden to the earth; but a good book... [has] a life beyond life," which affirms both statement I and statement III. Lines 35-36 say, "books are...some of good, some of evil substance," which contradicts statement II. Therefore, the only correct answer is (A) "I and III only."

28. **(B)** The passage says that the significance of God's command was "leaving the choice to each man's discretion" (lines 40-41). This choice does not support "...each man's task, not the government's, to destroy evil books" (A) because it concerns consumption as in eating or reading, not destruction as in killing or banning. "Read whatever books..." (C) ignores the choice by limiting the choosing to one— everything. (D) conveys an interesting idea that has nothing to do with the passage. (E), "...perils for the mind and soul," has the possibility of something with which the author might agree; but he never suggests this point. The correct answer "men should be able to choose" (B) is exactly the argument made by the passage.

29. **(C)** The passage says, "he who destroys a good book...kills reason itself, kills the image of God," (lines 22-23) verifying (D) and (A), respectively. Lines 16-18 say books "do preserve as in a vial...that living intellect that bred them," which verifies option (E) "a vial of living intellect." A less direct connection is made in lines 19-20, "[Books] are...may spring up armed men," verifying (B). The word *vault* does not occur anywhere in the passage, so the answer is "a vault" (C).

30. **(E)** The author makes a warning in lines 7-11 that does not suggest (A), "...a ban on all books," or (B), "...a black market." He worries that regulation will "hinder...discovery...in religious and civil wisdom," but to hinder is not the same as to "discourage..." (C). To make something more difficult is not automatically the same as to make it less desirable. The author is not concerned that religion will be a target as "suppress the word of God" (D) suggests. One of his concerns is that regulation will "[blunt] our abilities in what we know already," as in (E), "inhibit the distribution of knowledge."

31. **(C)** The author seems to be addressing a legislative body and is very tactful and diplomatic. He is not (A), "scolding," or (B), "sarcastic." The author does not

concede any agreement (E) until the following paragraph. Although he is making an appeal (D), the author should not be characterized as "pleading," which implies self-deprecation. His tone maintains his own personal audience's "love of truth [and]… uprightness of…judgment" (lines 3-4).

32. **(A)**   The author begins the second paragraph by not only acknowledging the dangers of books, "I deny not…" (line 12), but also by agreeing that some books should be "confine[d], imprison[ed]" (line 14). "Acknowledgment to denial" (C) and "acknowledgment to justification" (D) are incorrect because "acknowledgment" is not strong enough to describe the author's concession. "Concern to wariness" (E) is inaccurate because line 12's "it is of concernment to the church" is not the author's concern, but the author's acknowledgment of the church's concern. The paragraph proceeds to suggest that by killing books, one also kill good books. The author's position is not distant enough to be "disagreement" (B). The answer is "agreement to warning" (A).

33. **(D)**   The author's true feelings about censorship are expressed in the beginning of the second paragraph, "it is of the greatest concernment in the church and com-monwealth to have a vigilant eye how books demean themselves, as well as men; and thereafter to confine…and do sharpest justice on them as malefactors" (lines 12-15). He is not "…against it in every form" (A) nor does he find it "…a necessary evil" (E). He has an approval of censorship that is not limited to religion as "…apply to blasphemous texts" (B) and "…determine by the church" (C) suggest. His belief is most accurately expressed by (D): "it should occur after the books exists, not before the book is first circulated." The ordinance that the author is reacting to forbids the publishing of books that have not been "approved" by the state.

34. **(B)**   The sentence beginning, "And yet on the other hand…," does not "flat-ter…" (A) anyone; nor does it "introduce the first metaphor" (E) or the second or the third. This sentence begins a change, but not to (D), "…an unrelated topic." It begins to show the potential hazards of regulation, not by "contradict[ing] the preceding…" (C), but by explaining the consequences of improper banning. The sentence serves primarily to (B), "introduce the author's departure from agreement."

35. **(D)**   Any group that would ban books is not likely to be influenced by (A), "quote[d] prominent publishers." The topic is too serious to approach it with "… puns and satire" (C). Because the issue is truly a matter of principle rather than sci-ence or commerce, "…graphs…" (B) is not advisable. It is inaccurate to characterize the introduction as (E) "…transparently flattering…"; and, as it is, the introduction cannot harm the argument. The best proposed change to the essay is (D), "use historic examples instead of religious ones," which would release the limitation of appealing to only Christian faiths.

36. **(C)**   The passage in lines 24-25 says, "a good book is the precious life-blood of a master-spirit, embalmed and treasured up on purpose to a life beyond life." The attitude conveyed is certainly positive, eliminating "envy" (A),"apathy" (B),

and "hatred" (E), but we must now distinguish between worship and respect. The lines refer to a purpose without specifying or even remotely describing it. Usually one respects a power, an ability or an authority, but these lines do not emphasize these concepts. The lines have images of death and afterlife, emphasizing religion and suggesting a tone of (C) "reverence."

37. **(D)** The closing lines address what men get out of reading, eliminating (A), "...reading is not man's only pastime," and (B), "...more ways to learn than from books." Similarly, the author is not (C), "...emphasizing that readers are more socially active..." (E) implies that all experience, like all reading, can be positive, but the author would rather emphasize that evil reading can be reacted to in a constructive way. (D), "the author points out that reading is not passive, that men read and react according to their natures," is correct because reading does not "happen" to men. Men are in action when they read.

38. **(A)** The passage only briefly uses the metaphors of "dragon's teeth" (B), "mummies" (D) and "reason itself" (E). While the metaphor of "meat" (C) is used throughout the third paragraph, "men" (A) is used in more lines and in more ways: as the offspring of men, as armed men, as the image of God, and the running metaphor describing the death of men with images of homicide, martyrdom, and massacre.

39. **(D)** In lines 47-48, the passage says, "Prohibition is the act of the community, the State, the majority, which is the State...," verifying "the State" (D). The passage does not use the words of "the right" (A) or "the Godfearing populace" (B). "[S]ociety" (C) is never used as a synonym for the majority. While the passage tends toward gender bias, the author does not go so far as to equate the majority with "men" (E).

40. **(E)** The author never goes so far as to denounce the legitimacy of personal rights. He does not annihilate all of them by saying they "...are a fiction...." (C). He does not depopulate personal rights by saying they "...must be agreed upon..." (A) or that they "...are forfeit when abused" (D). The author does not restrict personal rights "...to the privacy of the home" (B); he simply argues that "Personal rights do not justify all social acts" (E)—namely, that the right to eat rotting meat does not create the right to sell rotting meat.

41. **(C)** Paragraph 5 uses examples, not metaphors, eliminating "a series..." (A) and "a sustained..." (B). The examples are in earnest, not "satirical..." (D); but they are not "point by point counter-examples" (E). The examples of paragraph 5, while many, only make one point among them; so, they cannot be said to be point by point. They are "repetitious legal examples" (C).

42. **(B)** The sentence beginning "You have a personal right..." (line 29) serves primarily to "associate liquor with putrid meat" (B). The paragraph "distinguish[es] between personal rights and public acts" (A) again and again, but never with so extreme an example as putrid meat. The sentence does not "emphasize the difference between reader and author" (C) because the "you" and the "I" are examples, not distinctions

of roles. "[A]ssociate the author…" (D) is incorrect because the author is in no way seeking to distance himself from his audience. "[M]irandize the reader" (E) is incorrect because, for the same reason just stated, the author does not assume any authority over the reader.

43. **(B)** The author's tone in the paragraph 2 is neither "annoyed" (A) nor "bored" (E). There is no sense of him being (D), "impatient," rather there is an atmosphere that a moment's explanation will clear the air. The author's reference to "many good men" dispels the idea that he is being (C), "condescending." The overall tone that simple explanation will convince the many good men that there is no assault on personal liberty is best described as "corrective" (B).

44. **(D)** Line 49 describes "traffic" (D) as immoral, "denying to an immoral and dangerous traffic the right of public sale," not "right" (A), "sale," (B), ("liberty" (E) or "public" (C), which is an adjective.

45. **(D)** Certain differences exist between paragraphs 1 and 5, such as (A), "…religious/literary [vs] legal…," (B), "…takes liberties [vs] not," and (E), "…fruit [vs] meat." However, these differences, while true, do not necessarily mean there is a conflict. Because the paragraphs do not undermine each other's points, they do not truly conflict. "the first paragraph associates prohibition with eating, while the fifth associates it with sale" (D) as eating or consumption. Paragraph 5 labors to convey the idea that prohibition does not limit the personal right to eat, while paragraph 1 calls God's forbiddance of eating the fruit of the tree of knowledge "prohibition." (C) is incorrect because in using varying examples, the author does not assume anything about the reader.

46. **(B)** The first paragraph alternately refers to Satan as "Beelzebub" (A), "the devil" (C) and "a brewer" (E). Paragraph 2 refers to those against prohibition as (D), "the enemy," but there is a secondary meaning implying that "the enemy" is Satan and that he is also against prohibition. The answer is (B), "a liar," which occurs in the first paragraph but is Satan's reference to God.

47. **(C)** The purpose of the sentence beginning, "Whether a man drinks" (lines 19-23), is "to demonstrate that even a personal liberty can become a social concern" (C). The sentence is not guilty of (B), "exaggerat[ion]," nor of implying the inevitability of (E), "…personal liberties are inherently a social burden." The sentence is almost comical in its lengthy list, but it does not go so far as "to ridicule drinkers…" (A). The sentence does demonstrate "…the pervasiveness of personal liberties," but its primary purpose is (C).

48. **(A)** The passage never claims that the law should or does "limit hazardous personal liberties." (B) While allowing people to drink, but not allowing the sale of liquor, may seem to intend (E), "eliminate the profit…," the passage never makes that statement. Nor does the passage outwardly claim that prohibition (D), "enforce(s) the will of God on weak men." The passage claims that prohibition (C), "den[ies] public sale to immoral and dangerous traffic," but this statement is a definition, not its

purpose. The purpose of prohibition, as taken from lines 48-49, is to "conserve social and civic liberty" (A).

49. **(D)** In the first paragraph, the author, to a limited degree, characterizes Satan as a lawyer, but never truly implies that "Satan is a lawyer" (A). The concessions of later paragraphs may suggest that (B), "Satan was correct," but the first paragraph does not. The author uses the Eden story as a form of truth without necessarily implying that "the Eden story is historic fact" (C). Paragraph 1 may imply that Eden was abstinence, but it does not imply that paradise can be regained by avoiding alcohol, that "Eden is abstinence" (E). The author definitely implies that (D), "the fruit is analogous to alcohol," that drinking alcohol is another fall, when he refers to the devil as "a brewer" (line 4).

50. **(D)** Lines 42-43 state, "total abstinence…relates to…personal conduct, and prohibition…relates to social conduct," which verifies statement I. Lines 44-45 state, "one is the act of the individual; the other is the act of the State," which verifies statement II. Lines 46-48 state, "abstinence…recognizes…personal liberty… Prohibition…is a matter of public policy," which verifies statement III. The answer is (D), all of the above.

51. **(D)** The passage does not define *dry* as "…sober" (A) or as "to thirst for alcohol" (E). The passage specifically distinguishes between "[having] signed a temperance pledge" (B) and "dry" in paragraph 4. Also, the passage never refers to "to not offer alcohol" (C). Lines 26-27 state, "when he votes dry—to prohibit liquor traffic." The answer is (D), "to outlaw the sale of alcohol."

52. **(C)** The author's belief or disbelief in God is not referred to in the closing lines of the passage, eliminating (B), "He has a strong belief in God." Nowhere does the passage suggest that the author "…wants drinkers to brew their own intoxicants" (D). In the closing lines, the author uses the will of the majority to justify prohibition, but does not "…maint[ain that] the majority is always right" (E). The author expresses "…concern…[for] the safety of the public" (A), but this concern is not implied to be primary. Line 49 refers to "an immoral and dangerous traffic," which implies that the immorality of the product is a reason to restrain it from public sale. The correct answer is (C), "…believes laws should uphold morality."

Section 2

Model Student Response to Essay Question 1:

We all have many influences in our lives, and those influences may change as we grow and develop. However, parents almost always play a major role in a person's life. The influences of a parent in a child's life are numerous, and they can be both positive and negative.

Parents affect our performance at school. Schools expect all students to get along with one another; however, children whose parents are antisocial are not likely to possess adequate skills to meet those expectations (Source B) since children almost always imitate their parent's behavior (Source G). Additionally, a parent's level of education may affect a child's academic performance. The ChildStats web site correlates mothers' education level with young children's proficiency in the skills they need even at the kindergarten level (Source F). One can speculate from these figures that the less-educated mother may simply not have the knowledge to help her children learn what they need to know, but other factors (e.g., home environment) may also be involved. Children who come from unhappy homes are not likely to care much about doing well at school—and may not be able to perform well even if they do care.

Parents influence the way we look at the world and what we expect in life. Maslow pointed out that children expect and need some type of predictable schedule (Source A). When parents fail to provide an orderly routine, the child may learn to perceive the world as chaotic and unpredictable, even as an adult. Orderliness and predictability encompass parental supervision and rules. Those who lack parental supervision are probably not going to feel as successful or secure about themselves because they will feel uncertain about what may happen.

Parents influence the type of person an individual becomes. President George W. Bush reminded Americans of "the values that bind families from one generation to the next" (Source G). However, these values are not always positive. Little good can come from having weak or abusive parents. As Source B indicates, the child who has a weak bond with parents and suffers abuse may become violent as an adult. And physical abuse as we grow up may cause us to feel life-long rejection. Children learn more from what a parent does than what he or she says (Source E). Obviously, the way our parents treat us affects our self-image, and our self-image plays a key role in the type of individuals we become.

In his press release, President Bush referred to children as "a source of joy, pride, and fulfillment" (Source G). His viewpoint is idealistic and sometimes unrealistic. Although parents are undoubtedly major influences in our lives, not every parent welcomes the responsibility of raising a child; in that case, the child may not be successful in school, and he or she may grow up to be insecure and have low self-esteem. In contrast, the individual who is fortunate enough to have educated, warm, and caring parents is likely to be success-oriented and secure.

Analysis of Student Response to Essay Question 1:

The student's response addresses the main challenge of the question (a synthesis of at least three sources for support and a position that defends, challenges, or qualifies the claim that a parent influences the physical and emotional development of a child). The writer begins with an introductory paragraph that starts with the broad topic of influences in our lives, and narrows to the specific topic of parental influences. The writer addresses three ways parents influence a child's life, and devotes one paragraph to each of those ways. The writer effectively synthesizes the sources to support the position of the essay by quoting or paraphrasing the sources to prove each point. For example, the second paragraph paraphrases, " . . . children whose parents are antisocial are not likely to possess adequate skills to meet those expectations (Source B), since children almost always imitate their parent's behavior (Source G)." And in the fourth paragraph the writer quotes a source: "Bush reminded Americans of 'the values that bind families from one generation to the next' (Source G)." Each reference is clearly attributed. The conclusion echoes the main ideas of the essay's body. The essay's language and development are effective, and the writer's position is supported with well-chosen examples (some drawn from the writer's own viewpoint rather than the sources). Overall, this essay is an effective response to the prompt.

Model Student Response to Essay Question 2:

Prejudice is still a continuing issue in society today. Slavery was one of the biggest acts of national discrimination in United States history. In Frederick Douglass's *Narrative of the Life of Frederick Douglass, an American Slave,* the speaker uses syntax, diction, and metaphor to distinguish the hopeful third paragraph from the rest of the sad, discouraging passage.

Douglass uses syntax to differentiate the third paragraph from the rest of the passage with a passionate outcry to explain his desire to be free. For example, the paragraph opens with "You are loosed from your mooring, and are free; I am fast in my chains, and am a slave!" Here Douglass uses coordination and parallel structure to connect the freedom that the ship has as the antithesis of the enslaved boy's bondage. The speaker uses this comparison to emphasize the boy's despair and desire by comparing his slavery to the freedom he longs for. Douglass's true desire is revealed with his urgent plea to God for answers, "God, deliver me! Is there any God? Why am I a slave?" He is calling out to God with a broken heart because he is in such a horrible condition. The dire situation calls his core beliefs into question. He uses an exclamatory sentence when he says, "Only think of it; one hundred miles straight north, and I am free!" This emotional statement shows the seriousness of his desire to be a free man. Without modern conveniences of transportation, one hundred miles is quite a long distance. He is willing to do whatever it takes to shake off the chains of slavery. Douglass is hopeful instead of complaining about his wretched conditions as he does in the first two paragraphs.

The speaker's word choice also distinguishes the optimistic third paragraph from the pessimist opening. He emphasizes his depression by comparing himself to a brute at the end of the first paragraph. The use of "brute" indicates his feelings of worthlessness as a human being. When white men look at him, they see only a work animal needing to be tamed and harnessed, not the valuable member of society he wishes to be. He juxtaposes the movements of the free with those of the slave by saying, "You move merrily before the gentle gale, and I sadly before the bloody whip." The adverbs "merrily" and "sadly" show the stark contrast of one who is free and one who is enslaved.

Finally, Douglass uses metaphors to compare the freedom he desires to the position in which he currently finds himself. He describes freedom in the passage, "You are freedom's swift-winged angels, that fly around the world." The angels represent the peace and happiness available to all free men—something for which Douglass desperately is striving. He knows of no other description for his current state than that of "the hottest hell of unending slavery." He is treated as one who is damned for all eternity. His spirit is broken, but his desires are still strong.

Douglass emphasizes the desire to be a free man through his hopefulness in the third paragraph as opposed to the sad, melancholy tone of the rest of the passage.

Analysis of Student Response to Essay Question 2:

This essay effectively analyzes how Frederick Douglass's change in style reinforces the rhetorical effect through a careful examination of the stylistic elements that distinguish paragraph 3 from the rest of the passage. The student recognizes how syntax, figurative language, and selection of detail shift in paragraph 3 and how the shift strengthens Douglass's overall message. The student also refers to the passage both directly and indirectly to support the specific thesis that the tone of the third paragraph is hopeful and optimistic as opposed to the melancholy of the first and second paragraphs. The essay moves beyond summary into analysis of the devices. The student employs a variety of sentence structure and a mature vocabulary. The prose demonstrates an ability to control a wide range of elements of effective writing but is not necessarily flawless.

Model Student Response to Essay Question 3:

Survival is the basic human need. People will go to great lengths to survive. The recent movie *127 Hours* illustrates this basic instinct. A hiker, trapped by a boulder, makes the heart-wrenching choice to cut off his own arm in order to free himself and live to see another day. For most, just surviving is not good enough. People also want to live a life with meaning and filled with flourishing relationships among family and friends. C.S. Lewis is correct in his assertion that friendship is not necessary for survival but gives value to the human existence.

Throughout history, men and women from all races, social classes, and various circumstances have found ways to survive in spite of overwhelming odds. In most cases, these people did not just survive but found a way to thrive in spite of their difficulties. How? Through friendships. In Mark Twain's classic American novel *The Adventures of Huckleberry Finn*, Huck Finn runs away from an abusive father. He goes as far as to fake his own death to escape and survive on his own. He seems happy to float down the river on a skiff and camp out on an island without anyone to accompany him. Even Huck doesn't seem to realize how much he needs a companion until he encounters Jim, the runaway slave. The two strike up an unlikely friendship (especially for the pre-Civil War South) and face their difficulties together, each relying on the other for support and camaraderie. Through every challenge, they stick together and find freedom.

Popular culture is also filled with tales of lone survivors. One thing most of these loners have in common is the connection to a loved one somewhere out there waiting for their safe return. Take the movie *Castaway*, for example. Tom Hanks' character is stranded on a deserted island after a plane crash. After he realizes that no one is going to rescue him, he sets out to survive. He makes a shelter. He lights a fire. He sharpens a stick for spear fishing. All the while, he continually opens the pocket watch his fiancé gave him during their last meeting. With his fiancé's picture included, the watch reminds him of what he has to live for. If he had no loved ones waiting for him, would he have fought so hard to survive? He spent years trying to get home. After building a raft to get off of the island and finally getting rescued by a freighter, he discovers his fiancé gave up on him and married someone else. Even though he loses the one that motivated him to survive, he seeks out other relationships to add value and meaning to his new life.

A person can't survive on friendships alone. However, a person cannot thrive without those relationships that provide value and meaning to life. Having friends is like wearing glasses. Sometimes a person doesn't even know that he has a vision problem until a friend brings life into focus.

Analysis of Student Response to Essay Question 3:

This cogent, well-supported, and carefully reasoned essay demonstrates both sophisticated argument and particularly impressive control of language. The student musters considerable and variable proofs for his or her claims and demonstrates an ability to make a point economically and compellingly before moving swiftly on to the next part of his or her carefully constructed argument. The evidence ranges widely from Mark Twain to a character played by Tom Hanks, and the student carefully qualifies his or her claim to point out that surviving is not the same thing as thriving. While most students would write an essay taking the same stance, this essay's success is certainly based upon its persuasive argument, but the writer's language is equally impressive with its demonstration of fluency, expressive vocabulary, and syntactical variety.

END OF PRACTICE TEST 3

APPENDICES
AP English Language & Composition

Punctuation

Try to read this paragraph.

take some more tea the march hare said to alice very earnestly ive had nothing yet alice replied in an offended tone so i cant take more you mean you cant take less said the hatter its very easy to take more than nothing lewis carroll

Now try again.

> *"Take some more tea," the March Hare said to Alice, very earnestly.*
> *"I've had nothing yet," Alice replied in an offended tone, "so I can't take more."*
> *"You mean you can't take less," said the Hatter. "It's very easy to take more than nothing."*
>
> *—Lewis Carroll*

This example illustrates to what extent punctuation helps the reader understand what the writer is trying to say. The most important role of punctuation is clarification.

In speech, words are accompanied by gesture, voice, tone, and rhythm that help convey a desired meaning. In writing, it is punctuation alone that must do the same job.

There are many rules about how to use the various punctuation marks. These are sometimes difficult to understand, because they are described with so much grammatical terminology. Therefore, this discussion of punctuation will avoid as much terminology as possible. If you still find the rules confusing, and your method of punctuation is somewhat random, try to remember that most punctuation takes the place of pauses in speech.

Keeping this in mind, read your sentences aloud as you write; if you punctuate according to the pauses in your voice, you will do much better than if you put in your commas, periods, and dashes either at random or where they look good.

Stops

There are three ways to end a sentence:

1. a period

2. a question mark

3. an exclamation point

The Period

Periods end all sentences that are not questions or exclamations. In speech, the end of a sentence is indicated with a full pause. The period is the written counterpart of this pause.

Go get me my paper. I'm anxious to see the news.

Into each life some rain must fall. Last night some fell into mine.

The moon is round. The stars look small.

Mary and Janet welcomed the newcomer. She was noticeably happy.

When a question is intended as a suggestion and the listener is not expected to answer or when a question is asked indirectly as part of a sentence, a period is also used.

Mimi wondered if the parade would ever end.

May we hear from you soon.

Will you please send the flowers you advertised.

We'll never know who the culprit was.

Periods also follow most abbreviations and contractions.

Wed.	Dr.	Jr.	Sr.
etc.	Jan.	Mr.	Mr.
Esq.	cont.	a.m.	A.D.

Periods (or parentheses) are also used after a letter or number in a series.

a. apples	1. president
b. oranges	2. vice president
c. pears	3. secretary

Errors to Avoid

Be sure to omit the period after a quotation mark preceded by a period. Only one stop is necessary to end a sentence.

She said, "Hold my hand." (no period after the final quotation mark)

"Don't go into the park until later."

"It's not my fault," he said. "She would have taken the car anyway."

After many abbreviations, particularly those of organizations or agencies, no period is used (check in a dictionary if in doubt).

AFL-CIO	NAACP	GM
FBI	NATO	IBM
TV	UN	SEC

The Question Mark

Use a question mark to end a direct question even if it is not in the form of a question. The question mark in writing denotes the rising tone of voice used to indicate a question in speech. If you read the following two sentences aloud, you will see the difference in tone between a statement and a question composed of the same words.

Mary is here.

Mary is here?

Here are some more examples of correct use of the question mark. Pay special attention to the way it is used with other punctuation.

Where will we go next?

Would you like coffee or tea?

"Won't you," he asked, "please lend me a hand?"

"Will they ever give us our freedom?" the prisoner asked.

"To be or not to be?" was the question asked by Hamlet.

Who asked, "When?"

Question marks indicate a full stop and lend a different emphasis to a sentence than do commas. Compare these pairs of sentences.

Was the sonata by Beethoven? or Brahms? or Chopin?

Was the sonata by Beethoven, or Brahms, or Chopin?

Did they walk to the park? climb the small hill? take the bus to town? or go skating out back?

Did they walk to town, climb the small hill, take the bus to town, or go skating out back?

Sometimes question marks are placed in parentheses. This indicates doubt or uncertainty about the facts being reported.

The bombing started at 3 a.m. (?)

She said the dress cost $200,000 (?)

Hippocrates (460(?)-(?)377 B.C.) is said to be the father of modern medicine.

The Exclamation Point

An exclamation point ends an emphatic statement. It should be used only to express strong emotions, such as surprise, disbelief, or admiration. If it is used too often for mild expressions of emotion, it loses its effectiveness.

Let go of me!

Help! Fire!

It was a wonderful day!

Who shouted "Fire!" *(Notice no question mark is necessary)*

Fantastic!

"Unbelievable!" she gasped. *(Notice no comma is necessary)*

Where else can I go! *(The use of the exclamation point shows that this is a strong statement even though it is worded like a question.)*

Do not overuse exclamation points. The following is an example of the overuse of exclamation points:

Dear Susan,

I was so glad to see you last week! You looked better than ever! Our talk meant so much to me! I can hardly wait until we get together again! Could you believe how long it has been! Let's never let that happen again! Please write as soon as you get the chance! I can hardly wait to hear from you!

Your friend,
Nora

INTERJECTIONS

An interjection is a word or group of words used as an exclamation to express emotion. It need not be followed by an exclamation point. Often an interjection is followed by a comma (see **The Comma**) if it is not very intense. Technically, the interjection has no grammatical relation to other words in the sentence; yet it is still considered a part of speech.

Examples:

Oh dear, I forgot my keys again.

Ah! Now do you understand?

Ouch! I didn't realize that the stove was hot.

Oh, excuse me. I didn't realize that you were next on line.

Pauses

There are five ways to indicate a pause shorter than a period.

1. dash

2. colon

3. parentheses

4. semicolon

5. comma

The Dash

Use the dash (—) to indicate a sudden or unexpected break in the normal flow of the sentence. It can also be used in place of parentheses or of commas if the meaning is clarified. Usually the dash gives special emphasis to the material it sets off. On a typewriter, two hyphens (--) indicate a dash.

Could you—I hate to ask!—help me with these boxes?

When we left town—a day never to be forgotten—they had a record snowfall.

She said—we all heard it—"The safe is not locked."

These are the three ladies—Mrs. Jackson, Miss Harris, and Ms. Forrest—you hoped to meet last week.

The sight of the Andromeda Galaxy—especially when seen for the first time—is astounding.

That day was the longest in her life—or so it seemed to her.

A dash is often used to summarize a series of ideas that have already been expressed.

Freedom of speech, freedom to vote, and freedom of assembly—these are the cornerstones of democracy.

Carbohydrates, fats, and proteins—these are the basic kinds of food we need.

Jones, who first suggested we go; Marshall, who made all the arrangements; and Kline, who finally took us there—these were the three men I admired most for their courage.

James, Howard, Marianne, Angela, Catherine—all were displeased with the decision of the teacher.

The dash is also used to note the author of a quotation that is set off in the text.

Nothing is good or bad but thinking makes it so.
> —William Shakespeare

Under every grief and pine
Runs a joy with silken twine.
> —William Blake

The Colon

The colon (:) is the sign of a pause about midway in length between the semicolon and the period. It can often be replaced by a comma and sometimes by a period. Although used less frequently now than it was 50 to 75 years ago, the colon is still convenient to use, for it signals to the reader that more information is to come on the subject of concern. The colon can also create a slight dramatic tension.

It is used to introduce a word, a phrase, or a complete statement (clause) that emphasizes, illustrates, or exemplifies what has already been stated.

He had only one desire in life: to play baseball.

The weather that day was the most unusual I'd ever seen: It snowed and rained while the sun was still shining.

In his speech, the president surprised us by his final point: the conventional grading system would be replaced next year.

Jean thought of only two things the last half hour of the hike home: a bath and a bed.

Notice that the word following the colon can start with either a capital or a small letter. Use a capital letter if the word following the colon begins another complete sentence. When the words following the colon are part of the sentence preceding the colon, use a small letter.

May I offer you a suggestion: don't drive without your seat belts fastened.

The thought continued to perplex him: Where will I go next?

When introducing a series that illustrates or emphasizes what has already been stated, use the colon.

Only a few of the graduates were able to be there: Jamison, Mearns, Linkley, and Commoner.

For Omar Khayyam, a Persian poet, three things are necessary for a paradise on earth: a loaf of bread, a jug of wine, and one's beloved.

In the basement, he kept some equipment for his experiments: the test tubes, some chemical agents, three sunlamps, and the drill.

Long quotations set off from the rest of the text by indentation rather than quotation marks are generally introduced with a colon.

The first line of Lincoln's Gettysburg address is familiar to most Americans:

> Four score and seven years ago our fathers brought forth on this continent a new nation, conceived in liberty and dedicated to the proposition that all men are created equal.

I quote from Shakespeare's *Sonnets*:

> When I do count the clock that tells the time,
> And see the brave day sunk in hideous night;
> When I behold the violet past prime,
> And sable curls all silver'd o'er with white ...

It is also customary to end a business letter salutation with a colon.

> Dear Senator Jordan:
> To Whom It May Concern:
> Gentlemen:
> Dear Sir or Madam:

In informal letters, use a comma.

> Dear Chi-Leng,
> Dear Father,

The colon is also used in introducing a list.

Please send the following:

1. 50 index cards
2. 4 typewriter ribbons
3. 8 erasers

Prepare the recipe as follows:

1. Slice the oranges thinly.
2. Arrange them in a circle around the strawberries.
3. Pour the liqueur over both fruits.

At least three ladies will have to be there to help:

1. Mrs. Goldman, who will greet the guests;
2. Harriet Sacher, who will serve the lunch; and
3. my sister, who will do whatever else needs to be done.

Finally, the colon is used between numbers when writing the time, between the volume and number or volume and page number of a journal, and between the chapter and verse in the Bible.

> 4:30 P.M.
> The Nation, 34:8
> Genesis 5:18

Parentheses

To set off material that is only loosely connected to the central meaning of the sentence, use parentheses [( )].

Most men (at least, most that I know) like wine, women, and song but have too much work and not enough time for such enjoyments.

On Tuesday evenings and Thursday afternoons (the times I don't have classes), the television programs are not too exciting.

Last year at Vail (we go there every year), the skiing was the best I've ever seen.

In New York (I've lived there all my life and ought to know), you have to have a license for a gun.

What must be done to think clearly and calmly (is it even possible?) and then make the decision?

Watch out for other punctuation when you use parentheses. Punctuation that refers to the material enclosed in the parentheses occurs inside the marks. Punctuation belonging to the rest of the sentence comes outside the parentheses.

I thought I knew the poem by heart (boy, was I wrong!).

For a long time (too long as far as I'm concerned), women were thought to be inferior to men.

We must always strive to tell the truth. (Are we even sure we know what truth is?)

When I first saw a rose (don't you think it's the most beautiful flower?), I thought it must be man-made.

The Semicolon

Semicolons (;) are sometimes called mild periods. They indicate a pause midway in length between the comma and the colon. Writing that contains many semicolons is usually in a dignified, formal style. To use them correctly, it is necessary to be able to recognize main clauses—complete ideas. When two main clauses occur in a single sentence without a connecting word *(and, but, or, nor, for)*, the appropriate mark of punctuation is the semicolon.

It is not a good idea for you to leave the country right now; you should actually try to stay as long as you possibly can.

Music lightens life; literature deepens it.

In the past, boy babies were often dressed in blue; girls, in pink. *("Were often dressed" is understood in the second part of the sentence.)*

Can't you see it's no good to go on alone; we'll starve to death if we keep traveling this way much longer.

Burgundy and maroon are very similar colors; scarlet is altogether different.

Notice how the use of the comma, period, and semicolon gives a sentence a slightly different meaning.

Music lightens life; literature deepens it.

Just as music lightens life, literature deepens it.

Music lightens life. Literature deepens it.

The semicolon lends a certain balance to writing that would otherwise be difficult to achieve. Nonetheless, you should be careful not to overuse it. A comma can just as well join parts of a sentence with two main ideas; the semicolon is particularly appropriate if there is a striking contrast in the two ideas expressed.

Ask not what your country can do for you; ask what you can do for your country.

It started out as an ordinary day; it ended being the most extraordinary of her life.

Our power to apprehend truth is limited; to seek it, limitless.

If any one of the following words or phrases is used to join together compound sentences, it is generally preceded by a semicolon.

then	however	thus	furthermore
hence	indeed	consequently	also
that is	nevertheless	anyhow	in addition

in fact	on the other hand	likewise	moreover
still	meanwhile	instead	besides
otherwise	in other words	henceforth	for example
therefore	at the same time	even now	

For a long time, people thought that women were inferior to men; *even now* it is not an easy attitude to overcome.

Being clever and cynical, he succeeded in becoming president of the company; *meanwhile,* his wife left him.

Cigarette smoking has never interested me; *furthermore,* I couldn't care less if anyone else smokes or not.

Some say Bach was the greatest composer of all time; *yet* he still managed to have an ordinary life in other ways: he and his wife had twenty children.

We left wishing we could have stayed much longer; *in other words,* they showed us a good time.

When a series of complicated items is listed or if there is internal punctuation in a series, the semicolon is sometimes used to make the meaning clearer:

You can use your new car for many things: to drive to town or to the country; to impress your friends and neighbors; to protect yourself from rain on a trip away from home; and to borrow against should you need money right away.

The scores from yesterday's games came in late last night: Pirates-6, Zoomers-3; Caterpillars-12, Steelys-8; Crashers-9, Links-8; and Greens-15, Uptowns-4.

In October a bag of potatoes cost 69¢; in December, 99¢; in February, $1.09; and in April, $1.39. I wonder if this inflation will ever stop.

The semicolon is placed outside quotation marks or parentheses, unless it is a part of the material enclosed in those marks.

I used to call him "my lord and master"; it made him laugh every time.

The weather was cold for that time of year (I was shivering wherever I went); nevertheless, we set out to hike to the top of that mountain.

The Comma

Of all the marks of punctuation, the comma (,) has the most uses. Before you tackle the main principles that guide its usage, be sure that you have an elementary understanding of sentence structure. There are actually only a few rules and conventions to follow when using commas; the rest is common sense. The worst abuse of commas comes from those who overuse them or who place them illogically. If you are ever in doubt as to whether or not to use a comma, do not use it.

IN A SERIES

When more than one adjective (an adjective series) describes a noun, use a comma to separate and emphasize each adjective.

the long, dark passageway

another confusing, sleepless night

an elaborate, complex plan

the haunting, melodic sound

the old, gray, crumpled hat

In these instances, the comma takes the place of "and." To test if the comma is needed, try inserting "and" between the adjectives in question. If it is logical, you should use a comma. The following are examples of adjectives that describe an adjective-noun combination that has come to be thought of almost as one word. In such cases, the adjective in front of the adjective-noun combination needs no comma.

a stately *oak tree*	my worst *report card*
an exceptional *wine glass*	a borrowed *record player*
a successful *garage sale*	a porcelain *dinner plate*

If you insert "and" between the adjectives in the above examples, it will not make sense.

The comma is also used to separate words, phrases, and whole ideas (clauses); it still takes the place of "and" when used this way.

an apple, a pear, a fig, and a banana

a lovely lady, an indecent dress, and many admirers

She lowered the shade, closed the curtain, turned off the light, and went to bed.

John, Frank, and my Uncle Harry all thought it was a questionable theory.

The only question that exists about the use of commas in a series is whether or not one should be used before the final item. Usually "and" or "or" precedes the final item, and many writers do not include the comma before the final "and" or "or." However, it is advisable to use the comma, because often its omission can be confusing—in such cases as these, for instance.

NO: Would you like to shop at Saks, Lord and Taylor and Macy's?

NO: He got on his horse, tracked a rabbit and a deer and rode on to Canton.

NO: We planned the trip with Mary and Harold, Susan, Dick and Joan, Gregory and Jean and Charles. *(Is it Gregory and Jean or Jean and Charles or Gregory and Jean and Charles?)*

WITH A LONG INTRODUCTORY PHRASE

Usually if a phrase of more than five or six words precedes the subject at the beginning of a sentence, a comma is used to set it off.

After last night's fiasco at the disco, she couldn't bear the thought of looking at him again.

Whenever I try to talk about politics, my husband leaves the room.

When it comes to actual facts, every generation makes the same mistakes as the preceding one.

Provided you have said nothing, they will never guess who you are.

It is not necessary to use a comma with a short sentence.

In January she will go to Switzerland.

After I rest I'll feel better.

At Grandma's we had a big dinner.

During the day no one is home.

If an introductory phrase includes a verb form that is being used as another part of speech (a "verbal"), it must be followed by a comma. Try to make sense of the following sentences without commas.

NO: When eating Mary never looked up from her plate.

YES: When eating, Mary never looked up from her plate.

NO: Because of her desire to follow her faith in James wavered.

YES: Because of her desire to follow, her faith in James wavered.

NO: Having decided to leave Mary James wrote her a letter.

YES: Having decided to leave Mary, James wrote her a letter.

Above all, common sense is the best guideline when trying to decide whether or not to use a comma after an introductory phrase. Does the comma make the meaning clearer? If it does, use it; if not, there is no reason to insert it.

TO SEPARATE SENTENCES WITH TWO MAIN IDEAS (COMPOUND SENTENCES)

To understand this use of the comma, you need to have studied sentence structure and be able to recognize compound sentences.

When a sentence contains more than two subjects and verbs (clauses) and the two clauses are joined by a connecting word *(and, but, or, yet, for, nor),* use a comma before the connecting word to show that another clause is coming.

I thought I knew the poem by heart, but he showed me three lines I had forgotten.

Are we really interested in helping the children, or are we more concerned with protecting our good names?

Jim knows you are disappointed, and he has known it for a long time.

Living has its good points to be sure, yet I will not mind when it is over.

If the two parts of the sentence are short and closely related, it is not necessary to use a comma.

He threw the ball and the dog ran after it.

Jane played the piano and Charles danced.

Errors to Avoid

Be careful not to confuse a compound sentence with a sentence that has a compound verb and a single subject. If the subject is the same for both verbs, there is no need for a comma.

> NO: Charles sent some flowers, and wrote a long letter explaining why he had not been able to come.

> NO: Last Thursday we went to the concert with Julia, and afterward dined at an old Italian restaurant.

> NO: For the third time, the teacher explained that the literacy level of high school students was much lower than it had been in previous years, and, this time, wrote the statistics on the board for everyone to see.

TO SET OFF INTERRUPTING MATERIAL

There are so many different kinds of interruptions that can occur in a sentence that a list of them all would be quite lengthy. In general, words and phrases that stop the flow of the sentence or are unnecessary for the main idea are set off by commas.

Abbreviations after names

Did you invite John Paul, Jr., and his sister?

Martha Harris, Ph.D., will be the speaker tonight.

Interjections: An exclamation added without grammatical connection.

Oh, I'm so glad to see you.

I tried so hard, alas, to do it.

Hey, let me out of here.

No, I will not let you out.

Direct address

Roy, won't you open the door for the dog?

I can't understand, Mother, what you are trying to say.

May I ask, Mr. President, why you called us together?

Hey, lady, watch out for the car!

Tag questions: A question that repeats the helping verb and is in the negative.

I'm really hungry, aren't you?

Jerry looks like his father, doesn't he?

You'll come early, won't you?

We are expected at nine, aren't we?

Mr. Jones can chair the meeting, can't he?

Geographical names and addresses

The concert will be held in Chicago, Illinois, on August 12.

They visited Tours, France, last summer.

The letter was addressed to Ms. Marion Heartwell, 1881 Pine Lane, Palo Alto, California 95824. *(No comma is used before a zip code.)*

Transitional words and phrases

On the other hand, I hope he gets better.

In addition, the phone rang six times this afternoon.

I'm, nevertheless, going to the beach on Sunday.

You'll find, therefore, no one more loyal to you than I.

To tell the truth, I don't know what to believe.

Parenthetical words and phrases

You will become, I believe, a great statesman.

We know, of course, that this is the only thing to do.

In fact, I planted corn last summer.

The Mannes affair was, to put it mildly, a surprise.

Bathing suits, generally speaking, are getting smaller.

Unusual word order

The dress, new and crisp, hung in the closet. *(Normal word order: The new, crisp dress hung in the closet.)*

Intently, she stared out the window. *(Normal word order: She stared intently out the window.)*

NONRESTRICTIVE ELEMENTS (NOT ESSENTIAL TO THE MEANING)

Parts of a sentence that modify other parts are sometimes essential to the meaning of the sentence and sometimes not. When a modifying word or group of words is not vital to the meaning of the sentence, it is set off by commas. Since it does not restrict the meaning of the words it modifies, it is called "nonrestrictive." Modifiers that are essential to the meaning of the sentence are called "restrictive" and are not set off by commas. Compare the following pairs of sentences:

The girl *who wrote the story* is my sister. (essential)

My sister, *the girl who wrote the story,* has always been drawn to adventure. (nonessential)

John Milton's famous poem *"Paradise Lost"* tells a remarkable story. (essential—Milton has written other poems)

Dante's great work, *"The Divine Comedy,"* marked the beginning of the Renaissance and the end of the Dark Ages. (nonessential—Dante wrote only one great work)

My parakeet *Simian* has an extensive vocabulary. (essential—because there are no commas, the writer must have more than one parakeet)

My parakeet, *Simian,* has an extensive vocabulary. (nonessential—the writer must have only one parakeet, whose name is Simian)

The people *who arrived late* were not seated. (essential)

George, *who arrived late,* was not seated. (nonessential)

She always listened to her sister *Jean.* (essential—she has more than one sister)

She always listened to her husband, *Jack.* (nonessential—obviously, she has only one husband)

TO SET OFF DIRECT QUOTATIONS

Most direct quotes or quoted materials are set off from the rest of the sentence by commas.

"Please read your part more loudly," the director insisted.

"I won't know what to do," said Michael, "if you leave me now."

The teacher said sternly, "I will not dismiss this class until I have silence."

Mark looked up from his work, smiled, and said, "We'll be with you in a moment."

Be careful not to set off indirect quotations or quotes that are used as subjects or complements.

"To be or not to be" is the famous beginning of a soliloquy in Shakespeare's *Hamlet.* (subject)

Back then my favorite song was *"A Summer Place."* (complement)

She said she would never come back. (indirect quote)

"Place two tablespoons of chocolate in this pan" were her first words to her apprentice in the kitchen. (subject)

TO SET OFF CONTRASTING ELEMENTS

Her intelligence, *not her beauty,* got her the job.

Your plan will take you further from, *rather than closer to,* your destination.

It was a reasonable, *though not appealing,* idea.

James wanted an active, *not a passive,* partner.

IN DATES

Both forms of the date are acceptable.

She will arrive on April 6, 1992.

He left on 5 December 1990.

In January 1987 he handed in his resignation.

In January 1987, he handed in his resignation.

Appendix B

Spelling

At first glance, one would expect *blew* and *sew* to rhyme. Instead, *sew* rhymes with *so*. If words were spelled the way they sound, one would expect *so* to rhyme with *do* instead of *dough* and would never expect *do* to rhyme with *blew*. Confusing, isn't it?

Words are not always spelled phonetically, and it sometimes seems that spelling is totally illogical. However, in spelling there is usually only one correct form.

It is important to learn to spell properly. Poor spelling is usually a sign of haste or carelessness, and it is often taken as a sign of ignorance or illiteracy. Yet learning to spell correctly is indeed more difficult for some people than for others. In any case, it can be mastered with time and patience.

There are many helpful practices to improve spelling: using the dictionary, keeping a list of words that cause difficulty, familiarizing oneself with word origin, and studying the word list and the rules in this chapter.

If a writer has absolutely no idea how to spell a word, he or she obviously cannot look it up. Yet in most spelling problems, the writer has a general idea of the spelling but is not certain. Even if only the first few letters of the word are known, the writer should be able to find it in the dictionary.

Example: To check the spelling of the word *miscellaneous.*

The writer probably knows that *misc-* compose the first four letters of the word and might even know a few more by sounding the word out. Although phonetics is not a reliable source for spelling, it can be helpful when using the dictionary. In this particular problem, it most likely is the ending *-aneous* that gives the writer difficulty. Since in the English language there are few words beginning with the letters *misc-,* the writer should have little trouble finding *miscellaneous* in the dictionary.

Example: To check the spelling of *occasionally.*

Here, the writer is probably concerned with the number of *c*'s and *s*'s. If one looks up the word with the beginning *oca-,* there is no listing. The next logical choice is to check the word with two *c*'s, which will be found a few entries later. One can even skim the page when a general idea of the spelling is known.

When using the dictionary, be sure also that you have found the desired word, not a homonym or a word with a similar form, by checking the word's definition.

So checking spelling is a matter of trial and error; use the dictionary when you are not sure—and even when you feel certain.

Word Analysis

A basic knowledge of the English language, especially familiarity with its numerous prefixes, can help build vocabulary and also strengthen spelling skills. For example, if one knows that *inter-* means *between* and that *intra-* means *within,* one is not likely to spell *intramural* as *intermural.* (The former means within the limits of a city, a college, etc.)

The following table lists some common Latin and Greek prefixes, which form part of the foundation of the English language.

PREFIX	MEANING	ENGLISH EXAMPLE
ab-, a-, abs-	away, from	abstain
ad-	to, toward	adjacent
ante-	before	antecedent
anti-	against	antidote
bi-	two	bisect
cata-, cat-, cath-	down	cataclysm
circum-	around	circumlocution
contra-	against	contrary
de-	down, from	decline
di-	twice	diatonic
dis-, di-	apart, away	dissolve
epi-, ep-, eph-	upon, among	epidemic
ex-, e-	out of, from	extricate
hyper-	beyond, over	hyperactive
hypo-	under, down, less	hypodermic
in-	in, into	instill
inter-	among, between	intercede
intra-	within	intramural
meta-, met-	beyond, along with	metaphysics
mono-	one	monolith
non-	no, not	nonsense
ob-	against	obstruct
para-, par-	beside	parallel
per-	through	permeate
pre-	before	prehistoric
pro-	before	project
super-	above	superior
tele-, tel-	far	television
trans-	across	transpose
ultra-	beyond	ultraviolet

Spelling Lists

There are some words that consistently give writers trouble. The list below contains about 100 words that are commonly misspelled. In studying this list, readers will find that certain words are more troublesome than others. These in particular should be reviewed.

100 COMMONLY MISSPELLED WORDS

accommodate	February	professor
achievement	height	prominent
acquire	immediately	pursue
among	interest	quiet
apparent	its, it's	receive
arguing	led	procedure
argument	lose	profession
athletics	losing	receiving
belief	marriage	recommend
believe	mere	referring
beneficial	necessary	remember
benefited	occasion	repetition
bureau	occurred	rhythm
business	occurrence	sense
category	occurring	separate
comparative	opinion	separation
conscious	opportunity	similar
controversial	parallel	studying
define	particular	succeed
definitely	performance	succession
definition	personal	surprise
describe	personnel	technique
description	possession	than
despair	possible	their, they're, there
disastrous	practical	then
effect	precede	thorough
embarrass	prejudice	to, too, two
environment	prepare	tomorrow
exaggerate	prevalent	transferred
existence	principal	unnecessary
existent	principle	villain
experience	privilege	write
explanation	probably	writing
fascinate	proceed	

As a handy reference, it is a good idea to set aside an area in a notebook to list problem words. Add to it any new words that are persistent spelling problems.

Spelling Rules

Prefixes

Prefixes (such as *dis-*, *mis-*, *in-*, *un-*, and *re-*) are added to words without doubling or dropping letters.

dis + appear = disappear
dis + service = disservice
dis + solved = dissolved
dis + satisfied = dissatisfied
mis + information = misinformation
mis + spelled = misspelled
mis + understand = misunderstand
in + capable = incapable
in + definite = indefinite
in + numerable = innumerable
un + usual = unusual
un + seen = unseen
un + named = unnamed
re + elect = reelect
re + search = research

Suffixes

When forming adverbs from adjectives ending in *al,* the ending becomes *ally.*

normal	normally	real	really
occasional	occasionally	legal	legally
royal	royally		

Words ending in *n* keep the *n* when adding *ness.*

openness stubbornness suddenness brazenness

All words ending in *ful* have only one *l.*

cupful	cheerful
forgetful	doleful
mouthful	graceful
helpful	meaningful
spoonful	handful

Add *ment* without changing the root word's spelling.

> adjust + ment = adjustment
> develop + ment = development
> amaze + ment = amazement

Silent *e*.

When a suffix beginning with a vowel is added, a word ending in a silent *e* generally drops the *e*.

Example:

> admire + able = admirable
> allure + ing = alluring
> believe + able = believable
> come + ing = coming
> dare + ing = daring
> deplore + able = deplorable
> desire + ous = desirous
> explore + ation = exploration
> fame + ous = famous
> imagine + able = imaginable
> move + able = movable
> note + able = notable

However, the word retains the *e* when a suffix beginning with a consonant is added.

Example:

> arrange + ment = arrangement
> glee + ful = gleeful
> like + ness = likeness
> spite + ful = spiteful
> time + less = timeless

With *judgment, acknowledgment,* and other words formed by adding *ment* to a word with a *dge* ending, the final *e* is usually dropped, although it is equally correct to retain it.

When adding *ous* or *able* to a word ending in *ge* or *ce*, keep the final *e* when adding the suffix. The *e* is retained to keep the soft sound of the *c* or *g*.

courageous	manageable	outrageous
changeable	advantageous	traceable

IE + EI

In words with *ie* or *ei* in which the sound is e, (long *ee*), use *i* before *e* except after *c*.

Examples: i before *e:*

believe	pier	shield	wield
chief	priest	siege	yield
niece	reprieve		

Examples: Except after *c:*

ceiling   conceit   conceive   deceive   perceive   receive

The following words are some exceptions to the rule and must be committed to memory.

either	conscience	weird	reign
leisure	height	freight	weigh
neither	forfeit		
seize	neighbor		

Except before *ing,* final *y* usually changes to *i.*

rely + ance = reliance
study + ing = studying
modify + er = modifier
modify + ing = modifying
amplify + ed = amplified
amplify + ing = amplifying

When preceded by a vowel, final *y* does not change to *i.*

annoying, annoyed
destroying, destroyed, destroyer
journeyman, journeyed, journeyer

Doubling the Final Consonant

In one-syllable words that end in a single consonant preceded by a single vowel, double the final consonant before adding a suffix that begins with a vowel.

Example:

drop + ing = drop(p)ing
clap + ed = clap(p)ed
man + ish = man(n)ish
snap + ed = snap(p)ed
quit + ing = quit(t)ing

However, when a suffix begins with a consonant, do not double the final consonant before adding the suffix.

Example:

> man + hood = manhood
> glad + ly = gladly
> bad + ly = badly
> fat + ness = fatness
> sin + ful = sinful

This is also the case in multisyllabic words that are accented on the final syllable and have endings as described above.

Example:

> admit + ed = admitted
> begin + ing = beginning
> commit + ed = committed
>   BUT
> commit + ment = commitment

However, in words with this type of ending, in which the final syllable is not accented, the final consonant is not doubled.

Example:

> happen + ing = happening
> profit + able = profitable
> comfort + ed = comforted
> refer + ence = reference
> confer + ence = conference

Only three words end in *ceed* in English. They are *exceed, proceed,* and *succeed.* All other "seed-sounding" words (except *supersede*) end in *cede.*

intercede	recede
concede	accede
secede	precede

Proofreading

The best way to improve spelling is to reread what has been written. In fact, many other writing problems can be avoided as well if the writer carefully rereads and revises. Remember, poor spelling is not something that must be tolerated. With a little work, it can be greatly improved.

Appendix C

Representative Authors and Texts

In the Course Description, the College Board acknowledges that there is "no recommended or required reading list for an AP English Language and Composition course." However, the College Board does publish a list of authors that is "designed to illustrate the possibilities of nonfiction prose."

The list below will give you a sense of the diversity of literature you will encounter on the AP English Language exam. When preparing for the exam, try to read a variety of texts, even if you only read partial texts. Select a few authors from each major category and read—some old, some new. Read a variety of topics.

Choose 6-8 works to read and study. Think about not only the authors' ideas, but more importantly, the rhetorical strategies and techniques they used to get their point across to their reader. Study their style, their use of language, syntax, and diction. Study their effectiveness. These writers are listed here for a reason—they're respected for what they say and how they say it.

While many of the writers listed are known for more than what is shown in representative works, this list shows those works that seem most suited to the exam or what is generally thought to be that writer's most accomplished or famous work.

PRE-TWENTIETH CENTURY

Writer	Representative Work(s)
Joseph Addison (1672–1719) English essayist, poet, playwright and politician	Founded *The Spectator* magazine with Richard Steele
Francis Bacon (1561–1626) English philosopher, statesman, scientist, lawyer, jurist and author	*The Advancement of Learning; Novum Organum*
James Boswell (1740–1795) Scottish lawyer, diarist, author	*The Life of Samuel Johnson,* a biography, and his journals
Thomas Carlyle (1795–1881) Scottish satirist, essayist, and historian	*Sartor Resartus; Signs of the Times*

Continued ➜

Writer	Representative Work(s)
Samuel Taylor Coleridge (1722–1834) English poet, literary critic and philosopher	*Biographia Literaria*
Charles Darwin (1809–1882) English naturalist	*On the Origin of Species*
Frederick Douglass (circa 1818–1895) American abolitionist, editor, orator, author, and statesman	*A Narrative of the Life of Frederick Douglass, an American Slave*; *My Bondage and My Freedom*; *Life and Times of Frederick Douglass*
Ralph Waldo Emerson (1803–1882) American philosopher, essayist, and poet	Various essays can be found at *http://www.rwe.org/*
Benjamin Franklin (1706–1790) one of the Founding Fathers of the United States, also a leading author and printer, satirist, political theorist, politician, and diplomat	*The Autobiography of Benjamin Franklin*
Margaret Fuller (1810–1850) American journalist, critic, and women's rights advocate	*Woman in the Nineteenth Century*
Edward Gibbon (1737–1794) English historian and member of Parliament	*The History of the Decline and Fall of the Roman Empire*
Thomas Hobbes (1588–1679) English political philosopher	Leviathan
Harriet Jacobs (Linda Brent) (1813–1897) American writer, abolitionist speaker and reformer	*Incidents in the Life of a Slave Girl*
Thomas Jefferson (1743–1826) third President of the United States, philosopher, and writer (among numerous other things)	primary author of the *Declaration of Independence*; *Declaration of the Causes and Necessity of Taking Up Arms*
Samuel Johnson (1709–1784) British author, poet, essayist, literary critic, biographer, and editor	*Dictionary of the English Language*; *Lives of the Most Eminent English Poets*
Charles Lamb (1775–1834) English essayist	*Specimens of English Dramatic Poets who Lived About the Time of Shakespeare*; *Essays of Elia*
John Locke (1632–1704) English philosopher	*An Essay Concerning Human Understanding*
Niccolò Machiavelli (1469–1527) Italian philosopher and writer, considered one of the main founders of modern political science	*The Prince*

Writer	Representative Work(s)
John Stuart Mill (1806–1873) British philosopher	His collected works are easily accessed online: *http://www.gutenberg.org/browse/authors/m#a1705*
John Milton (1608–1674) English poet, author	*Areopagitica*; *Paradise Lost*
Michel de Montaigne (1533–1592) French writer, essayist	His collected essays (Montaigne is considered to be the father of the modern essay).
Thomas More (1478–1535) English lawyer, social philosopher, author, and statesman	*Utopia*
Thomas Paine (1737–1809) American author, pamphleteer, radical, intellectual, revolutionary, one of the founding fathers of the United States	*Common Sense*; *The American Crisis*; *The Rights of Man*
Francis Parkman (1823–1893) American historian	*The Oregon Trail: Sketches of Prairie and Rocky-Mountain Life*; *France and England in North America*
Walter Pater (1839–1894) English essayist, critic, and fiction writer	*The Renaissance*, especially *The Conclusion*
George Bernard Shaw (1856–1950) Irish playwright, critic, journalist; Nobel Prize in Literature	*The Intelligent Woman's Guide to Socialism and Capitalism*; *Treatise on Parents and Children*; *Pygmalian*
Richard Steele (1672–1729) Irish writer and politician, remembered as co-founder, with his friend Joseph Addison, of the magazine *The Spectator*	*The Tatler*; *The Spectator*
Jonathan Swift (1667–1745) Anglo-Irish satirist, essayist	*Gulliver's Travels*; *A Modest Proposal*; *A Tale of a Tub*; *Drapier's Letters*
Henry David Thoreau (1817–1862) American author, naturalist, critic	*Walden*; *Civil Disobedience*
Alexis de Tocqueville (1805–1859) French political thinker and historian	*Democracy in America*; *The Old Regime and the Revolution*
Oscar Wilde (1854–1900) Irish writer, poet, and playwright	*Intentions*; *De Profundis*
Mary Wollstonecraft (1759–1797) British writer, philosopher, and feminist	*A Vindication of the Rights of Woman*

Continued →

20TH CENTURY TO THE PRESENT

Writer	Representative Work(s)
Edward Abbey (1927–1989) American author and essayist noted for his advocacy of environmental issues and criticism of public land policies	*The Monkey Wrench Gang*; *Desert Solitaire*
Diane Ackerman (1948–) American author, poet, and naturalist	*A Natural History of the Senses*
Paula Gunn Allen (1939–2008) Native American poet, literary critic, lesbian activist, and novelist	*The Sacred Hoop: Recovering the Feminine in American Indian Traditions*
Natalie Angier (1958–) American nonfiction writer and a science journalist for the *New York Times*; also a contributor to *Time* magazine	*Natural Obsessions*
Margaret Atwood (1939–) Canadian author, poet, critic, essayist, feminist and social campaigner	*Writing with Intent: Essays, Reviews, Personal Prose—1983–2005*; *Second Words: Selected Critical Prose*
James Baldwin (1924–1987) American novelist, writer, playwright, poet, essayist and civil rights activist	*Notes of a Native Son*; *The Fire Next Time*; *No Name in the Street*; *The Devil Finds Work*; *The Evidence of Things Not Seen*; *The Price of the Ticket*
Dave Barry (1947–) Pulitzer Prize-winning American author and columnist; humorist	*The World According to Dave Barry*; *Dave Barry is NOT Making This Up*
Melba Patillo Beals (1941–) American journalist and member of the Little Rock Nine, a group of African-American students who were the first to integrate Central High in Little Rock, Arkansas	*Warriors Don't Cry*; *White is a State of Mind*
Simone de Beauvoir (1908–1986) French existentialist philosopher and writer	*The Ethics of Ambiguity*; *The Second Sex*
Lerone Bennett Jr. (1928–) American scholar, author and social historian	*When the Wind Blows*; *History of Us*
Wendell Berry (1934–) American writer, fiction, nonfiction, and poetry	Essay collections: *Citizenship Papers*; *The Way of Ignorance*
Susan Bordo (1947–) modern feminist philosopher and writer	*Unbearable Weight: Feminism, Western Culture, and the Body*
Jacob Bronowski (1908–1974) British mathematician and biologist	*The Ascent of Man*; *A Sense of the Future*; *Magic Science & Civilization*; *The Origins of Knowledge and Imagination*

Writer	Representative Work(s)
William F. Buckley (1925–2008) American author, commentator, editor	Online @ *http://cumulus.hillsdale.edu/ buckley/Standard/index.html*
Judith Butler (1956–) American feminist philosopher and writer	*Gender Trouble: Feminism and the Subversion of Identity*
Rachel Carson (1907–1964) American marine biologist and nature writer	*Silent Spring*
G. K. Chesterton (1874–1936) British journalist, novelist, essayist	*Eugenics and Other Evils*
Winston Churchill (1874–1965) British Prime Minister, historian, and writer	*The Second World War*; *A History of the English-Speaking Peoples*
Judith Ortiz Cofer (1952–) Puerto Rican author	*Sleeping with One Eye Open: Women Writers and the Art of Survival*; *The Myth of the Latin Woman*
Richard Dawkins (1941–) British ethologist, evolutionary biologist and popular science author	*The Selfish Gene*
Joan Didion (1934–) American novelist, essayist, memoir writer	*Slouching Towards Bethlehem*; *The Year of Magical Thinking*
Annie Dillard (1945–) Pulitzer Prize-winning American author and artist, best known for her narrative nonfiction	*Pilgrim at Tinker Creek*
Maureen Dowd (1952–) columnist for the *New York Times* and best-selling author	*Are Men Necessary?: When Sexes Collide*; also see current and archived columns in the *New York Times*
Elizabeth Drew (1935–) American political journalist and author	Washington Journal: *The Events of 1973–74*; *Portrait of an Election: The 1980 Presidential Campaign*; *On the Edge: The Clinton Presidency*; *Citizen McCain*; *George W. Bush's Washington*
W. E. B. Du Bois (1868–1963) American civil rights activist, historian, and author	*The Souls of Black Folk* and much more
Richard Ellmann (1918–1987) American literary critic and biographer	*Four Dubliners: Wilde, Yeats, Joyce, and Beckett*
Nora Ephron (1941–) American film director, producer, screenwriter, novelist, and journalist	Various screenplays: *Silkwood*, *When Harry Met Sally*, *Julie and Julia*

Continued →

Writer	Representative Work(s)
Timothy Ferris (1944–) American science writer	*The Science of Liberty; Coming of Age in the Milky Way*
M. F. K. Fisher (1908–1992) American writer	*Map of Another Town: A Memoir of Provence; To Begin Again: Stories and Memoirs*
Frances Fitzgerald (1940–) American journalist and author, known for her journalistic account of the Vietnam War	*America Revised; Cities on a Hill; Way Out There in the Blue: Reagan, Star Wars and the End of the Cold War; Rewriting American history, a short article in The Norton Reader; and Vietnam: Spirits of the Earth*
Tim Flannery (1956–) Australian palaeontologist and environmental activist	*The Weather Makers: The History & Future Impact of Climate Change*
Shelby Foote (1916–2005) American novelist and historian of the American Civil War	*The Civil War: A Narrative*
John Hope Franklin (1915–2009) United States historian	*Racial Equality in America; My Life and an Era: The Autobiography of Buck Colbert Franklin; Runaway Slaves: Rebels on the Plantation; Mirror to America: The Autobiography of John Hope Franklin*
Antonia Frasert (1932–) Anglo- Irish author	*The Weaker Vessel: Woman's Lot in Seventeenth-Century England; The Warrior Queens: Boadicea's Chariot; The Gunpowder Plot*
Thomas L. Friedman (1953–) American journalist, columnist and Pulitzer Prize-winning author	*The Lexus and the Olive Tree; The World Is Flat; Longitudes and Attitudes*
Paul Fussell (1924–) American cultural and literary historian, professor of literature	*The Great War and Modern Memory; Thank God for the Atom Bomb and Other Essays*
John Kenneth Galbraith (1908–2006) Canadian-American economist, writer	*A Life in Our Times*
Henry Louis Gates Jr. (1950–) American literary critic, educator, scholar, writer, editor	*Colored People; Tradition and the Black Atlantic: Critical Theory in the African Diaspora; Personal History: Family Matters*
Ellen Goodman (1941–) American journalist and Pulitzer Prize-winning syndicated columnist	*Making Sense; Value Judgments; Paper Trail*

Writer	Representative Work(s)
Nadine Gordimer (1923–) South African writer, political activist and Nobel laureate	*The Conservationist; The Pickup; The Essential Gesture: Writing, Politics and Places*
Stephanie Elizondo Griest (1974–) Chicana author and activist from South Texas	*Around the Bloc: My Life in Moscow, Beijing, and Havana; 100 Places Every Woman Should Go*
David Halberstam (1934–2007) American Pulitzer Prize-winning journalist and author; known for his early work on the Vietnam War	*Summer of '49; The Next Century; The Fifties; October 1964*
Elizabeth Hardwick (1916–2007) American literary critic, novelist, and short-story writer.	*A View of My Own* (1962), *Seduction and Betrayal* (1974), *Bartleby in Manhattan* (1983), and *Sight-Readings* (1998).
Elva Trevino Hart Mexican-American writer	*Barefoot Heart: Stories of a Migrant Child* (memoir)
John Hersey (1914–1993) Pulitzer Prize-winning American writer and journalist	*Hiroshima*
Edward Hoagland (1932–) American author best known for nature and travel writing.	*Compass Points; Hoagland on Nature; Early in the Season*, plus numerous essays
Richard Holmes (1945–) British biographer	*Shelley: The Pursuit; Coleridge: Early Visions*
Bell Hooks (1952–) American author, feminist, and social activist	*Ain't I a Woman?: Black Women and Feminism; Yearning: Race, Gender, and Cultural Politics*
Zora Neale Hurston (1891–1960) American folklorist, anthropologist, and author	*Mules and Men; Their Eyes Were Watching God*
Evelyn Fox Keller (1936–) American author and physicist	*The Century of the Gene, Making Sense of Life: Explaining Biological Development with Models, Metaphors, and Machines*
Helen Keller (1880–1968) American author and lecturer	*The Story of My Life*
Martin Luther King Jr. (1929–1968) American clergyman and political leader	various speeches, letters, essays
Barbara Kingsolver (1955–) American novelist, author	*Animal, Vegetable, Miracle; Small Wonder: Essays, High Tide in Tucson*
Maxine Hong Kingston (1940–) Asian American author	*The Woman Warrior*

Continued →

Writer	Representative Work(s)
Paul Krugman (1953–) American columnist, author and Nobel Prize-winning economist	Op-ed columns for the *New York Times*; various books and articles
Alex Kuczynski (1967–) American author and reporter for the *New York Times*, columnist for the *New York Times Magazine*	*Beauty Junkies*
Lewis H. Laphamn (1935–) American author, journalist	*Waiting for the Barbarians; Theater of War; Gag Rule; and Pretensions to Empire*
T. E. Lawrence (1888–1935) British army officer, known also as Lawrence of Arabia	*Seven Pillars of Wisdom; Revolt in the Desert*
Gerda Lerner (1920–) American historian and author	*Why History Matters; The Creation of Feminist Consciousness; Fireweed: A Political Autobiography*
Phillip Lopate (1943–) American author and media critic	*Waterfront: A Walk Around Manhattan; Against Joie de Vivre*
Barry Lopez (1945–) American environmental author and social critic	*Home Ground: Language for an American Landscape*
Norman Mailer (1923–2007) American writer, co-founder of "new journalism"	*The Executioner's Song; The Big Empty: Dialogues on Politics, Sex, God, Boxing, Morality, Myth, Poker and Bad Conscience in America*
Nancy Mairs (1943–) American author, writes about her experiences with multiple sclerosis	*Waist High in the World*
Peter Matthiessen (1927–) American writer and environmental activist	*In the Spirit of Crazy Horse, Travelin' Man, Shadow Country*
Mary McCarthy (1912–1989) American author and political activist	*Memories of a Catholic School Girl, Vietnam, Ideas and the Novel*
Frank McCourt (1930–2009) Irish-American writer	*Angela's Ashes*
Bill McKibben (1960–) American environmentalist and writer	*The Bill McKibben Reader: Pieces from an Active Life, Eaarth: Making a Life on a Tough New Planet*
John McPhee (1931–) American writer and pioneer of creative nonfiction	*Annuls of the Former World, Encounters with the Archdruid, Silk Parachute*
Margaret Mead (1901–1978) American anthropologist	*Sex and Temperament in Three Primitive Societies, Male and Female*

Writer	Representative Work(s)
Jan Morris (1926–) Welsh historian and travel writer	*Locations, O Canada!, Contact! A Book of Glimpses*
John Muir (1838–1914) Scottish-born American naturalist, author, and early advocate of preservation of wilderness in the United States, co-founder of the Sierra Club	*The Story of My Boyhood and Youth*
Donald M. Murray (1923–2006) American journalist and teacher	*My Twice-Lived Life: A Memoir, The Lively Shadow: Living with the Death of a Child*
V. S. Naipaul (1932–) Trinidadian novelist and essayist, awarded the Nobel Prize in literature in 2001 for his life's work	*The Writer and the World: Essays,* or anything by this writer
Joyce Carol Oates (1938–) American novelist and essayist	*Where I've Been, And Where I'm Going: Essays, Reviews, and Prose*
Barack Obama (1961–) 44th President of the United States, president of *Harvard Law Review*	Keynote address at the Democratic National Convention in 2004
George Orwell (1903–1950) English author and journalist	*Politics and the English Language; 1984*
Cynthia Ozick (1928–) Jewish American writer	*Fame & Folly: Essays, Quarrel & Quandary, The Din in the Head: Essays*
Francine Prose (1947–) American writer	*Blue Angel; The Lives of the Muses: Nine Women & the Artists They Inspired*
David Quammen (1948–) award-winning science, nature and travel writer	*Monster of God: The Man-Eating Predator in the Jungles of History and the Mind*
Arnold Rampersad (1941–) biographer and literary critic, born in Trinidad	*Days of Grace: A Memoir, Jackie Robinson: A Biography*
Ishmael Reed (1938–) American poet, essayist, and novelist	*Barack Obama and the Jim Crow Media: The Return of the "Nigger Breakers," Mixing It Up: Taking on the Media Bullies and Other Reflections*
David Remnick (1958–) American journalist and Pulitzer Prize-winning writer	*Lenin's Tomb: The Last Days of the Soviet Empire.*
Mordecai Richler (1931–2001) Canadian author, screenwriter and essayist	*Oh Canada! Oh Quebec! Requiem for a Divided Country, Dispatches from the Sporting Life*

Continued ➞

Writer	Representative Work(s)
Sharman Apt Russell (1954–) American nature and science writer	*An Obsession with Butterflies: Our Long Love Affair with a Singular Insect, Anatomy of a Rose: Exploring the Secret Life of Flowers*
Carl Sagan (1934–1996) American astronomer, astrophysicist, and author	*Pale Blue Dot: A Vision of the Human Future in Space, Cosmos*
Edward Said (1935–2003) Palestinian-American literary theorist	*Out of Place*
George Santayana (1863–1952) Spanish-American philosopher and author	*The Sense of Beauty, The Life of Reason*
Arthur M. Schlesinger (1917–2007) Pulitzer Prize-winning American historian and social critic	*A Thousand Days: John F. Kennedy in the White House, The Disuniting of America: Reflections on a Multicultural Society, A Life in the 20th Century, Innocent Beginnings, 1917–1950*
David Sedaris (1956–) American humorist and writer	*Naked; Holidays on Ice; Me Talk Pretty One Day, Dress Your Family in Corduroy and Denim*
Richard Selzer (1928–) American surgeon and author	*The Exact Location of the Soul: New and Selected Essays; Raising the Dead: A Doctor's Encounter with His Own Mortality*
Leslie Marmon Silko (1948–) Native American author	*Yellow Woman and a Beauty of the Spirit: Essays on Native American Life Today*
Barbara Smith (1946–) American lecturer, author, and lesbian feminist	*Writings on Race, Gender and Freedom: The Truth That Never Hurts*
Red Smith (1905–1982) American sportswriter	*Views of Sport; Out of the Red*
Shelby Steele (1946–) American author and documentary film maker, specializing in the study of race relations	*The Content of Our Character*
Lincoln Steffens (1866–1936) American journalist, lecturer, and political philosopher, a famous muckraker	*The Shame of the Cities*
Ronald Takaki (1939–2009) American author	*Debating Diversity: Clashing Perspectives on Race and Ethnicity in America*
Lewis Thomas (1913–1993) American physician, researcher, and writer	*The Lives of a Cell: Notes of a Biology Watcher*

Writer	Representative Work(s)
Barbara Tuchman (1912–1989) American historian and Pulitzer Prize-winning author	*The Guns of August*
Cynthia Tucker (1955–) American journalist and Pulitzer Prize-winning columnist	Her blog can be found at *http://blogs.ajc.com/cynthia-tucker/*
Laurel Thatcher Ulrich (1938–) Harvard University professor and women's historian	*Good Wives: Image and Reality in the Lives of Women in Northern New England, 1650–1750, A Midwife's Tale: The Life of Martha Ballard based on her diary, 1785–1812*
John Updike (1932–2009) American novelist and critic	*The Clarity of Things: What's American About American Art?, Due Considerations: Essays and Criticism, Still Looking: Essays on American Art*
Gore Vidal (1925–) American author and political activist	*Gore Vidal: Snapshots in History's Glare, Imperial America: Reflections on the United States of Amnesia*
Alice Walker (1944–) American author	*In Search of Our Mothers' Gardens: Womanist Prose, We Are the Ones We Have Been Waiting For*
Jonathan Weiner (1953–) American journalist, science writer	*Long For This World; The Next One Hundred Years: Shaping the Fate of Our Living Earth; The Beak of the Finch: A Story of Evolution in Our Time* (Pulitzer Prize)
Cornel West (1953–) African American philosopher, author, and civil rights activist	*The African-American Century: How Black Americans Have Shaped Our Century; Restoring Hope: Conversations on the Future of Black America; The War Against Parents: What We Can Do For America's Beleaguered Moms and Dads*
E. B. White (1899–1985) American writer	Essays of E.B. White
George Will (1941–) U.S. newspaper columnist, journalist, author, and baseball fan	Will has published numerous books, but search online for his editorials and columns in *Newsweek, The Washington Post*, and ABC News. He is syndicated across the nation.

Continued ➡

Writer	Representative Work(s)
Terry Tempest Williams (1955–) American author, naturalist, and environmental activist	*Mosaic: Finding Beauty in a Broken World*
Garry Wills (1934–) American historian and Pulitzer Prize-winning author	*Lincoln at Gettysburg: The Words That Remade America; Inventing America: Jefferson's Declaration of Independence*
E. O. Wilson (1929–) American biologist, researcher, and Pulitzer Prize-winning author, specializing in the study of ants	*On Human Nature, The Ants, The Future of Life*
Edmund Wilson (1895–1972) American writer, literary and social critic	*The American Earthquake: A Documentary of the Twenties and Thirties, The Bit Between My Teeth: A Literary Chronicle of 1950–1965*
Tom Wolfe (1930–) American author and journalist, one of the founders of the New Journalism movement	*The Electric Kool-Aid Acid Test, The Right Stuff,* and 35th Jefferson Lecture in the Humanities titled "The Human Beast"
Virginia Woolf (1882–1941) English author	*A Room of One's Own, Women And Writing, Collected Essays*
Richard Wright (1908–1960) American author	*American Hunger, Black Boy*
Malcolm X (1925–1965) African-American Muslim minister, public speaker, and human-rights activist	*The Speeches of Malcolm X at Harvard, The Autobiography of Malcolm X*
Anzia Yezierska (circa 1880–1970) Polish-American novelist	*Red Ribbon on a White Horse; Bread Givers*

ANSWER SHEETS

AP English Language & Composition

ANSWER SHEETS

AP English Language & Composition

Exam 1

Section 1

1. Ⓐ Ⓑ Ⓒ Ⓓ Ⓔ
2. Ⓐ Ⓑ Ⓒ Ⓓ Ⓔ
3. Ⓐ Ⓑ Ⓒ Ⓓ Ⓔ
4. Ⓐ Ⓑ Ⓒ Ⓓ Ⓔ
5. Ⓐ Ⓑ Ⓒ Ⓓ Ⓔ
6. Ⓐ Ⓑ Ⓒ Ⓓ Ⓔ
7. Ⓐ Ⓑ Ⓒ Ⓓ Ⓔ
8. Ⓐ Ⓑ Ⓒ Ⓓ Ⓔ
9. Ⓐ Ⓑ Ⓒ Ⓓ Ⓔ
10. Ⓐ Ⓑ Ⓒ Ⓓ Ⓔ
11. Ⓐ Ⓑ Ⓒ Ⓓ Ⓔ
12. Ⓐ Ⓑ Ⓒ Ⓓ Ⓔ
13. Ⓐ Ⓑ Ⓒ Ⓓ Ⓔ
14. Ⓐ Ⓑ Ⓒ Ⓓ Ⓔ
15. Ⓐ Ⓑ Ⓒ Ⓓ Ⓔ
16. Ⓐ Ⓑ Ⓒ Ⓓ Ⓔ
17. Ⓐ Ⓑ Ⓒ Ⓓ Ⓔ
18. Ⓐ Ⓑ Ⓒ Ⓓ Ⓔ
19. Ⓐ Ⓑ Ⓒ Ⓓ Ⓔ
20. Ⓐ Ⓑ Ⓒ Ⓓ Ⓔ

21. Ⓐ Ⓑ Ⓒ Ⓓ Ⓔ
22. Ⓐ Ⓑ Ⓒ Ⓓ Ⓔ
23. Ⓐ Ⓑ Ⓒ Ⓓ Ⓔ
24. Ⓐ Ⓑ Ⓒ Ⓓ Ⓔ
25. Ⓐ Ⓑ Ⓒ Ⓓ Ⓔ
26. Ⓐ Ⓑ Ⓒ Ⓓ Ⓔ
27. Ⓐ Ⓑ Ⓒ Ⓓ Ⓔ
28. Ⓐ Ⓑ Ⓒ Ⓓ Ⓔ
29. Ⓐ Ⓑ Ⓒ Ⓓ Ⓔ
30. Ⓐ Ⓑ Ⓒ Ⓓ Ⓔ
31. Ⓐ Ⓑ Ⓒ Ⓓ Ⓔ
32. Ⓐ Ⓑ Ⓒ Ⓓ Ⓔ
33. Ⓐ Ⓑ Ⓒ Ⓓ Ⓔ
34. Ⓐ Ⓑ Ⓒ Ⓓ Ⓔ
35. Ⓐ Ⓑ Ⓒ Ⓓ Ⓔ
36. Ⓐ Ⓑ Ⓒ Ⓓ Ⓔ
37. Ⓐ Ⓑ Ⓒ Ⓓ Ⓔ
38. Ⓐ Ⓑ Ⓒ Ⓓ Ⓔ
39. Ⓐ Ⓑ Ⓒ Ⓓ Ⓔ
40. Ⓐ Ⓑ Ⓒ Ⓓ Ⓔ

41. Ⓐ Ⓑ Ⓒ Ⓓ Ⓔ
42. Ⓐ Ⓑ Ⓒ Ⓓ Ⓔ
43. Ⓐ Ⓑ Ⓒ Ⓓ Ⓔ
44. Ⓐ Ⓑ Ⓒ Ⓓ Ⓔ
45. Ⓐ Ⓑ Ⓒ Ⓓ Ⓔ
46. Ⓐ Ⓑ Ⓒ Ⓓ Ⓔ
47. Ⓐ Ⓑ Ⓒ Ⓓ Ⓔ
48. Ⓐ Ⓑ Ⓒ Ⓓ Ⓔ
49. Ⓐ Ⓑ Ⓒ Ⓓ Ⓔ
50. Ⓐ Ⓑ Ⓒ Ⓓ Ⓔ
51. Ⓐ Ⓑ Ⓒ Ⓓ Ⓔ
52. Ⓐ Ⓑ Ⓒ Ⓓ Ⓔ
53. Ⓐ Ⓑ Ⓒ Ⓓ Ⓔ
54. Ⓐ Ⓑ Ⓒ Ⓓ Ⓔ
55. Ⓐ Ⓑ Ⓒ Ⓓ Ⓔ
56. Ⓐ Ⓑ Ⓒ Ⓓ Ⓔ
57. Ⓐ Ⓑ Ⓒ Ⓓ Ⓔ
58. Ⓐ Ⓑ Ⓒ Ⓓ Ⓔ

Section 2

Use the following page to prepare your essays. During the official exam, you will be given 12 lined pages for your essays.

_____

_____

_____

_____

_____

_____

_____

_____

_____

_____

_____

_____

_____

_____

_____

_____

ANSWER SHEETS

AP English Language & Composition

Exam 2

Section 1

1. Ⓐ Ⓑ Ⓒ Ⓓ Ⓔ	20. Ⓐ Ⓑ Ⓒ Ⓓ Ⓔ	39. Ⓐ Ⓑ Ⓒ Ⓓ Ⓔ
2. Ⓐ Ⓑ Ⓒ Ⓓ Ⓔ	21. Ⓐ Ⓑ Ⓒ Ⓓ Ⓔ	40. Ⓐ Ⓑ Ⓒ Ⓓ Ⓔ
3. Ⓐ Ⓑ Ⓒ Ⓓ Ⓔ	22. Ⓐ Ⓑ Ⓒ Ⓓ Ⓔ	41. Ⓐ Ⓑ Ⓒ Ⓓ Ⓔ
4. Ⓐ Ⓑ Ⓒ Ⓓ Ⓔ	23. Ⓐ Ⓑ Ⓒ Ⓓ Ⓔ	42. Ⓐ Ⓑ Ⓒ Ⓓ Ⓔ
5. Ⓐ Ⓑ Ⓒ Ⓓ Ⓔ	24. Ⓐ Ⓑ Ⓒ Ⓓ Ⓔ	43. Ⓐ Ⓑ Ⓒ Ⓓ Ⓔ
6. Ⓐ Ⓑ Ⓒ Ⓓ Ⓔ	25. Ⓐ Ⓑ Ⓒ Ⓓ Ⓔ	44. Ⓐ Ⓑ Ⓒ Ⓓ Ⓔ
7. Ⓐ Ⓑ Ⓒ Ⓓ Ⓔ	26. Ⓐ Ⓑ Ⓒ Ⓓ Ⓔ	45. Ⓐ Ⓑ Ⓒ Ⓓ Ⓔ
8. Ⓐ Ⓑ Ⓒ Ⓓ Ⓔ	27. Ⓐ Ⓑ Ⓒ Ⓓ Ⓔ	46. Ⓐ Ⓑ Ⓒ Ⓓ Ⓔ
9. Ⓐ Ⓑ Ⓒ Ⓓ Ⓔ	28. Ⓐ Ⓑ Ⓒ Ⓓ Ⓔ	47. Ⓐ Ⓑ Ⓒ Ⓓ Ⓔ
10. Ⓐ Ⓑ Ⓒ Ⓓ Ⓔ	29. Ⓐ Ⓑ Ⓒ Ⓓ Ⓔ	48. Ⓐ Ⓑ Ⓒ Ⓓ Ⓔ
11. Ⓐ Ⓑ Ⓒ Ⓓ Ⓔ	30. Ⓐ Ⓑ Ⓒ Ⓓ Ⓔ	49. Ⓐ Ⓑ Ⓒ Ⓓ Ⓔ
12. Ⓐ Ⓑ Ⓒ Ⓓ Ⓔ	31. Ⓐ Ⓑ Ⓒ Ⓓ Ⓔ	50. Ⓐ Ⓑ Ⓒ Ⓓ Ⓔ
13. Ⓐ Ⓑ Ⓒ Ⓓ Ⓔ	32. Ⓐ Ⓑ Ⓒ Ⓓ Ⓔ	51. Ⓐ Ⓑ Ⓒ Ⓓ Ⓔ
14. Ⓐ Ⓑ Ⓒ Ⓓ Ⓔ	33. Ⓐ Ⓑ Ⓒ Ⓓ Ⓔ	52. Ⓐ Ⓑ Ⓒ Ⓓ Ⓔ
15. Ⓐ Ⓑ Ⓒ Ⓓ Ⓔ	34. Ⓐ Ⓑ Ⓒ Ⓓ Ⓔ	53. Ⓐ Ⓑ Ⓒ Ⓓ Ⓔ
16. Ⓐ Ⓑ Ⓒ Ⓓ Ⓔ	35. Ⓐ Ⓑ Ⓒ Ⓓ Ⓔ	54. Ⓐ Ⓑ Ⓒ Ⓓ Ⓔ
17. Ⓐ Ⓑ Ⓒ Ⓓ Ⓔ	36. Ⓐ Ⓑ Ⓒ Ⓓ Ⓔ	55. Ⓐ Ⓑ Ⓒ Ⓓ Ⓔ
18. Ⓐ Ⓑ Ⓒ Ⓓ Ⓔ	37. Ⓐ Ⓑ Ⓒ Ⓓ Ⓔ	56. Ⓐ Ⓑ Ⓒ Ⓓ Ⓔ
19. Ⓐ Ⓑ Ⓒ Ⓓ Ⓔ	38. Ⓐ Ⓑ Ⓒ Ⓓ Ⓔ	57. Ⓐ Ⓑ Ⓒ Ⓓ Ⓔ

Section 2

Use the following page to prepare your essays. During the official exam, you will be given 12 lined pages for your essays.

ANSWER SHEETS

AP English Language & Composition

Exam 3

Section 1

1. Ⓐ Ⓑ Ⓒ Ⓓ Ⓔ
2. Ⓐ Ⓑ Ⓒ Ⓓ Ⓔ
3. Ⓐ Ⓑ Ⓒ Ⓓ Ⓔ
4. Ⓐ Ⓑ Ⓒ Ⓓ Ⓔ
5. Ⓐ Ⓑ Ⓒ Ⓓ Ⓔ
6. Ⓐ Ⓑ Ⓒ Ⓓ Ⓔ
7. Ⓐ Ⓑ Ⓒ Ⓓ Ⓔ
8. Ⓐ Ⓑ Ⓒ Ⓓ Ⓔ
9. Ⓐ Ⓑ Ⓒ Ⓓ Ⓔ
10. Ⓐ Ⓑ Ⓒ Ⓓ Ⓔ
11. Ⓐ Ⓑ Ⓒ Ⓓ Ⓔ
12. Ⓐ Ⓑ Ⓒ Ⓓ Ⓔ
13. Ⓐ Ⓑ Ⓒ Ⓓ Ⓔ
14. Ⓐ Ⓑ Ⓒ Ⓓ Ⓔ
15. Ⓐ Ⓑ Ⓒ Ⓓ Ⓔ
16. Ⓐ Ⓑ Ⓒ Ⓓ Ⓔ
17. Ⓐ Ⓑ Ⓒ Ⓓ Ⓔ
18. Ⓐ Ⓑ Ⓒ Ⓓ Ⓔ

19. Ⓐ Ⓑ Ⓒ Ⓓ Ⓔ
20. Ⓐ Ⓑ Ⓒ Ⓓ Ⓔ
21. Ⓐ Ⓑ Ⓒ Ⓓ Ⓔ
22. Ⓐ Ⓑ Ⓒ Ⓓ Ⓔ
23. Ⓐ Ⓑ Ⓒ Ⓓ Ⓔ
24. Ⓐ Ⓑ Ⓒ Ⓓ Ⓔ
25. Ⓐ Ⓑ Ⓒ Ⓓ Ⓔ
26. Ⓐ Ⓑ Ⓒ Ⓓ Ⓔ
27. Ⓐ Ⓑ Ⓒ Ⓓ Ⓔ
28. Ⓐ Ⓑ Ⓒ Ⓓ Ⓔ
29. Ⓐ Ⓑ Ⓒ Ⓓ Ⓔ
30. Ⓐ Ⓑ Ⓒ Ⓓ Ⓔ
31. Ⓐ Ⓑ Ⓒ Ⓓ Ⓔ
32. Ⓐ Ⓑ Ⓒ Ⓓ Ⓔ
33. Ⓐ Ⓑ Ⓒ Ⓓ Ⓔ
34. Ⓐ Ⓑ Ⓒ Ⓓ Ⓔ
35. Ⓐ Ⓑ Ⓒ Ⓓ Ⓔ
36. Ⓐ Ⓑ Ⓒ Ⓓ Ⓔ

37. Ⓐ Ⓑ Ⓒ Ⓓ Ⓔ
38. Ⓐ Ⓑ Ⓒ Ⓓ Ⓔ
39. Ⓐ Ⓑ Ⓒ Ⓓ Ⓔ
40. Ⓐ Ⓑ Ⓒ Ⓓ Ⓔ
41. Ⓐ Ⓑ Ⓒ Ⓓ Ⓔ
42. Ⓐ Ⓑ Ⓒ Ⓓ Ⓔ
43. Ⓐ Ⓑ Ⓒ Ⓓ Ⓔ
44. Ⓐ Ⓑ Ⓒ Ⓓ Ⓔ
45. Ⓐ Ⓑ Ⓒ Ⓓ Ⓔ
46. Ⓐ Ⓑ Ⓒ Ⓓ Ⓔ
47. Ⓐ Ⓑ Ⓒ Ⓓ Ⓔ
48. Ⓐ Ⓑ Ⓒ Ⓓ Ⓔ
49. Ⓐ Ⓑ Ⓒ Ⓓ Ⓔ
50. Ⓐ Ⓑ Ⓒ Ⓓ Ⓔ
51. Ⓐ Ⓑ Ⓒ Ⓓ Ⓔ
52. Ⓐ Ⓑ Ⓒ Ⓓ Ⓔ

Section 2

Use the following page to prepare your essays. During the official exam, you will be given 12 lined pages for your essays.

Index

A

American Psychological Association (APA), 29
AP English Language and Composition
      examination
  annotation, 7
  composition test score range, 5
  content change, 4
  defined, 4
  grade distribution and scoring, 5
  materials needed, 5–6
  scoring change, 4
  synthesis essay, directions for, 4
  test format and content
    argument essay, 6–7
    rhetorical/language analysis essay, 6
    synthesis essay, 7
  timing, 7–8
Argument essays
  defined, 61–62
  questions, 62–63

C

Council of Science Editors (CSE), 29

D

Documentation and citation
  annotated material, 30–31
  styles
    APA, 29
    CSE, 29
    MLA, 29
    Turabian/Chicago, 29

E

Essays
  defined, 55
  preparing for
    research, 67
    writing practice, 68
  scoring, 55–57
  strategies for answering questions
    five-paragraph structure, 67
    ideas, 66–67

    quotation and example, 67
    reading of, 66
    response planning, 66
    revision, 67
    time, 66
    transition, 67
  types of
    argument, 61–63
    rhetorical analysis, 63–65
    synthesis, 57–61

F

Footnotes and documentation
  nonprint, 30
  print, 29–30

M

Modern Language Association (MLA), 29
Multiple-choice questions
  formation of
    content, change, 36
    scoring, change, 36
  grammar
    dependent clause, 39–40
    independent clause, 39
    phrases, 41
    pronoun reference, 40–41
    punctuation, 41
    subject and verb, 39
  passages
    academic writing on, 36–37
    criticism, 36
    test, 37
  practice, 37
    audience, 38
    Canassatego craft, 38–39
    letter, purpose of, 38
  tricky format
    "EXCEPT" world, 48–49
    "three possibilities," 49
  types of
    author/audience, 42–43
    conclusions, 48
    development, 47

NOTES

NOTES

NOTES

NOTES

NOTES

NOTES

NOTES

NOTES

Installing REA's TestWare®

System Requirements

Pentium 75 MHz (300 MHz recommended) or a higher or compatible processor; Microsoft Windows 98 or later; 64 MB Available RAM; Internet Explorer 5.5 or higher.

Installation

1. Insert the AP English Language & Composition TestWare® CD-ROM into the CD-ROM drive.
2. If the installation doesn't begin automatically, from the Start Menu choose the RUN command. When the RUN dialog box appears, type d:\ setup (where *d* is the letter of your CD-ROM drive) at the prompt and click OK.
3. The installation process will begin. A dialog box proposing the directory "Program Files\REA\APEnglishLang" will appear. If the name and location are suitable, click OK. If you wish to specify a different name or location, type it in and click OK.
4. Start the AP English Language & Composition TestWare® application by double-clicking on the icon.

REA's AP English Language & Composition TestWare® is **EASY** to **LEARN AND USE**. To achieve maximum benefits, we recommend that you take a few minutes to go through the on-screen tutorial on your computer. The "screen buttons" are also explained there to familiarize you with the program.

SSD Accommodations for Students with Disabilities

Many students qualify for extra time to take the AP exams, and our TestWare® can be adapted to accommodate your time extension. This allows you to practice under the same extended-time accommodations that you will receive on the actual test day. To customize your TestWare® to suit the most common extensions, visit our website at *www.rea.com/ssd*.

Technical Support

REA's TestWare® is backed by customer and technical support. For questions about **installation or operation of your software**, contact us at:

Research & Education Association
Phone (732) 819-8880 (9 a.m. to 5 p.m. ET, Monday–Friday)
Fax: (732) 819-8808
Website: *www.rea.com*
E-mail: *info@rea.com*

Note to Windows XP Users: In order for the TestWare® to function properly, please install and run the application under the same computer-administrator level user account. Installing the TestWare® as one user and running it as another could cause file-access path conflicts.